THE OFFICIAL RED BOOK®

A Guide Book of UNITED STATES TOKENS AND MEDALS

Featuring Illustrations From the American Numismatic Society's Collection

Katherine Jaeger

Foreword by
Q. David Bowers

Valuations Editors
Steve Tanenbaum and Steve Hayden

A Guide Book of
UNITED STATES TOKENS AND MEDALS

www.whitmanbooks.com

© 2008 by Whitman Publishing, LLC
3101 Clairmont Road, Suite C, Atlanta, GA 30329

THE OFFICIAL RED BOOK is a trademark of Whitman Publishing, LLC.

All rights reserved, including duplication of any kind and storage in electronic or visual retrieval systems. Permission is granted for writers to use a reasonable number of brief text excerpts and quotations in printed reviews and articles, provided credit is given to the title of the work and the author. Written permission from the publisher is required for other uses of text, illustrations, and other content, including in books and electronic or other media.

Photographs from the American Numismatic Society's collection are used with permission; all rights are reserved and ©2008 American Numismatic Society.

Correspondence concerning this book may be directed to the publisher, Attn: Tokens and Medals, at the address above.

ISBN: 0794820603
Printed in China

Disclaimer: Expert opinion should be sought in any significant numismatic purchase. This book is presented as a guide only. No warranty or representation of any kind is made concerning the completeness of the information presented. The author and valuations editors sometimes buy, sell, or hold certain of the items discussed in this book.

Caveat: The value estimates given are subject to variation and differences of opinion. Before making decisions to buy or sell, consult the latest information. Past performance of the numismatic market or any medal or token within that market is not necessarily an indication of future performance, as the future is unknown. Such factors as changing demand, popularity, grading interpretations, strength of the overall market, and economic conditions will continue to be influences.

> *About the cover:* Four fascinating pieces of Americana grace the cover—a tiny sampling of the thousands of tokens and medals issued in the United States since the 1700s. The 1860 Washington cabinet medal (top left; see also page 206) is one of the most impressive of all medals struck at the Philadelphia Mint in the 19th century. The Pioneer Base Ball Club medal (top right; see also page 263) is regarded as the first medal to specifically commemorate the national game. The charming "Good For a Cent" design (bottom left; see also page 78) was used on several commercial tokens during the Civil War. The "American Beaver" medal (bottom right) shows America symbolized as an industrious, diligent beaver nibbling at the oak of British power in 1776.

If you enjoy the *Guide Book of United States Tokens and Medals*, you will also enjoy *100 Greatest American Medals and Tokens*, by Katherine Jaeger and Q. David Bowers, also available from Whitman Publishing.

For a complete catalog of numismatic reference books, supplies, and storage products, visit Whitman Publishing online at www.whitmanbooks.com.

WCG™ Pricing Grid
OCG™ Collecting Guide

TABLE OF CONTENTS

ABOUT THE AUTHOR vi
FOREWORD vii
PREFACE ix
CREDITS AND ACKNOWLEDGMENTS xi
INTRODUCTION: WELCOME TO EXONUMIA 1

PART I: TOKENS OF EXCHANGE, ACCOUNTING, AND ADVERTISING 19

Chapter 1: Merchant Tokens 22
   Early America, Through 1831 22
   Merchant Issues of 1845–1860 23
   After the Civil War 24
   The 20th Century and Today 26

Chapter 2: Hard Times Tokens (1832–1844) 61
   Satirical Issues 63
   Merchant Issues 66

Chapter 3: Civil War Tokens (1860–1865) 68
   Encased Postage Stamps 68
   Token Currency 69
   Patriotic Tokens 71
   Store Cards, by State 75
   Sutlers' Tokens 87

Chapter 4: Company Store and Commissary Tokens 88
   Mining-Company Tokens 88
   Lumber-Company Tokens 90
   Farm and Factory Checks 90
   Commissary Tokens 92

Chapter 5: Amusement Tokens 94
   Gambling-Machine Tokens 94
   Arcade Tokens 95
   Music-Machine Tokens 96

Chapter 6: Gaming Chips and Tokens 98
   Play Money and Game Counters 98
   Board-Game Money 99
   Casino Chips 100
   Casino Tokens 102

Chapter 7: Transportation Tokens 106
   Stage, Omnibus, and Hack Tokens 106
   Horsecar Tokens 107
   Cable-Car and Electric Streetcar Tokens 107
   Subway and Bus Tokens 108
   Ferry Tokens 108
   Tokens for Passage 109

Chapter 8: Government-Sponsored Tokens 113
   Civilian Conservation Corps Tokens 113
   Alaska Rural Rehabilitation Corps Tokens 114
   State Sales-Tax and Emergency-Relief-Tax Tokens 114
   OPA Ration Tokens 116
   Internment-Camp Tokens 117
   Food-Stamp Change Tokens 117

PART II: SOUVENIR AND COMMEMORATIVE MEDALS AND TOKENS 119

Chapter 9: Contemporary Medals and Tokens 120
   Pre-Federal Medals 120
   National Medals 124
   Major-Event Medals 130
   Celebration Souvenirs 137
   Tourist-Site Souvenirs 142
   Performance Souvenirs 146
   Medals of the Space Program 150

Chapter 10: Exposition Souvenirs 154

Chapter 11: Personal Medals and Tokens 158
   Arras Tokens 161

Chapter 12: The Historical Commemorative Craze of 1858–1861 163
   Diesinkers and Coin Dealers 165
   Augustus B. Sage Token Series 167
   Odd Mulings 169

Chapter 13: Coin Medals of the Franklin Mint 170

PART III: POLITICAL AND PRESIDENTIAL EXONUMIA 178

Chapter 14: Presidential Campaign Medals and Tokens 180
   Supportive Pieces 180
   Satirical Pieces 188
   Ferrotypes 191

Chapter 15: Political-Cause Medals and Tokens 193
   Abolition Pieces 193
   Temperance Pieces 194

Chapter 16: Contemporary Presidential Commemoratives 196
   Inaugural Medals 196
   Indian Peace Medals 199

Chapter 17: Post-Presidency Commemoratives 204
   Life, Death, and Accomplishment Pieces 204
   Presidential Series 209

PART IV: ART MEDALS 213

Chapter 18: Art and Exhibition Medals 214
    The American Numismatic Society Exhibition of 1910 214
    The Circle of Friends of the Medallion 217
    The Society of Medalists 220
    Evolving Medallic Art Today 226

PART V: PRIZE MEDALS 229

Chapter 19: Academic Medals 230

Chapter 20: Major Institutional Medals 234

Chapter 21: Fair and Exposition Medals 239
    Agricultural and Mechanics' Society Medals 239
    National Prize Fairs and Expositions 244

Chapter 22: Lifesaving and Heroism Medals 249

PART VI: FRATERNAL AND MEMBERSHIP-THEMED MEDALS AND TOKENS 255

Chapter 23: Fraternal, Incentive, and Membership Medals and Tokens 256
    Firefighters' Medals 256
    Military and Other Challenge Coins 259
    Membership Medals 261

PART VII: TOOLED AND ALTERED COINS 267

Chapter 24: Merchant Advertising on Coins 268
    Countermarked Coins 268
    Encased Coins 270
    Capped Coins 272
    Stickered Coins 272

Chapter 25: Carved Coins 274
    Hobo Nickels 274

Chapter 26: Elongated Coins 276

Chapter 27: Love Tokens and Other Engraved Coins 278

Chapter 28: Enameled, Cut-Out, and Pop-Out Coins 281

BIBLIOGRAPHY 284
NOTES 287

About the Author

Katherine Jaeger earned a B.A. from Allegheny College in 1979, and spent each of her college summers working at archaeological digs in Israel. There she first heard the peculiar term *numismatics*, and began to view coins as archaeological dating tools and as pieces of the historical record. From 1979 to 1986, she worked in New York City as a copyeditor and then managing copyeditor; later, while raising a family with her husband, Tom, she switched to freelance editing. In 1999 she began writing history features for magazines such as *American History* and *American Heritage*. The "hook" into exonumia came when she found a clipping of an 1885 newspaper interview with diesinker George H. Lovett, her great-great-grandfather. Immersed in the study of medals and tokens since then, she has authored several features for *The Numismatist* and *Coin World* and is the coauthor (with Q. David Bowers) of Whitman's *100 Greatest American Medals and Tokens*. In 2006 she received the American Numismatic Association's Heath Literary Award, and, in 2007, the ANA's Wayte and Olga Raymond Literary Award.

About the Foreword Author

Q. David Bowers became a professional numismatist as a teenager in 1953, later earning a B.A. in finance from the Pennsylvania State University (1960), which in 1976 bestowed its Distinguished Alumnus Award on him. He served as president of the Professional Numismatists Guild (PNG) from 1977 to 1979 and president of the ANA from 1983 to 1985. He is a recipient of the Founder's Award and Farran Zerbe Award, the highest honors of the PNG and the ANA. He is the author of over 50 books and has received more honors from the Numismatic Literary Guild than has any other person. His column, "The Joys of Collecting," has been a feature of *Coin World* for more than 40 years and is the longest-running column by any author in the history of numismatics.

About the Valuations Editors

Steve Tanenbaum of New York is a researcher, consultant, collector, and dealer in tokens, medals, and colonials. He was introduced to exonumia in 1972, and 10 years later became a full-time dealer. Among his specialties are early U.S. tokens, Civil War and Hard Times tokens, shell cards, counterstamps, New England and mid-Atlantic states tokens, and Connecticut colonials.

Steve Hayden has been buying and selling tokens and medals for nearly 25 years—the last 10 of them as a full-time Internet and show dealer. The specialties featured on his Web site, civilwartokens.com, are Hard Times tokens, art and historical medals, and, of course, Civil War tokens. Steve was born and raised in Michigan and now resides in Charleston, South Carolina.

FOREWORD

"The Token: America's Other Money" was the title of the Coinage of the Americas conference held by the American Numismatic Society in 1994. And, indeed, tokens have been an important type of money for a long time, but not as much in our own era as in the past. A "token of affection," perhaps appropriate in romance or on Valentine's Day, could also relate to the feeling numismatists have for these interesting pieces. Diversity is to the extreme—ranging from admission tokens to museums and theaters, to use in paying turnpike tolls, to playing music, ordering a glass of beer, or actually substituting for federal coins that were nowhere to be seen (such as in the Panic of 1837 and during the Civil War).

As to medals, nearly all were created for special occasions or purposes, miniature sculpted remembrances of events, accomplishments, or perhaps distinguished lives. Having a display of medals is like having an art museum in your own home.

Some years ago the president of the Medallic Art Company told me why his customers liked medals, and why they were excellent for awards and also as advertising: "No one ever throws a medal away," he noted. "Plaques, certificates, and other such things are here today and gone tomorrow, but medals are kept forever." Actually, that is not always the case, as Katherine Jaeger points out in this book. Sometimes when the prices of precious metals such as silver and gold rise, mementos are brought out of cabinets and drawers and melted, such as happened with untold millions of Franklin Mint medals during the great "silver rush" of the late 1970s. Similarly, we can only speculate that the dozens of gold award medals given by the American Institute in the 19th century have long since disappeared, as their intrinsic value trumped their original significance when such pieces were passed on to later generations and their sentiment faded. Although Jaeger relates that 50 gold versions of the Erie Canal medal were struck in 1826, today in the early 21st century only a handful are known to survive.

Within the numismatic hobby, tokens and medals are here, there, and everywhere. The Civil War Token Society, the Token and Medal Society, the American Vecturist Association (do you know what a vecturist is?), and other groups are birds of a collecting feather that flock together. Dozens of guides and reference books can be found, most of them out of print, all interesting in one way or another. However, before this book there was no single introductory guide, no passport to the series.

Now, Katherine Jaeger brings it all together, and in a fascinating way—a truly "good read" for experienced collectors, and a marvelous introduction for those who are entering the specialty. Familiar topics such as Civil War, Hard Times, and good-for tokens are discussed, as are national, Indian peace, award, presidential, life-saving, casino, academic, and other medals.

In reading the text I appreciated for the first time the depth and breadth of interest in such modern series as casino chips, challenge coins, and medals associated with the space program. All too often I tend to bury myself in the depths of history—sometimes forgetting that, indeed, the 20th century is perhaps richer with medals and tokens than is the more extensively studied 19th century.

As you contemplate the rarity and beauty of certain examples, you will probably pause to wonder why beautiful art medals, with productions only in the hundreds of pieces, issued by the Circle of Friends of the Medallion from 1909 to 1915, and the Society of Medalists from 1930 to recent times, are so inexpensive. Each one is a piece of sculptured art you can hold in your hand or display in a cabinet. Original works by many sculptors such as Isadore Konti, John Flanagan, Paul Manship, Hermon A. MacNeil, Laura Gardin Fraser, Chester Beach, or A.A. Weinman are apt to cost many thousands of dollars (indeed if you can find them at all). Medals by the same people are easily affordable, with several hundred dollars being a typical price for each of the 12 in the Circle of Friends set and with many of the Society of Medalists issues selling for $100 to $200. A small budget can go a long way, quite unlike collecting federal coins of comparable rarity.

Part of the reason for this remarkable opportunity is that medals are lightly chronicled in readily available numismatic publications. I believe that the present book offers the first listing of the more than 100 Society of Medalists issues to appear in a modern book with popular distribution.

Of course, this might also sound an alert. Series have a way of becoming popular once people learn about them. Fair warning! Indeed, knowledge is everything. Similarly, I can relate that in the 1950s, when I began collecting copper coins issued by Vermont, Connecticut, and other states, the number of enthusiasts with whom I could correspond could be numbered on the fingers of my hands. Today, information is readily available, and there are thousands of people interested. Colonial coins that used to cost $50 are more apt to cost $1,000.

Up to now, tokens have been more extensively chronicled than medals. Still, there are many opportunities to collect within a specialty for which interesting pieces can be acquired for just a few dollars. Many good-for, Ingle, saloon, and other tokens are very inexpensive.

Katherine Jaeger was my coauthor in the *100 Greatest American Medals and Tokens* book, published by Whitman. Working with her was a great pleasure. A descendant of famed die cutter George H. Lovett, Jaeger has embraced numismatics with a passion, combined with a rare combination of research ability and writing talent.

How fortunate we all are that she created the present *Guide Book of United States Tokens and Medals*. I enjoyed immensely the opportunity to contribute to her effort and, especially, to read the finished work. With this book in your hand you have a passport to a new world of collecting pleasure.

Q. David Bowers
Wolfeboro, New Hampshire

Preface

United States tokens and medals comprise a field of collectibles that is both broad and deep. There are many in-depth reference books that offer encyclopedic studies of individual subcategories (such as Civil War tokens), but the hobby has long felt the need for an *overview* reference book, one with high-quality illustrations and a representative sampling of market valuations. The *Guide Book of United States Tokens and Medals*, illustrated largely from the collections of the American Numismatic Society, is that reference book. Its goal is to introduce the newcomer to the diversity of tokens and medals, while educating and refreshing the experienced collector.

Exclusions

Several categories of exonumia have been excluded from this work—the largest being that of U.S. military medals, orders, and decorations, because of certain legal limitations on trading in these items. According to Title 18, Section 4, of the United States Code:

> Whoever knowingly wears, manufactures, or sells any decoration or medal authorized by Congress for the armed forces of the United States, or any of the service medals or badges awarded to the members of such forces, or the ribbon, button or rosette of any such badge, decoration or medal, or any colorable imitation thereof, except when authorized under regulations made pursuant to law, shall be fined under this title or imprisoned not more than six months, or both. . . . [If] the medal involved in such offense is the Congressional Medal of Honor, not only the sale, but also the trade, barter or exchange of such medal for anything of value, is prohibited and punishment shall be imprisonment not greater than one year.

This rule, of course, does not apply to the numerous military medals awarded by states, municipalities, and military associations such as the Grand Army of the Republic. America's first military medal was presented by the City of Philadelphia to participants in the 1756 battle in which American/British forces under Colonel John Armstrong defeated French-allied Indian forces at Kittanning, Pennsylvania. Engraved by watchmaker Edward Duffield and struck by silversmith Joseph Richardson Sr., this medal was the forerunner of many historic military medals eagerly sought by collectors. The best source of information for collectors of these items is the many organizations, newspapers, magazines, and Internet sites dedicated to the field of militaria, as opposed to numismatics.

Since there were no coining presses available in 1756, America's first military medal was struck by hand, with a sledgehammer, in the manner of ancient coiners.

The orders and decorations of clubs, fraternal societies, and civic organizations have been excluded from this guide (though souvenir and commemorative pieces of such groups are covered in Part VI). These items frequently employ pinbacks, jewels, enameling, hinged sections, and other features that take them away from the definition of medals and tokens as "coin-like objects." Likewise, slave tags, clothing buttons, badges, dog tags, bracelet charms, watch fobs, and the like, even when struck from dies, are excluded.

Due to space considerations, the huge category of sports medals, awarded for achievement in baseball, football, golf, swimming, Olympic events, and myriad other athletic contests, are excluded. Die-struck medals for feats of marksmanship and archery, and for winners of yacht races and bicycle runs, proliferated toward the end of the 19th century. In the early 20th century, beautifully made kennel-club and horse-show prizes came into vogue. These may appear in a future edition. Another huge category excluded for space reasons is religious medals, such as Catholic medals of St. Christopher, Protestant Sunday school attendance medals, communion tokens, and the broad category of Judaic exonumia.

ORGANIZATION

No one book on U.S. medals and tokens spanning colonial times to the present could cover everything. The Civil War years alone produced almost 11,000 varieties of patriotics and store cards! This guide is an introduction to each category, sampling what it has to offer and suggesting avenues for further exploration

Items are assigned to different parts of the book according to their original purpose. Each part is divided into categories that may have nothing else in common but that shared purpose. Examples in each category are presented chronologically, along with mint and artist information, descriptions, and valuations by grade. Also provided are references to pertinent in-depth publications such as standard catalogs, books, and monographs, and listings of collector organizations for each category.

Part I is devoted to tokens of exchange, accounting, and advertising. What all of these objects have in common is their commercial purpose: they were intended to circulate from hand to hand and be spent like coins, not to be kept or displayed. **Part II** includes tokens and medals that were *not* designed to be exchanged as money. It features souvenirs, historical commemoratives, medals struck for collectors, and so forth. **Part III** is for political-campaign pieces and items related to the U.S. presidency. These can be medals or tokens, might have circulated as money, or could have been held as keepsakes. They have been given their own section because of the strong tradition of collecting these items as a separate group. **Part IV** covers the medal as an art form. **Part V** covers award medals and prizes sponsored by local, national, and international organizations on U.S. soil. **Part VI** introduces a relative newcomer to the numismatic scene, the 20th-century challenge coin, and incorporates older items that have a nature similar to challenge coins, such as firemen's medals, membership medals, and items having a fraternal theme. **Part VII** covers the fascinating arena of tooled and altered coins: items which began as coins of government mints, and were either countermarked, carved, engraved, encased, elongated, or otherwise changed to become something else.

Katherine Jaeger
Shamokin, Pennsylvania

Comments and recommendations for future editions of this book may be addressed to the publisher, Whitman Publishing, Attn: Tokens and Medals, 3101 Clairmont Road, Suite C, Atlanta, GA 30329.

Credits and Acknowledgments

A good number of the tokens and medals illustrated in this book—more than 500 pieces, including many rarities—are from the collections of the American Numismatic Society.

The **American Numismatic Association** library staff offered patient and efficient help. The **American Numismatic Society** provided many medal and token images. The **Buffalo and Erie County Historical Society** provided a medal image. The late **Charles Andes** gave an interview and helpful communications. **Anne Bentley** of the Massachusetts Historical Society made items available for photography, including the gold Manly medal. **David Baldwin** contributed a token image and historical research. **Columbia University** provided images of a 1928 Pulitzer Prize medal. **Keith Baron** shared transportation token images. **Felix Blanco** reviewed parts of the text. Many thanks to **Q. David Bowers** for the opportunity to write this book, great encouragement, and hundreds of images, and for contributing chapter 12. **Kenneth Bressett** reviewed the manuscript, made many helpful comments, and provided token images. **John Coffee** shared information on transportation tokens. **Miguel Colón Ortiz** reviewed parts of the text and provided images. **Paul Cunningham** provided insight, shared tokens for photography, and assisted with valuations. Thanks to **Eugene Daub** for his interview and images. **Ray Dillard** and **Sandra Marxen** provided elongated token images. **Bill Fivaz** contributed to the coverage of hobo nickels. **Clark Fogg** photographed Weinberg collection items. **EvAngelos Frudakis** contributed an interview and images. Thanks to **Rosalie and Zenos Frudakis** for sculptor contacts and encouragement. **Kay O. Freeman** conducted historical research along several lines, especially pertaining to Tiffany & Co. Thanks to **David Gladfelter** for his interview, and many helpful comments and additions. **Ken Goldman** contributed photos of music-machine and amusement tokens. The Carnegie Hero medal photos came from **Hugo Greco**. **Rick Gross** provided token images. **Andrew Harkness** made research contributions. **Rich Hartzog** provided exonumia for photography, including pop-out coins, and shared information from his research. **Steve Hayden** provided valuations, as well as encased coins and various tokens and medals for photography. **Tom Hoffman** provided photographs and valuations for Columbian Exposition elongated coins. **Dick Johnson** graciously and frequently shared his knowledge and research. **R.W. Julian** reviewed the manuscript, made helpful comments, and offered historical additions. **Ellen Kadin** gave editorial advice. **John Kallman** contributed military token images and content. **Sylvia Karges** of the American Numismatic Society staff assisted in many ways. **Les Layser** (Eagle Scout) provided medal images. **Bob Leonard** reviewed the manuscript, gave many helpful comments, and provided tokens for photography. **Harold Levi** reviewed the manuscript and offered helpful comments. **Joseph Levine** gave an interview and provided medal images. **Charles McSorley** shared his knowledge and research, and furnished reference books. **Michael McAllister** contributed challenge-coin information. Thanks to **Clifford Mishler** for his manuscript review, helpful comments, and images of CCC tokens and stickered coins. **Roger Moore** contributed medal images. **Leonard Opanashuk** provided FBI challenge-coin images. **Oded Paz** shared information on pop-out-coin-making technology. **David Pietrowski** provided a medal for photography. **Russ Rulau** shared his knowledge and research, and encouraged my study of medals and tokens in the first place. **Peter G. Scott** contributed information and updates on the Life Saving Benevolent Association. **Joseph Segel** gave an interview, hospitality, and access to multiple research materials. **Stack's Rare Coins** provided many medal and token images. **Forrest Stevens** provided arras tokens for photography. **Elena Stolyarik** facilitated photography of the American Numismatic Society collection. **Greg Susong** shared casino chip images. **Steve Tanenbaum** provided valuations and numerous tokens and medals for photography. **Anthony Terranova** contributed valuations and insight. **Michael Tucker** provided a military challenge coin. **Ute Wartenberg-Kagan** of the American Numismatic Society was very helpful in many ways. **Alan Weinberg** provided numerous tokens and medals for photography. **Howard Weinberger** provided images and valuations for Robbins medals, and reviewed content. **Benjamin Weiss** provided historical medal images. **Cindy Wibker** gave an interview. **Karen Worth** gave an interview.

Market values in this book were compiled by valuations editors **Steve Hayden** and **Steve Tanenbaum,** with assistance mainly from **Anthony Terranova** and **Alan Weinberg.** Valuations assistance also came from **Paul Cunningham.** Others who assisted are listed above.

Thanks to **Tom, Wendy, Fred,** and **Pam Jaeger** for their love and support, and for letting me have the computer *all the time.* **John Whelan** and **Aine Brazil** offered warm hospitality and excellent company, facilitating many research trips in New York City.

I dedicate this book to my parents, George A. and Anne S. Moller.

MY BEST WISHES

My best wishes to you. I hope you enjoy reading the book you now hold in your hands.

In connection with my long-time interest in medals and tokens as well as in other areas of numismatics, I am interested in corresponding with anyone with information to share. In particular, I seek pre-1870 articles, newspaper notices, advertisements, and other ephemera relating to the issuing and distribution of coins, tokens, medals, and paper money.

Special focal points include: Jacob Perkins of Newburyport, Mass. • Documents, ledgers, paper money (rarer varieties), correspondence pertaining to state-chartered and national banks in New Hampshire up to 1900. • Advertisements, trade cards, broadsides, etc., issued by merchants whose names appear on encased postage stamps and Civil War tokens. • Tokens and medalets issued by George Merriam, and ditto for those by John A. Bolen. • 31 mm (approximate) size medalets issued for the numismatic trade 1858–1861, by Robinson, the Lovetts, et al. • Rare varieties of Feuchtwanger tokens. • Wealth of the South tokens (1860) and newspaper advertisements for them, including related campaign tokens. • Tokens, usually nickel size, once used to play music boxes, slot machines with musical attachments, and coin-operated pianos. These usually have inscriptions such as GOOD FOR ONE TUNE, GOOD IN THE PIANO, etc. A new book (successor to my 1975 study) on these is in progress. • Counterstamped large cents 1793–1857 with merchants' names or otherwise identifiable for attribution as to the location of the issuer. • Civil War tokens of rare merchants (I only need a handful); also, separately, rare die combinations with THE PRAIRIE FLOWER obverse. Advertisements, invoices, etc., by CWT issuers such as Stanton, True, Lanphear, Lovett, et al.

*Do you have something interesting to me?
I would love to hear from you!*

Q. David Bowers

c/o Stack's New Hampshire Office
Box 1804 • Wolfeboro, N.H. 03894
e-mail: qdbarchive@metrocast.net

Author of more than 50 books (including by Whitman Publishing LLC); partner in Stack's; fellow of the American Antiquarian Society, American Numismatic Society, and Massachusetts Historical Society; past president of both the American Numismatic Association and the Professional Numismatists Guild.

Introduction: Welcome to Exonumia

Ever since the dawn of coin collecting interest in this country in the mid-19th century, Americans have acquired and studied medals and tokens alongside coins. In 1960, eminent U.S. token cataloger Russell Rulau gave us the name *exonumia* for this companion branch to numismatics. Exonumia encompasses all items related to but outside *(exo-)* the study of coins *(-numia)*. It begins with metallic tokens and medals, but includes all kinds of money-like items, made from many different materials. Such diverse collectibles as die-struck badges and buttons, counterstamped, tooled, and elongated coins, watch fobs, key tags, and stamped ingots fall under its umbrella. Coin jewelry, postage stamps encased in metal, casino chips, play money, and certain bracelet charms are all considered exonumia. So are wooden nickels, cardboard and fiber ration coupons, hard rubber tokens, plaquettes, medalets, art bars, and all manner of identification tags. The main focus of this guide is on "coin-like objects," and the vast majority studied are made of metal.

Why Collect and Study Coin-Like Objects Made of Metal?

Imagine how you might feel if you could have the privilege of examining an original Pulitzer Prize medal. Wouldn't you be touched with awe? This object is not just a pretty disc of gold bearing designs and words. Its illustrious history has given it many levels of meaning. Publisher Joseph Pulitzer's bequest to establish an organization to encourage achievement in journalism and letters was first executed in 1917. Renowned sculptors Daniel Chester French and Augustus Lukeman created the award medal, which was produced by the Medallic Art Company, a medal manufacturer of New York City. The biographies of Pulitzer and the sculptors, and the histories of the Pulitzer organization and the Medallic Art Company, are all facets of this object's story. Then there are the winners—nearly a century of writers whose talent and dedication brought them to the height of achievement in their profession. Examples of awarded Pulitzer Prize medals seldom come into the hands of collectors. But every medal, great and ordinary, contains fascinating stories and layers of meaning, and to collectors, every medal can be as interesting as a Pulitzer.

Medals have been issued to commemorate historic events, to serve as souvenirs of a location or occasion, to honor important individuals, to be offered as diplomatic gifts, and strictly for art's sake. For the past two centuries, at private studios, commercial mints, and the United States Mint, America's greatest engravers and sculptors have been putting their best efforts into the creation of these pleasing and durable works

The Pulitzer committee awards only one struck medal per year, the gold medal for public service. Authors who win Pulitzers in other categories may receive medals privately commissioned by their publishers. Actual size 71 mm.

of art. Collecting medals of all kinds is a practical and affordable way to obtain very fine art by very fine artists, for display in a small space for a relatively small price. You don't need a princely income to boast ownership of 20th-century sculpture by art-world icons the likes of Victor David Brenner, Paul Manship, James Earle Fraser, and Adolph Weinman, or 19th-century engravings by greats such as John Reich, C.C. Wright, Christian Gobrecht, and Anthony Paquet. Affordable medallic art is available at coin shows, at flea-market tables, at estate auctions and antiques fairs, on Internet auction and coin-dealer Web sites, and in the classified sections of hobby newspapers and magazines. There may even be some in your grandpa's cigar box or your mom's curio cabinet.

Tokens have much in common with medals. Certainly, they can feature delightful designs and high-quality workmanship; this is particularly true of 19th-century tokens. They hold the same "history in your hand" mystique, and generate just as many stories for the gratification of research lovers. Tokens, however, were issued as substitutes for money, to be used as a medium of exchange, and as such they do not often bear heavy symbolism or carry profound meanings. Tokens advertised the shops of merchants, carried patriotic or political messages, paid for shows, games, and rides, and even took the place of coins when national economic conditions created coin shortages.

With access to a few token catalogs, you can probably locate interesting issues from every city you have lived in. In the author's case, from Hoboken, New Jersey, came America's first ferry token, that of the 1829 John Stevens steam ferry. From Howell, New Jersey, came the "Howell Works Garden" company-store coppers of the 1830s. There were department-store trade tokens from Linden, New Jersey, and tavern tokens from Shamokin, Pennsylvania. Danville had bus and railroad tokens, and Lock Haven produced a token stamped DISCOVER FLYING IN A PIPER—good for one introductory flying lesson.

While medals tell the stories of statesmen, generals, presidents, scientists, scholars, and heroes, tokens recall ordinary people: their entertainments, travel, work, and wagers; their dining and shopping; the brands of soap they used; even their incarcerations. A collection of tokens and medals together can illustrate the whole scope and sweep of American life. Because they have traditionally been acquired from the same places in the same ways, they have often been cataloged and studied together. But what are the differences between tokens and medals?

MEDAL VS. TOKEN VS. COIN

Many of the items Russell Rulau lists in his indispensable *Standard Catalog of United States Tokens, 1700–1900*, were called *medals* by their makers. For example, he includes a great many store cards, struck as advertising pieces for businesses to hand out like today's business cards. Other pre-1900 items (e.g., membership medals, souvenir medals, and political campaign pieces) had no monetary or exchange value, yet were small, inexpensive, and the same size as the tokens of their era. These items might be collected along with tokens, but should be termed *medalets*.

Throughout history, the uses of coins, tokens, and medals have overlapped somewhat, as this book will show. Most collectors agree with Kenneth Bressett's terminology:

> I always use *token* to mean something that has a value, or is a substitute for some other form of money. *Medals* (in all their various sizes and forms) are commemorative, artistic, or instructive pieces, with no intended monetary value. A *coin* must be authorized by a governing body for use as money.[1]

Factors of quality and size also come into play when defining objects as tokens or medals. Generally, if a great deal of care and expense went into producing the item, if it has high relief and a thick planchet (that is, the blank disc of metal on which the designs are struck), and if it is made of precious metal, it is a medal. Medals almost always featured a high level of workmanship. If the item is thin, lightweight, made of an inexpensive metal or alloy, and bears a simple, single-struck design, it is probably a token.

In his token catalog, Rulau includes items 33 millimeters in diameter and smaller, and most tokens do fall within that range. American medals expert D. Wayne Johnson and political-exonumia specialist Edmund Sullivan set the cutoff between medal and medalet at 25.4 mm (one inch). Broadly speaking, medals are bigger than tokens, and as longtime numismatic writer Clifford Mishler says, "Collectors tend to be expansive of size within their specialty to embrace the issues they favor."

Very large medals—round *medallions* and square or rectangular *plaquettes* (up to eight inches in diameter)—are easy to distinguish from tokens. Some medal dealers stock sculpted bas-relief *plaques* (greater than eight inches in diameter), especially if a smaller version has been struck and sold as a plaquette, but such large items really do not fall into the category of exonumia. They present storage problems for people set up for collecting tokens and medals, and they are too large to have been struck from dies. Exonumists generally take greatest interest in die-struck objects.

How Medals and Tokens were Made

The procedures for designing and producing medals and tokens in the United States have evolved along with technology. In the 18th and 19th centuries, the artisans who produced these objects called themselves *diesinkers*, because they intaglio-engraved or "sank" their designs directly onto the steel of a medal or token die with a sharp instrument. In the 20th century, medallic artists called themselves *sculptors*, and used traditional bas-relief modeling processes to create designs that were later mechanically engraved onto dies.

The Art of Sinking Dies

One of the 19th century's most prolific diesinkers was George H. Lovett of New York City (1824–1894). Alongside two brothers in the same trade, George created his earliest items in 1838, in the workshop of his father, Robert Sr., a renowned stone-seal engraver. Lovett's shop churned out medals honoring George Washington; historical commemorative medals; award medals for colleges, fraternal organizations, fairs, and expositions; souvenir medals; membership medals; merchant tokens; Civil War tokens; lifesaving medals; political campaign medals; and numismatic series designed specifically for sale to collectors. His work was the centerpiece of many an award banquet, anniversary dinner, and exposition finale.

After 45 years in the business, George explained his procedures in an interview with a reporter from the *New York Sun*. In the opening of the piece entitled "The Art of Sinking Dies: A Talk with one of the Oldest New York Medallists," published August 16, 1885, the journalist describes making his way up to a little office on the third floor of a Broadway building. Once inside, the first thing to attract his attention was "a large screw cutter. Near by it lay sheets of white metal, out of which numerous small circular pieces had been cut. Seated at a long, narrow table near the window, and peering through a magnifying glass adjusted so that a circular piece of steel held by clamps was within its focus, was a man busily at work on the steel with a small instrument. His face was partially turned away, but his gray hair showed him to be well advanced in years."

The reporter asked Lovett if there had been any changes in methods over his years in the profession. Said Lovett:

> We formerly cut [our dies] on steel bound with iron, so that if the steel cracked the iron would hold the pieces together. But since then the quality of steel has been greatly improved, so that the binding can be dispensed with. The metal for our work now comes in round or octagon-shaped bars from six to fifteen feet long. We saw off a piece of the bar for each design we have to cut. Medals, of course, require two dies. We strike off the medals on powerful screw presses. Hard metals we are obliged to anneal [and strike] from six to ten times before we can get a clear impression.

"In what metals do you generally strike off your medals?" asked the man from the *Sun*.

> Most commonly in white metal, which closely resembles silver and retains its luster for a long time. For presidential campaigns or any important celebration, die sinkers get out little white metal medals with the busts of the candidates or some design commemorative of the celebration. We strike these medals off by the thousands. They are hawked about on the street and sold by fancy dealers. You will see many Grant medals between now and the General's funeral. Thousands of medals were struck off for the Evacuation Day Centennial, but the rain spoiled the sale. Besides white metal we use bronze, or more properly stated, bronze-stained copper. The precious metals are not often called for.

When the reporter asked Lovett if he devoted much time to the striking of medals, he replied:

> Yes. When the medal is a fine one and careful work is required, I rarely strike off more than four or five a day. But that kind of work isn't called for very often now. The demand for medals has increased wonderfully, but people want them small and cheap. Work has to be done quickly now. Orders are coming in from all over the country, I am constantly sinking dies for medals to be distributed as prizes at agricultural fairs, college commencements, musical prize contests, and prize drills, or to be sold as memorials at centennial celebrations. Here for instance, is a medal I have cut for the Alabama State Fair. The obverse represents the arms of the state, the reverse a scene on a cotton plantation. The wreath around it is composed of wheat, corn and rice. Formerly, orders were fewer, but the designs were more elaborate. Most of the designs that come to me now, I can cut in a week—many of them in a day or two.
>
> Contrast that with the two months and a half I spent on the cable medal. That medal was ordered by the [New York] Chamber of Commerce to commemorate the successful laying of the Field [Atlantic telegraph] cable. I should think that $10,000 worth of gold was put into the limited number of gold copies struck off. They were presented to Mr. Field, the officers of the vessels which took part in laying the cable, and others prominently concerned in the enterprise. The obverse showed a globe between the figures of America and Britannia, holding each an end of the cable. At the feet of Britannia was the British lion, and at the feet of America the American eagle. The reverse showed the vessels parting in mid-ocean and an appropriate inscription.

"Is there any favorite line of designs?" asked the reporter. "Formerly, it was considered the thing to put a head of Washington on a medal if you could find any pretext for so doing. Now, the arms of the state in which the fair or celebration occurs is most frequently included in the designs." The journalist closed his interview with the statement, "Mr. Lovett thinks that the Government, in allowing orders for medals to be taken at the Mint, competes unfairly with diesinkers." (George's brother, Robert Lovett Jr., and others who operated out of the Mint's hometown of Philadelphia, must have felt particularly bitter about this state of affairs. Private medal producers, led by New York's Medallic Art Co. in 1908 and 1909, continued to lobby against this practice until the Mint ceased taking new commercial orders in 1910, and ceased striking commercial medals from "grandfathered" dies in the late 1940s.)[2]

Lovett's own screw press, surrounded by goddesses, is seen on this 1850 silver award medal of the Ohio State Board of Agriculture.

Lovett also felt strongly about the public perception of the die-sinking profession as a whole. He told the reporter: "You see, people go to these jewelry firms with their orders for medals, and the jewelers employ us. People, at least city people, don't seem to know that there are such beings as die-sinkers in existence." Often these firms did not allow the artists to sign their medals. His April 1894 obituary in the *American Journal of Numismatics* told how Lovett believed that diesinkers deserved better exposure, and in March 1873 had issued a circular amplifying his belief that "medal die sinking is a distinct branch of art."

Jewelry firms were not the only middlemen in the chain between the artist and the final customer. Coin dealers sometimes conceived designs for special medals or tokens they thought might attract buyers, and commissioned diesinkers to create them. Silverware manufacturers employed diesinkers to make dies for designs applied to spoon shanks. Die engravers took work where they could find it, and during slowdowns in demand for fancy medals, they struck tokens for upcoming political campaigns, as Lovett described above.

Overstriking was one way for diesinkers to economize. If a particular line of tokens and medals had not sold out, the diesinker could reuse the remainder as planchets for another line of the same size, rather than cutting new planchets from fresh metal stock. Often the artisans intentionally worked to the same sizes as existing U.S. and foreign coins, in order to be able to use old, worn-out coins as planchets. In other instances, coins were used to provide convenient planchets in metals not normally used, to create items for collectors. As an example, Civil War token dies were often impressed on copper-nickel Indian Head cents and Liberty Seated silver dimes to create special pieces. Collectors find it particularly gratifying when they detect a previously unnoticed "ghost" of a former design in the un-engraved field on a token or medal, because what may have started out as a common piece may now be classed as a rarity, by virtue of its being overstruck. (Today, it is illegal in the United States to manufacture any coin-like item in a size and weight identical to that of federal money.)

Another way diesinkers generated extra income from completed work was *die muling*, which created a fun aspect of medal and token collecting. Tokens and medals require two dies: an *obverse*, which is considered the front, and a *reverse*, which is considered the back. Reusing obverses and reverses in pairings different from the original was common. For example, in 1864 George Lovett muled a single 19 mm obverse token die bearing a bust of Abraham Lincoln, with 20 different reverse dies.[3] Some had reverses endorsing Lincoln as a candidate for the 1864 presidential election. Some had patriotic-themed reverses, originally for use as one-cent coin substitutes during the Civil War. Others had reverses advertising the shops of particular merchants, and were used both as advertising pieces and money substitutes. One token even had a reverse bearing a palm tree and YNGENIO ECUADOR, the name of a Cuban sugar plantation. This was struck to fill the coinage needs of the plantation's hacienda workers.

Diesinkers who were partners, like Bale and Smith of New York, often combined their artistic talents on a single object, with a reverse engraved by one artist and an obverse by the other.

Each diesinker had a selection of stock reverse dies to pair with made-to-order merchant advertising on the obverse. When a craze for collecting portraits of George Washington broke out in 1860 and 1861, diesinkers paired every imaginable obverse with their portraits of Washington. They even reused old obverses bearing busts of other presidents or statesmen, to create two-headed medals. From this period, it is not uncommon to find the works of different, competing diesinkers combined on one piece.

The Sculpted Medal

The greatest change in the medal-production process came with the introduction of a new technology: the reducing lathe. This mechanical concept, originally developed by a Frenchman named Contamin for button manufacture, was employed at the U.S. Mint for coining as early as 1837. It came into use for medallic applications in 1899, after various refinements in the technology resulted in a machine known as the *Janvier pantograph*. This invention by Frenchman Victor Janvier changed the medal maker's art from one of intaglio engraving on steel to one of bas-relief modeling in clay.

Janvier's machine copied the design from a nine-inch or larger model, called a *galvano*, onto a hub of any desired smaller size.[4] As the machine slowly rotated the two items side by side, a tracing point "read" the contours of the galvano, while a cutting point produced matching contours on the hub. The galvano was made the same way as any bas-relief sculpture in metal: First, the design was modeled in clay, wax, or plastilene. Then, a plaster negative was made of the model. The negative served as the form for the casting in metal, which became the galvano.

Prior to this innovation, the diesinker was the artist. Afterward, the sculptor was the artist. Die engraving still was no simple laborer's task—it required great delicacy and finesse, and a trained engraver's hand—but the artistic shift went toward the sculptor. This change also meant the creator of a medal did not need to own a medal press and annealing forge and all the other components of an engraver's shop. He or she could work anywhere, even devoting the better part of a career to other forms of sculpture, and have medal-making as a sideline. The artist's direct start-to-finish oversight was limited to the production of the galvano, a process that took place at a foundry and was already familiar to any classically trained sculptor. There was no longer a need for the artist's involvement with the actual striking of the medals in their final size. This function was taken over by commercial and government minting facilities with large staffs, multiple powered coining presses, and a highly efficient striking capacity.

According to present-day sculptor Eugene Daub of California, who is well known for his medallic work:

Since the advent of Janvier's machine, the process has not evolved or changed very much. Leonard Baskin gave an excellent lecture for the ANA [American Numismatic Association] in the 1980s, speaking of the "damage" to the art wrought by the pantograph: in terms of medal and coin design, what works on a nine-inch model will not necessarily work on a 39 mm (two-inch) medal or an even smaller coin. From ancient times through the 19th century, artists conceived and executed their designs in the same size as the final struck medal. The products of 20th-century mints often looked crowded or busy, because the reduction in size changed the effect of the design elements. The best medal sculptors have taken this into account.[5]

The computer age is revolutionizing the medal-making process once again. Daub says he "can count on one hand" the few remaining sculptors, like himself, who prefer to use entirely traditional sculpture methods to make models for medals. Free-form virtual-sculpture software programs are available to create designs, and several of the artists who submitted designs for the U.S. Mint's 50 States Quarters® Program created them on a computer. Says Daub, "I believe we are on the edge of the next metamorphosis of medal sculpting methods and technology."

Eugene Daub stands before the clay model for his 2005 Lewis and Clark relief panel entitled "We Proceeded On." Later cast in bronze, the 16x7–foot panel was installed on the wall of the Senate Chambers of the Montana State Capitol. To raise funds for historic preservation, the Montana Historical Society sold a limited edition of 75 bronze plaques in 14x9–inch size.

Obverse and reverse of Daub's Lewis and Clark bicentennial medallion. This bears the same design as on the medallions at the bottom center of the larger relief panel, in a diameter of 74 mm.

HISTORY AND MATERIAL CULTURE

For many people, the fun of investigating the provenance of medals and tokens—their historical background, production statistics, and resale history—is the main inspiration behind building a collection. Today's collector has access to a wonderful array of Internet research tools. Search engines can trace the terms borne on an item's legends and inscriptions, the name of the diesinker or sculptor who designed it, the person or firm who published it, and the event or purpose that inspired it. Web sites sponsored by museums, libraries, historical societies, genealogists, and numismatists furnish every sort of historical data, and point the way to America's vast collections of manuscript materials. Member-supported group web sites devoted to each particular collecting category unite like-minded people from around the world to archive their research. Some display crisp digital images of privately held items that might otherwise never be published. Best of all are the ever-growing online databases of full-text searchable historical documents that formerly could be seen only in libraries.

Not only is it informative to read historical manuscripts to learn more about tokens and medals, but it can also be informative to "read" tokens and medals to learn more about history. In the absence of written records, objects and physical remains—called *material culture*—provide concrete evidence about the past. In his 1988 book *Tippecanoe and Trinkets Too*, Roger Fischer lamented the fact that political historians traditionally confined their study to official documents, campaign literature, and the like, while ignoring the rich material culture of political campaigns. Someone who studies campaign tokens, for example, might be aware that there were not one but three people who made five separate runs for executive office. The obvious is Franklin D. Roosevelt, and the not so obvious, Richard M. Nixon and Eugene Debs.[6] The typical young American today remembers Richard Nixon for just one thing: his resignation over the Watergate scandal—and remembers Eugene Debs, perhaps, not at all. The student of campaign tokens and presidential medals has more information.

Mardi Gras "doubloons" offer an example of how historic events can affect the popularity of numismatic items. Before Hurricane Katrina flooded the city of New Orleans in 2005, there had been a long-established tradition of issuing souvenir tokens for the annual Mardi Gras celebrations. The best way to acquire examples was by attending the Fat Tuesday parades and catching them as they were thrown from floats into the delirious crowds. These colorful anodized aluminum pieces issued by individual groups of parade organizers, or *krewes*, were also available to less adventurous collectors at shops around the city. In either case, collecting them was a matter of "catch as catch can." The tokens in this series have taken on a new significance in the aftermath of the destruction of New Orleans. All the issues struck for the celebration of February 28, 2006, sold out before the date arrived.

THE COLLECTOR'S FOCUS

Civil War token collector Cindy Wibker of Florida says, "My theory is, someone either has the 'collecting gene' or they don't. Most collectors I know have a variety of collections, myself included." Many numismatists who start out collecting coins may branch out into exonumia. David Gladfelter of New Jersey, who collects and writes about coins, medals, tokens, and bank notes, says, "When one field starts to feel saturated to me, because so much research has been done by so many people, and so many things have been published on the subject, I may strike off in a new direction. I enjoy breaking new ground." For traditional coin collectors, the field of exonumia represents an attractive road less traveled. But there are so many types, categories, historical eras, purposes, and price ranges represented, it is generally most rewarding to select a collecting specialty.

The ways in which people specialize in medals differ somewhat from the ways they specialize in tokens.

Specializing in Medals

By Topic. Members of the Storer family of Massachusetts were medal collectors par excellence. In 1896, Horatio Robinson Storer published an article in *The Numismatist* titled "The Advantages of Specialization in Numismatics." "To become expert in any direction," he said, "it is necessary to have served an apprenticeship as an indiscriminate student and as a free collector . . . but to labor with any expectation of adding to numismatic knowledge, one must progressively confine oneself more and more to a single series of coins and medals." Horatio was a Harvard-educated physician who collected world coins, medals, and tokens having to do with the subject of medicine. He held portrait medals of physicians from Aesculapius and Hippocrates to Linnaeus, Jenner, and Pasteur, and famous nurses such as Clara Barton and Florence Nightingale, as well as tokens advertising pharmacist shops and patent medicines. His collection featured Red Cross medals, souvenir medals from hospital groundbreaking ceremonies, and medical school achievement awards. In 1931, Horatio's son Malcolm published the collection in a 1,200-page volume, *Medicina in Nummis*. This book even had token categories arranged alphabetically by disease (gonorrhea, gout, hernia, idiocy, indigestion. . .).

Malcolm's own specialized collecting was just as intense as his father's. As coins and medals curator of the Massachusetts Historical Society, he spent a decade furiously collecting Massachusetts pieces. Of special interest in his book on the series were the complete works of two renowned diesinkers, John Adams Bolen of Springfield and Joseph H. Merriam of Boston. The U.S. Naval Academy Museum in Annapolis, Maryland, is the repository for another of Malcolm's collections, consisting of 1,210 maritime pieces featuring boats from triremes to tall ships to steamships, obtained from more than 30 countries and reaching back as far as 342 B.C. Malcolm's older brother John Humphries Storer specialized in the numismatics of Mexico. The collections of all three Storers demonstrate how medals and tokens fit in with coins, when gathered in pursuit of a particular topic.

By Category. Some collectors prefer to accumulate medals that belong to a single category, such as souvenir medals or Indian peace medals. Collector Andrew Harkness of New York has focused on prize medals issued by the 19th-century agricultural societies that sponsored farmers' and mechanics' fairs around the country. The workmanship on some of these beautiful gold, silver, and bronze awards is among the finest this nation has produced. The category of World's Fair medals, particularly those of the 1893 Columbian Exposition in Chicago, which celebrated the 400th anniversary of the discovery of America, has recently seen an upsurge in collector interest.

By Set or Series. According to D. Wayne Johnson on the web site of the Medal Collectors of America, the first United States medals issued as a group were the trio of Seasons medals (The Shepherd, The Farmer, and The Family). These were Indian peace medals honoring George Washington and struck in Birmingham, England, in 1798. A *set* of medals has come to be defined as "two or more medals issued at once, which belong together." Joseph Sansom of Philadelphia launched the first American medal series in 1805, with his medal honoring GEORGE WASHINGTON, C.C.A.U.S.— Commander in Chief of the United States. Sansom's series was to be named "The Medallic History of the Revolution," but only four medals were completed by engraver John Reich before he was hired as assistant engraver at the U.S. Mint and could not complete the commissions. Private diesinker Charles Cushing Wright, of New York created the next series, from 1847 to 1849, for the American Art Union. These medals bore portraits of painters John Trumbull, Washington Allston, and Gilbert Stuart, but only three were issued before the art union was dissolved. The term *series* afterward came to be defined as "medals of a similar theme, issued over time, which belong together." In the 19th century Augustus B. Sage produced historical medals in series, and in the 20th-century the master of commemorative medal series was the Franklin Mint. Through a combination of effective advertising and a quality silver Proof medallic line called "coin medals," this firm drove an upwelling of collector interest in commemoratives between 1964 and 1980. Certain other pieces fall into series of their own accord. Examples on the national level are the Indian peace medals struck by the U.S. Mint; on the local level are Mardi Gras doubloons.

By Size. Ever since 1912, when New York City coin dealer Thomas L. Elder referred to the 1904 Louisiana Purchase Exposition souvenir medal as a *so-called dollar* in a catalog, some people have collected souvenir and commemorative medals by size. That is, they collected all souvenir medal and token items close in size to a silver dollar. In 1963, Harold Hibler and Charles Kappen "wrote the book" on so-called dollars. They confined their listing to items measuring between 33 and 45 mm (1-5/16 and 1-3/4 inches), and their research included a large number of commemorative and exposition medals, as well as Bryan money[7] and other coin-like items.

By Medallography. Collecting one example each of a single artist's entire medallic output is a possibility for those interested in art medals, or the career of a particular die-sinker. In the case of George H. Lovett, that could be an ambitious undertaking. In the case of Augustus Saint-Gaudens or Victor David Brenner, it could be an expensive one. For nearly every maker, there is no truly complete listing. New discoveries are often made, this being part of the challenge of collecting such a specialty, which might involve coins as well as medals and tokens.

Specializing in Tokens

By Geography. An easy way to begin a token collection is by concentrating on the items most readily available in one's home region. Coin shows, flea markets, yard sales, and favorite dealers are all within driving distance, and for trading, other collectors specializing in regional items will be in proximity too. There may even be a local coin club to join, to add social enjoyment to the hobby. Some collectors have endeavored to collect all the tokens pertaining to their home city, while others have broadened their search to include their entire home state. When a truly dedicated token collector devotes a long time to such a pursuit, he or she may decide to publish the result. At the turn of the 21st century, more than half the states of the U.S. were represented with catalogs, books, or at least monographs on their tokens. These publications constitute remarkable material culture records of the commerce of a region: in many cases, the only vestige left of the existence, name, and location of a long-defunct business or frontier ghost town is the tokens that were once struck to advertise it.

By Type. A beautiful aspect of token collecting is the multiplicity of types in which to specialize, such as transportation tokens, saloon tokens, theater tokens, dairy tokens, and magician's tokens, to name just a few.

By Historical Era. The fourth edition (2004) of Russell Rulau's *Standard Catalog of U.S. Tokens, 1700–1900,* classifies tokens chronologically, in the following groups: Early American Tokens (1694–1832), Hard Times Tokens (1832–1844), U.S. Merchant Tokens (1845–1860), Civil War Store Cards (1861–1865), Patriotic Civil War Tokens (1861–1865), U.S. Trade Tokens (1866–1889), and Tokens of the Gay Nineties (1890–1900). To date, no one has attempted to write a standard token catalog for the 20th century. Between 1700 and 1900, tokens were struck by hand, one at a time, so the output of each producer was limited by considerations of time and manpower. In the 20th century, with its mushrooming population and mechanically enhanced token production capacity, output increased exponentially, and cataloging of 20th century tokens generally must be done by category rather than by era.

By Topic. Some collectors choose a favorite topic, and buy everything they can find pertaining to that topic. Most collections of this nature, like the Storer collections mentioned above, feature coins and medals as well as tokens. For example, Princeton University houses the collections of Arthur L. Newman, who assembled more than 800 pieces on the theme of aviation, and C.C. Vermeule III, who gathered hundreds of die-struck objects depicting dogs. Horses, railroads, ships, slavery, and countless other themes are available to the imaginative collector.

Aspects of Shopping for Medals and Tokens

Generally, collectors acquire medals one at time. That is, they weigh all the factors that go into their decision to buy, on a case-by-case basis. The same is true for those who collect 19th-century and earlier tokens. Twentieth-century tokens, on the other hand, may be found in mixed lots, by the pound! Your medal collection might begin with a piece already in your hands, such as something you inherited or long ago found yourself compelled to buy at a flea market. For the person armed with patience and information, a collection of great quality can have such a modest origin. Cindy Wibker, for example, had always been interested in Civil War history, and was very excited when she purchased her first Civil War token in 1975. It was a common piece with an attempted drill hole, and she paid $1. She continued over the next 20 years to amass a marvelous collection of more than 4,000 Civil War tokens.

Opinions vary as to the best ways to shop for medals and tokens. One of David Gladfelter's favorite categories is what he calls numismatic self-portraits, or items designed by a diesinker or bank-note engraver to advertise his own business, and offered as a sample of his best output. Gladfelter's foremost sources for this collection are trusted dealers who understand what he wants and have the means to locate what he needs. He also enjoys trading with other collectors and bidding at auctions, either live, by mail, or online. He attends an occasional coin show, and keeps an eye on the classified advertising in numismatic periodicals. One place Gladfelter does not buy medals and tokens is on eBay. He is not comfortable dealing with "invisible" strangers in this marketplace, although he does know of some familiar dealers who have relocated their entire face-to-face businesses to eBay, and he would feel comfortable patronizing them.

Virginia presidential-medals dealer Joseph Levine has no problem with the idea of eBay shopping, and in fact recommends it as an easy way to acquire medals, for buyers who understand the dangers of anonymous shopping and take precautions. "Fakes and forgeries are not a significant problem in the medals market, so the risk of getting burned that way is still low. Interest in art medals, such as those of the Society of Medalists, has doubled since the advent of eBay. It used to be quite a challenge to fill in a missing piece from that series. The Internet has made it much easier, and has brought new exposure to all the sculptors who participated. Formerly, collecting medals was mostly a pastime for people who already collected coins and had long-established relationships with dealers. They gave these dealers their 'want lists' and waited patiently for their desired articles to be found. They also subscribed to numismatic periodicals, reviewed auction catalogs, and made bids by mail. The Internet has made it possible for any newcomer to begin collecting medals and tokens right away." Levine does not feel threatened by amateur eBay sellers as his competition, however. "There are so many new collectors out there because of the Internet, and a fresh customer base is constantly being generated. People will always need the expertise of an experienced dealer."

Elizabeth McSorley, daughter and partner of political campaign token and medal dealer Charles McSorley of New Jersey, says television programs about antiques have also been a factor in building today's customer base. "TV shows like *Antiques Road Show* on PBS and *Cash in the Attic* on BBC have made the public a lot more savvy. People know that those old items they found in great-grandpa's trunk are worth something. In the past, people would bring their cache to the nearest dealer, and accept whatever the dealer offered for them. Today, they bring it to us with a demand for the same price they saw on TV—not understanding that the prices quoted on TV shows are for *retail*, not what a dealer might pay for them." The average dealer in medals and tokens might only pay 50% of retail, increasing or decreasing that percentage based on the anticipated demand for an object, its condition and rarity, and the general desirability of the piece.

Education

The one piece of collecting advice offered by every knowledgeable numismatic writer, dealer, and collector is to *be informed*. Study. Become an expert in your category. There is a reason the phrase "buy the book before the coin" has become hackneyed: it is good advice. The accomplished collector of medals and tokens is a collector of numismatic books by default. Online, a world of free numismatic information is available, and Internet auction sites are a good place to learn about prices. Says Joseph Levine, "You can get a good idea of the going rates in your area of interest by tracking the eBay sales for a few months, and recording your observations of prices realized." Online and printed auction catalogs are also very informative in this regard, if you obtain the corresponding listing of hammer prices after the sale.

A subscription to a current numismatic newspaper, magazine, or e-zine is another essential to the educated collector, and many like to review numismatic periodicals of yesteryear, to take advantage of prior research. David Gladfelter says, "I stay abreast of what is out there, so if I see a piece that is unknown to me, I am likely to bid on it. If I don't know about it, then probably few others do, and there may be little competition for the piece. Even the foremost authorities can't know everything about the vast world of tokens. The best thing to do is read everything that has been published on your category. Be informed, study and learn, know what you are looking at, and know what you are looking for." Cindy Wibker advises, "If you're knowledgeable and willing to invest time and make an effort to visit local coin shops, flea markets, etc., you can pick up some bargains. Dealers do not have the time required to learn all areas of numismatics. In the 1970s and '80s it was fairly common to visit a coin show or coin shop and pick up a rare token at a common price."

Market Valuations and Grading

What are the factors affecting the cost of medals and tokens?

Popularity. In his book *The Expert's Guide to Collecting and Investing in Rare Coins*,[8] Q. David Bowers emphasizes the maxim, "Popularity is the single most important determinant of value." A hypothetical example: Forty years ago, collector "Jack" began collecting Civil War tokens because he liked them, the category contained a huge number of fascinating varieties, and the cost was well suited to his budget. He could find these in lots or singly, and he seldom had to pay more than $5 or $10 apiece for them. Soon, an expert published a useful and authoritative catalog. Now Jack had a roadmap to his category, but so did Jill and Bob and a host of newcomers. Hobby journalists noticed the swelling interest in Civil War tokens and published stories about them. The stories seduced more new collectors. Dealers began making special efforts to acquire and advertise the type, marking them up somewhat to recoup the extra effort and "strike while the iron is hot."

Presto! Civil War tokens began selling at $10 to $50 apiece, with rarities going far higher. A good way to determine how popular a particular series may be is to research the question, "How many books and articles have been published about this category?"

A glance at the photos and valuations in this guide can give an indication of relative popularity. For example, in chapter 1, ordinary good-for tokens from Western states and territories show far higher prices than do Eastern pieces of the same style, from the same decades. The differential is linked to the popularity of Western issues, sought by a large pool of eager collectors. Similarly, a token issued by a saloon or brothel may cost more than a similar one issued by a grocer, because there are more collectors of such issues.

Rarity. When there is a multitude of collectors vying in the same category, rarity becomes very important. As a rule, common pieces are priced lower, scarcer ones higher, and unique pieces highest. In the study of medals, rarity is quantifiable—based on known mintages and estimations of attrition of the original population through destruction and museum acquisition. Painstaking historical assessment of the number of times a medal type has appeared on the market also helps the determination. Rarity of tokens can be more difficult to establish. Token manufacturers seldom kept records of the quantities they struck, and the sudden appearance of hoards on the market is not uncommon. (Populations of early American and Hard Times tokens are fairly well fixed, however.) Often, the standard reference book for a particular token category will express rarity in a numerical range of R1–R8, with R1 pieces being the most common, and R8 pieces being unique.

Instances of historic token and medal rarities reaching five-figure prices are increasing in frequency, propelled by the series of record-smashing sales of the John J. Ford Jr. exonumia collections (held in 2005–2007 by Stack's Rare Coins). The highest prices obtained for U.S. medal and token rarities, however, are nowhere near the astounding rates being paid for U.S. coin rarities. Record prices include those set for the gold version of Augustus Saint-Gaudens's 1889 George Washington inauguration centennial medal ($391,000) and for an 1849 gold congressional medal presented to Major General Zachary Taylor ($460,000). In comparison, for U.S. coin rarities, auction records stand in the multiple millions of dollars. Currently, some contemporary medals of George Washington, Indian peace medals, and some presidential inaugural medals of the U.S. Mint are fetching wonderful sums.[9] This guide includes plenty of examples of the fascinating, historic, and sometimes unique pieces that cost a fortune to own, and seldom make their appearance on the market. It also illustrates hundreds of more commonly obtainable items. But, as experienced collector Bob Leonard advises, "Always keep chasing the rarities in your specialty, even if prices rise a lot. It is the 'keys' that dealers want to buy, not the commoner pieces. I have followed this plan up to the limit of my purse, even buying things on layaway from time to time."

Condition. The price of a medal or token is also tied to its condition. The rarest medal in the most popular series won't be a pearl of great price if it bears deep scratches, dents, abrasions, stains, corrosion, extensive wear, or unsightly polishing marks. Yet, in categories of high demand with a low population, exonumists will seriously consider just about any example, if it is one their collection lacks. When a better example becomes available, they can always replace the poorer one. Generally, token and medal collectors do not worry quite as much about condition as coin collectors, and hence the grading scales they employ may be somewhat less complicated. The scale chosen for this guide needed to be a simple catch-all system that could be applied to many collecting categories. The three grades our valuations editors chose are:

F (Fine)—The piece exhibits moderate to considerable even wear. The entire design is bold with an overall pleasing appearance.

EF (Extremely Fine)—Light wear is evident, but all lettering and most of the elements and details of the design are clearly evident.

MS-63 (Average Mint State or Uncirculated)—The piece shows no sign of wear but may have some distracting contact marks or blemishes in prime focal areas. Luster may be impaired.

When an item is unlikely to be found in a particular grade, the chart column for that grade is left blank.

In their pricing discussions, the valuations editors of this book (Steve Tanenbaum and Steve Hayden, assisted mainly by Anthony Terranova and Alan Weinberg) sometimes ascribed different cost estimates to the same piece. According to Weinberg:

> This is not at all unusual. Exonumia is not like coins or currency: medals and tokens cannot be "looked up" as to value in a certain condition. They are, in the main, far rarer than most coins, and they don't trade nearly as often. Value is still very much seat-of-your-pants instinct, gut feeling, and experience with the item. For instance, a certain unique medal came up for auction in 2007. I went to the auction feeling it could be acquired for $75,000. Others had guessed $50,000 to $75,000. (It had auctioned for $10,000 in 1984.) I surveyed the opinion of two highly regarded experts in the field. Independently, they both said it could go as high as $150,000. As the auction commenced and lots were bringing two to three times what everyone thought they were worth, I knew that even $150,000 was not going to take it. The piece sold for $316,250.

Are Tokens and Medals a Good Investment?

As Q. David Bowers is fond of saying, "Time vindicates most numismatic purchase decisions." Token and medal collectors of the past have generally done well when selling their collections, and there have been spectacular, well-publicized cases of yesterday's minor outlay turning into today's major return. Exonumia collectors' main motivation, however, is to enrich their lives, not their pocketbooks. Cindy Wibker cautions, "Generally medals do increase in value, but I would never use them as an investment tool. I'd probably do better with the stock market. I did make a profit when I sold my Civil War token collection. However, if I had invested that money in conventional ways over the same 20-year period, my profit might have been much greater. I collect for the love of the hobby and the 'thrill of the hunt.' If I happen to make a monetary profit, I consider that a bonus. If I look at the time I had invested in building and cataloging and organizing the collection versus the profit realized, it would be somewhere along the lines of 'slave labor.' I consider my thousands of hours of enjoyment as part of my profit, as I love every minute of it."

Joseph Segel of Pennsylvania founded the wildly successful Franklin Mint in 1964, as the General Numismatics Corporation. Over the next 16 years, his company sold hundreds of millions of dollars' worth of commemorative medals in the United States and abroad. Very early in the history of the mint, Segel realized that promoting commemorative medals as an investment was not a good idea, and imbued his marketing staff with the following maxim, which he calls "Segel's Law": *The more any product is promoted as an investment, the less likely it is to become a good investment, because too many people will buy it primarily to sell it for a profit rather than to hold on to it for its historical, educational, or aesthetic value.* Segel hired more accomplished sculptors than any minter in modern history. America's most distinguished authorities chose the subjects commemorated on the coin medals, whenever those subjects were not chosen by popular vote of the collectors themselves. The highest level of engraving, metallurgical, and minting technologies, and the brightest talents of the industry, were employed at every phase of production. Yet today, the inherent interest of Franklin Mint medals—as examples of sculptural medallic art—is overlooked, because too many people evaluate them on the basis of their resale value alone. Segel notes, "Collectors of all types of collectibles continue to operate on the flawed logic that they will eventually be able to sell their collections for a big profit."

Joseph Segel, left, and Charles Andes, right, share a smile after relating to the author their memories of operating the Franklin Mint. Andes passed away in August 2006.

Counterfeits, Restrikes, Copies, and Fantasies

Counterfeits. As described above, 19th-century and earlier medals took a great deal of time and effort to produce. Considerable engraving talent and a great deal of experience with the striking process were required to produce just one medal of quality. This level of difficulty has protected important medals from counterfeiting by striking from new dies. Counterfeits have, however, been made by the casting method. To an educated collector, cast copies make very poor imitations of struck originals. Before 1900, people with the means and determination to risk the legal penalties for counterfeiting hand-struck items generally focused on the more lucrative arena of coins. Single-struck tokens of simple design were, and still are, easy enough to counterfeit. There are instances of slave tags, Confederate dog tags, and Ku Klux Klan membership tokens being faked to dupe collectors, but most garage-shop "slug" producers favor production of casino tokens for slot machines and other tokens having a cash value.

Restrikes. It was the custom of some late-19th-century and early-20th-century coin dealers to buy original medal and token dies from the estates of deceased diesinkers, for the purpose of making restrikes for collectors. Their new versions usually did not mimic the original metallic content of a piece. For example, if the original token was made of copper, the dealer might strike his copies in silver or bronze. The purpose of making restrikes was not to deceive, but to make more examples of a scarce medal or token available to those who desired it. Identifying whether an old token or medal is an original or a later restrike can be difficult for today's collectors, and requires a certain amount of expertise.

Copies. Electrotyping—the process of copying an engraved original by electrically depositing metals from solutions of their salts—was in use in the United States by the 1850s. It infuriated diesinkers that there was no law preventing these very good copies of their artwork from being made and sold by others.[10] In January 1858, New York City's engravers and diesinkers banded together to place a memorial before the U.S. Congress to outlaw this practice, but in June 1869, the trade journal *Manufacturer and Builder* published a detailed "how-to" on the well-established art of electrotyping, so obviously it was still legal and widely used as of that time. Records of the U.S. Patent Office of the 1880s show that many diesinkers were by then applying for design patents on individual pieces, to protect their work from imitators. Reputable dealers will list 19th-century electrotype copies of medals as such. Collectors may buy them as lower-priced but nearly contemporary examples of the medals they seek, and with experience, can recognize an electrotype copy on sight.

Today, it is legal to manufacture an exact replica of any old medal or token, only as long as the word COPY is incused on the obverse or reverse (not on the edge) in a non-removable way. Near-replicas without the word COPY may also be made, as long as some other distinguishing variation from the original exists, such as in size, signature, or some design element.

Fantasies. Another way for producers of new exonumia products to avoid breaking any laws is by minting "fantasies," or objects that never existed in the past but give the appearance of being old. For the beginning collector, fantasies are the predominant pitfall to be avoided. Among the more common types are brothel tokens, saloon tokens, sheriff badges, and others with Wild West themes, and items of the Confederacy such as rebel-army dog tags, slave tags, merchant tokens, watch fobs, and the like. Fantasies of Southern bank notes and Confederate coinage are also plentiful.

Recording, Storing, and Cleaning Medals and Tokens

Note: See the *Expert's Guide to Collecting and Investing in Rare Coins* (Bowers) for detailed recommendations on these topics.

Human memory is imperfect, so it is best to document medal and token purchases as they happen. Methods vary from collector to collector. Some carry pocket-sized notebooks to coin shows and dealers' shops, and jot down on the spot the date, seller's name, and price paid. Some use numismatic computer software programs that have data-entry blanks for the name, type, metal, measurements, grade, rarity, verbal description, creator, creation date, and purchase information for each item. From these stored files, users can generate various kinds of statistical reports, or look up specific items in a matter of a few keystrokes. Other collectors design their own computer filing systems, or use looseleaf binders, recording entries in pencil so additions or removals can easily be made. Another traditional system is to create an index card for each item. Cards can be alphabetized or arranged according to category, type, diesinker, or geography, as desired. The means by which purchases are recorded is not crucial: what does matter is that they be recorded, with as much detail as possible.

Museum staffs go to great lengths to provide stable, secure environments for their numismatic holdings. They handle objects by the edge only, wearing cotton gloves to prevent scratches and fingerprints and to keep skin oils off metallic surfaces. They carefully regulate temperature, humidity, and light conditions to prevent oxidation, corrosion, and staining. The collector at home must provide, at the least, an environment that excludes bright light and extremes of temperature and humidity. For many years in the United States, the vogue among collectors was custom-made wooden storage cabinets with multiple velvet-lined, divided drawers. Unfortunately, many hardwoods can give off acid fumes that damage metal surfaces, and many velvets contain acidic dyes that have the same effect. Today, the accepted best fabrics for storing medals are undyed cotton and acid-free paper. Many collectors use 2x2–inch or larger paper envelopes on which they can jot notes about the object, and wrap their pieces in acid-free tissue or cotton sleeves before sliding them into the envelopes.

Plastics are safe for coin storage, too—with the exception of PVC, which should never be used for long-term numismatic storage. Many dealers display medals and tokens in 2x2–inch or larger square cardboard sleeves with round central windows of transparent Mylar®, for customers to view the objects without being able to touch them directly. Others use all-plastic "flips." These may be slid into looseleaf binder pages (similar to those used by postcard or sports-card collectors), or oblong cardboard boxes for upright storage, as in a card file. Professional grading services may place a medal or token into a sealed plastic holder nicknamed a *slab*, on which is printed the grading information.

Before attempting to clean a token or medal, make sure to educate yourself about the damage that can be done by improper cleaning. Many dipping, polishing, and rubbing processes used by amateur collectors can do more harm than good to an object and its resale value. Metal surfaces are far more delicate than the average person thinks. Any cleaning process can affect them adversely, and what is safe for one metal might damage another. Polishing is generally a no-no; even the gentlest of metal polishes remove a small amount of surface metal, and many will leave scratches. Cleaning of numismatic items should be attempted only after thorough research.

For the Collector of the Future

In the 21st century, the production of tokens as a money substitute might altogether cease. Many highway authorities, for their bridge, tunnel, and turnpike tolls, have switched from tokens to monthly passes or computerized identification-plate readers. Likewise, operators of city transit systems are switching to machine-readable fare cards—Boston's Massachusetts Bay Transportation Authority token was a casualty in 2007. Winners at casino slot machines no longer get the thrill of hearing a torrent of tokens or coins pouring out of the chute—now a redeemable total prints out on a paper slip. Manufacturers of video arcade games, token-operated pool tables, and the like are phasing out tokens as well—and users might do well to put some tokens away for the collector of the future.

The awarding of prize medals is following a similar path. Sponsors of agricultural fairs long ago switched from expensive gold, silver, and bronze medals to blue, red, and white ribbons as awards, and many long-established prize committees now award sums of cash instead of medals. A recent recipient of the Valentine Mott Medal of New York University, awarded since 1856, received $1,000 and a framed paper certificate. Medals are still given for sporting competitions—any five-year-old on a midget soccer team has one—but these are cheap, mass-produced trinkets that are unlikely to have any after-market value (unless the five-year-old grows up to be an international soccer star).

Fortunately, many truly important awards, like the Pulitzer Prize or the Carnegie Hero award, still involve the conferring of medals. Few of these, however, make it into the marketplace. According to Joseph Levine, they are "scarce as hen's teeth," and usually when he sees them, it is for appraisal prior to their donation to museums or libraries. Those not earmarked for donation will take a few generations to enter the marketplace. The Library of Congress "Living Legend" award for contributions to U.S. popular culture was inaugurated in the year 2000. The Springarn Medal of the NAACP, the Gottheil Medal for Services to American Jewry, the Dartmouth Medal of the American Library Association, and virtually any other major prize kicked off in the 20th century, may become collector's prizes in the 21st.

As stated multiple times above, the key to success and enjoyment as a medal and token collector is education. It is hoped that the information in this guide will be the starting point for a long and pleasurable journey of learning, through the rich and exciting world of exonumia.

How to Use This Book

As discussed in the preface, this book is divided into seven parts and twenty-eight chapters. The parts organize tokens and medals by their original functions, and the chapters discuss particular categories or types.

Determining Obverse and Reverse. In the study of coins, the portrait or pictorial side is considered the obverse. This is also true for award and commemorative medals, which generally have pictorial elements on one side and text elements on the other. In the study of merchant tokens, however, the side showing the merchant or business name is considered the obverse—so, very often, the pictorial side is the reverse. This rule is followed for countermarked coins, love tokens, hobo nickels, and similar items—the side with the marking or carving is always considered the obverse. Photo pairs in this book show the obverse on the left, and reverse on the right. Many items are uniface (that is, having a blank reverse), while others have the same design on both sides; in such cases, only one side is shown.

Image Sizes. Most objects in this book are shown at actual size, up to a diameter limit of 60 mm. For space considerations, all larger items are shown at 60 mm, with their actual sizes noted beneath the images.

Dates and Date Ranges. In many cases, the date on a token or medal is not its date of issue. Dates given in the charts are for year of issue. When the exact year is not known, the decade of issue is supplied. Most categories in this book are arranged chronologically. Hard Times and Civil War tokens are exceptions: they are arranged according to the catalog numbers taken from their standard references.

Material Abbreviations. In the coverage of Civil War Tokens, the metal column is eliminated because that information is included as part of the Fuld number (see chapter 3 for specifics). In the rest of the book, the following abbreviations are used.

Alum	aluminum	HR	hard rubber or vulcanite
Br	brass	Leath	leather
Bz	bronze	Mir	mirror
Card	cardboard	Nick	nickel
Cell	celluloid	Pew	pewter
Cop	copper	Silv	silver
C-N	copper-nickel	Ster	sterling silver
Enam	enamel	Svd Br	silvered brass
GS	German silver	Tin	tin
Gilt Br	gilded brass	WM	white metal
Gold	gold		

Part I
TOKENS OF EXCHANGE, ACCOUNTING, AND ADVERTISING

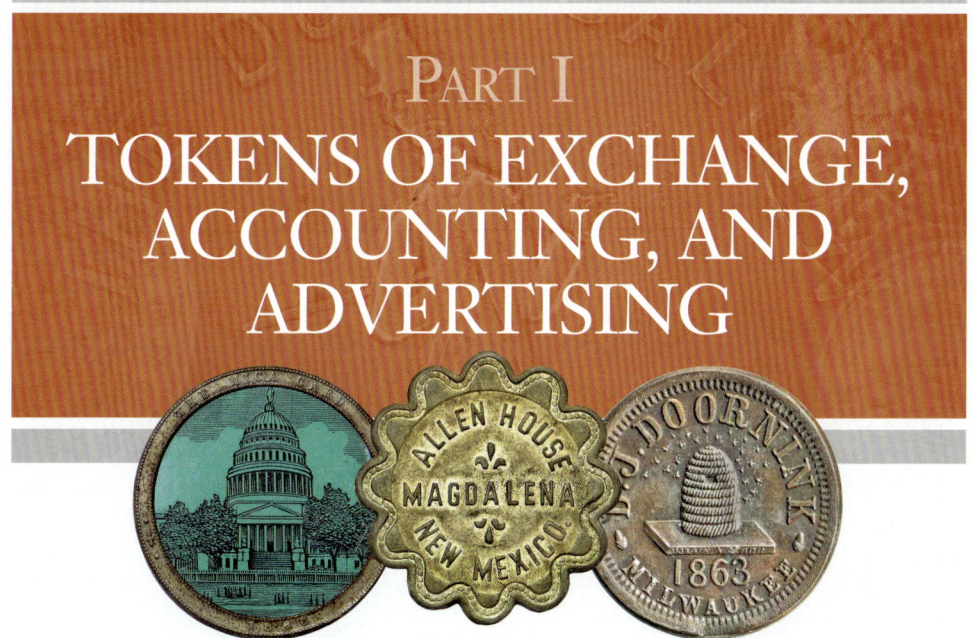

Of the multitude of token types issued in the United States, the vast majority were intended to have an exchange or monetary value, and most tokens listed in Part I have this characteristic. Some have a fixed value stated on the token, such as $1 or GOOD FOR 5¢. Some only imply their value, by being of a size and composition similar to a particular legal-tender coin, like the large-cent-sized copper tokens of the Hard Times era. Some tokens held values that were never coined as federal money, such as the 1920s 8¢ Rappahannock Bridge toll token of Fredericksburg, Virginia. Some made change for the smallest denomination coined, such as the sales-tax tokens issued by 12 states in the 1930s, in denominations of 1/4¢ and 1/5¢. Others had a value in commodities or services rather than a specific amount of money, such as the tavern token that was "good for one drink" or the drayage check that was "good for one 2-horse load."

Many tokens had no set monetary denomination, especially those struck after the Industrial Revolution, with its turnstiles, fare boxes, vending machines, music machines, and other coin-fed devices that accepted mass-produced tokens of a single size. Business owners could assign any values they wanted to non-denominated tokens, selling them, for example, at 20 for $1, 10 for $1, or even $1 apiece. Many transportation tokens, admission pass tokens, and amusement tokens are non-denominated.

Diesinkers and mints used inexpensive rather than precious metals, because the key to profitability in tokens was that the intrinsic value be considerably less than the face value. In the 19th century, copper, brass, white metal, German silver (a nickel alloy containing no silver), pewter, and, starting in the 1890s, aluminum were the favored materials. Other inexpensive compositions were alloys of iron, hardened rubber (vulcanite), cardboard, celluloid, and, rarely, lead. In the 20th century, Bakelite, plastic, bimetallic combinations, and brightly colored tints of anodized aluminum made their appearance. Precious-metal tokens do exist, but they were generally presentation pieces, collector strikes, or attempts at private coinage.

Purposes of These Tokens

Tokens in Part I are grouped into chapters according to purpose, beginning with merchant tokens, which had a dual benefit. The primary advantage was to keep customers returning to the one establishment where the token held value. To attract people to use them in the first place, merchants sold them in quantity at a small discount from face value. The secondary advantage was in advertising, to circulate the company name from hand to hand. Store cards were a type that did not have a fixed value stated on them.

Merchants who did not issue struck tokens often made their own by counterstamping their company or product name onto circulating coins. In the 20th century, merchant advertising was applied to coins in three other ways: with encasements, caps, and stickers. All merchant advertising on coins is covered in Part VII.

In the Hard Times era (1832 to 1844) and during the Civil War (1861 to 1865), merchant tokens took on a new purpose. During both of these financially unstable periods in American history, tokens circulated alongside (or, often, in place of) U.S. coins, and were spent as money. All kinds proliferated, and for a time direct service as small money was their primary purpose. Lyman Low made the first attempt at exhaustive cataloging of Hard Times tokens in 1886, and George Hetrich and Julius Guttag did the same for Civil War tokens in 1924. Since then, collectors have considered these series separate unto themselves, and Part I adheres to tradition by treating them individually in chapters 2 and 3.

Tokens have substituted for coins for other reasons. In the Western territories, fur trappers and Indian traders used tokens at their trading posts, because federal coinage was not readily available there. In other areas remote from banks and mercantile activity, such as logging camps deep in the forest or mining camps high in the mountains, tokens served as wages for workers to redeem at on-site supply outlets. Token coinage could also limit a certain population's spending to a particular area. Issuers with large workforces, such as plantation farmers or coal-mining companies, could advance wages in paper scrip and tokens (to make change for the scrip), and thereby confine spending to their own company-held stores. Military base commissaries, and even some boys' academies issued token coinage on the same principle.

Another type of token-based wage was the agricultural "picker check." Workers received one token for each crop unit harvested. At day's or week's end, they redeemed their tokens for wages or spent them at general stores that accepted them. Farmers tallied the paid-out tokens to inventory crop production and assess their workers' efficiency. Food-preparation industries such as fruit, vegetable, and seafood canneries, as well as meat-packing plants, used token tallies.

Tokens also worked as a security measure. Adult and juvenile prison wages were payable in tokens, giving incarcerated people no opportunity to employ their cash outside the penal system's control. Tokens were issued to workers at construction and mine sites, as inventory "checks" for individual sticks of dynamite or lots of gunpowder, assuring that no worker could obtain more explosive than needed for a particular job. Libraries issued checks for books, and hotels checks for towels, to ensure these items were returned at a patron's departure from the premises. Today, tokens discourage theft from outdoor vending machines, turnstiles, automatic car washes, and the like, because crowbar-wielding thieves generally want legal-tender money. In casinos, the use of chips and tokens precludes having gaming tables piled high with vulnerable cash. (And casino operators know well that gamblers will more readily place a $50 chip into play than a $50 bill, because it just doesn't look like real money!)

In Alaska, during the Great Depression, the government paid relocated farm workers in scrip and tokens. During World War II, tokens were employed in government rationing. Later, they aided in the regulation of welfare benefits, when food-stamp tokens were issued to make change for food stamps. Today, public welfare agencies may still distribute standard transportation tokens (bus, subway, etc.) to fund an employed welfare recipient's passage to work.

Flexible and fixed-value tokens have been used to sell products and inspire brand loyalty with scores of imaginative promotions. Starting in the 1920s, milk-route customers preferred dairies that issued tokens, because they did not need to worry about having the correct change for the milkman—they could simply leave a pre-purchased "good for one quart" token in the box for the dawn delivery. In the 1930s, consumers found tokens wrapped with bars of soap. Like today's newspaper coupons, these could be presented for a discount on future purchases of that brand, or for a free bar. An effective 1940s promotion of Atlanta, Georgia, placed a token inside each package of Capitola Flour, which was good for a free movie at participating theaters. Knowing this, what homemaker would buy token-free flour? In 2005, a token hunt was used to promote a children's book. Author Michael Stadther hid 12 tokens around the United States, leaving clues to their locations in his book *A Treasure's Trove*. Anyone who could find and return one of the tokens could exchange it for a piece of "treasure" (i.e., a gem-encrusted piece of jewelry) valued at $25,000. All 12 tokens were eventually found by the readers, and Stadther penned a sequel detailing the finders' stories.

1

MERCHANT TOKENS

This chapter covers merchant advertising on tokens. Merchant advertising on *coins*—including counterstamped, encased, capped, and stickered coins—is covered in part VII.

EARLY AMERICA, THROUGH 1831

In spite of the fact that there was no unified monetary system in the American colonies, and private, colonial, and European coin issues reigned until well after the United States authorized its first official coinage in 1792, few tokens that can strictly be defined as *merchant* issues were struck before 1800. Logically, merchant tokens should have proliferated when small coins were in short supply, but metals exploration and production capabilities were still in their infancy on the under-developed continent. Of the tokens that did exist, many were struck in Europe. There is a certain amount of debate regarding early American issues, as to whether each should rightly be called a token, a "private coin," or an authorized coin. Some items, like the New England and Carolina elephant tokens, the Kentucky Myddelton tokens, and the Franklin Press tokens, though they have American themes, did not circulate in America. Others, such as the tin American Plantations tokens of 1688, met the definition of tokens in that their intrinsic value was far less than their stated value, but they were authorized for official use as coins. The 1783 Annapolis, Maryland, store cards of silversmith John Chalmers, in values of threepence, sixpence, and one shilling, though clearly intended to circulate as money,[11] might be considered merchant issues because they bear a proprietor's name. Like Ephraim Brasher's famous gold doubloons or Standish Barry's Baltimore silver threepence, however, these pieces' precious-metal content precludes any legitimate classification as tokens.

Some exonumists identify the earliest domestic token as the 1714 Gloucester Courthouse token of Virginia, issued for an unknown purpose by the business partnership of Christopher Rigault, a courthouse-area landowner, and a Mr. Dawson.[12] Only two genuine specimens of this token are known. Other candidates are the well-known but rare Higley coppers from Connecticut, of 1737 to 1739, the product of copper mines at Simsbury, near the town of Granby. (The famous Mott token, once thought to be New York's earliest merchant issue, was in fact a 19th-century anniversary issue.) It wasn't until the 1790s that the first absolutely certain-to-be-merchant-token issues appeared. That decade saw a heightened flow of immigrants to the new republic, creating a demand for small change that could not quite be met by the coinage of the fledgling Mint. For example, the city of New York nearly quadrupled in population from 33,131 in 1790 to 123,706 in 1800, and the widely circulated 1794–1795 tokens of the India trading firm of Talbot, Allum, and Lee (struck in Birmingham, England) helped meet the increased coinage need.

Tokens giving admission to public events likely made their first appearance in 1793, in Philadelphia. George Washington himself may have spent a copper Ricketts's Circus token to see the equestrian antics of Scotsman Bill Ricketts, when he attended an April 1793 performance. (Ricketts's brick amphitheater had been built in 1792, and was the home of what has been credited as America's first circus. It featured an acrobat, a wire walker, and Tom Sully the English clown. Original Ricketts tokens are exceedingly rare, though restrikes made later at the U.S. Mint are more common.)[13]

Other wonderful tokens survive from the period when America's first theaters were being constructed. In 1796, William E. Burton of Philadelphia issued a "season ticket" engraved on silver, holed for suspension from a cord or chain, which could be shown at the door of his New National Theater to admit two people to its varied musical and dramatic offerings. In New York, the simple Park Theater ADMIT and PAID tokens of 1817 were followed by the beautiful oval "subscriber passes" for Rathbone & Fitch, proprietors of New York's Castle Garden in 1825. (These latter were the work of New York City diesinker Richard Trested.)

Another form of entertainment just being established in America was the museum. Charles Willson Peale, the renowned Philadelphia painter, opened his first museum in his own home in 1784. His collection of paintings and natural-history exhibits kept growing, prompting him to seek larger quarters, and in 1821, he lodged it at the State House and called it Peale's Philadelphia Museum. At this time he arranged for copper admission tokens, bearing his own portrait and engraved by Christian Gobrecht, to be struck at the U.S. Mint. In 1825, Peale's son Rubens established the Parthenon museum on lower Broadway in New York, and also issued copper admission tokens. At the Parthenon, visitors could see paintings and sculptures, snakes, lizards, a stuffed rhinoceros, and a real Egyptian mummy. They experienced the novelties of being weighed and "electrified" (i.e., charged with static electricity), and could also hear the comic recitals of a Dr. Valentine.[14]

Overall, merchant-token production was scant and issues were scattered until America's own diesinkers finally came to the fore in the late 1820s. The famous Scovill token plant at Waterbury, Connecticut, evolved from origins as a button maker in the early part of the 19th century, and embarked on the token trade in 1829, at first employing a succession of experienced European diesinkers. In New York, the unofficial center of the profession, Richard Trested established a shop in 1823, succeeded in 1829 by the partnership of James Bale and Charles C. Wright. Robert Lovett Sr. also opened a New York shop in the mid-1820s. The prominence of the U.S. Mint's home city, Philadelphia, in the engraving arts was established early in the century by greats such as John Reich and Christian Gobrecht, but their emphasis, when not making coins, was on medals.

THE HARD TIMES ERA: 1832–1844

Though Hard Times store-card issues are really part of the continuous production of merchant types, they are covered separately, in chapter 2, in deference to long-established collecting tradition.

MERCHANT ISSUES OF 1845–1860

In the period between the national monetary crises of the Hard Times era and the Civil War, there was no emergency need for merchant tokens to circulate as money, but a regular demand for them as promotional pieces sustained a workforce of token producers. Diesinkers' hearts' desire may have been in producing exquisite medals, but their bread and butter was in these everyday versions of their art. By 1860, diesinkers had set up shop not only in New York and Waterbury, but also in Newark, Springfield (Massachusetts), Philadelphia, Boston, Baltimore, Cincinnati, St. Louis, Chicago, and Milwaukee. For the most part, Southern merchants sent their token orders to Waterbury, New York, or Philadelphia, until the Civil War severed North/South business relationships. Collectors prize this period's merchant token output for its variety and quality of pleasing designs, emanating from the shops of greats such as William Bridgens, Frederick B. Smith, F.C. Key, Robert Lovett Jr., Joseph Merriam, and Benjamin True.

Another group having a marked impact on the nature of the token trade after 1857 were the handful of coin dealers who aggressively built up the token- and medal-collecting hobby. In order to offer the widest possible assortment and price range in their shops, they designed new tokens, ordered restrikes from old token dies in precious as well as common metals, and muled previously unmatched dies in new combinations. Dealers such as Edward Cogan, Augustus B. Sage, and William Idler were leaders in this effort.[15] The diesinkers, as they began to experience the new demand from collectors, also made restrikes and mulings to sell at their shops. The availability of uncirculated examples of mid-19th-century merchant tokens today is a testament to this phenomenon. Chapter 12, contributed by Q. David Bowers, explores these issues in some detail.

The period from 1793 to 1857 was ruled by copper tokens imitating the 27 mm size of the federal large cent. In the 1850s, Joseph Merriam of Boston produced a variety of numbered "counter checks" in this size, for use at restaurants and dining saloons throughout New England. Patrons received a numbered check from their waiter, for presentation (after dinner) to the cashier, who held the corresponding bill.

In 1857, federal one-cent coins were reduced in size from 27 to 19 mm, and token diameters followed suit. The California Gold Rush of 1849 had its impact on token manufacture, just as it had on all aspects of American commerce, ushering in brass as a popular composition, due to its resemblance to the color of gold. The Scovill plant struck many brass trade tokens imitating $10 gold pieces. The lucrative fur trade carried on throughout the U.S. territories created another new type of token, as hunters and trappers handed in their small animal pelts and buffalo hides for a token apiece, to be spent at trading posts that rarely remained in one location long enough for official federal coinage issues to reach them.

The Civil War: 1861–1865

Though Civil War store card issues are really part of the continuous production of merchant types, they are covered separately, in chapter 3, in deference to long-established collecting tradition.

After the Civil War

Even though federal law of 1864 forbade the manufacture of tokens in one- and two-cent denominations, the use of tokens continued to flourish in trade. They simply got larger: most post-war tokens were greater than 26 mm in diameter, and were valued higher than 2¢. In addition to struck metal types, the year 1866 saw the emergence of merchant "shell cards," which featured a paper advertisement encased in an embossed brass frame, similar in principle to campaign ferrotypes (chapter 14) and encased postage stamps (chapter 3). These most often imitated the Liberty Seated and silver trade dollars in size and design, and remained in use until about 1876. Some were brass on both sides and completely hollow, while others had a cardboard stiffener between the layers. Shell cards are scarce today, because the metal on which they were embossed was so thin that they were quite fragile.

During and after Reconstruction, two main forces drove token production: the "good for" gimmick, and the westward expansion of American settlement. Between 1866 and 1900, saloons across the country began issuing tokens good for drinks. Services like a shave or a shoeshine, a hotel room for the night, or a waltz in a dance hall could also be had for a token, along with commodities such as restaurant meals, blocks of ice, loaves of bread, and even barrels of slop. Advertising tokens bearing perpetual calendars or the Lord's Prayer on the reverse were popular as pocket pieces. The 1890s saw the emergence of the general-store token. Throughout America's farm belt, general-store owners paid farmers in tokens for deliveries of produce. Totaling paid-out tokens was an easy way for shopkeepers to keep track of inventory, and it ensured that farmers would do their shopping at the issuing store. These remote locations were usually short of cash and also relied on barter ("trading" at the store often really meant that).[16]

The inability of the U.S. Treasury to keep up, initially, with distributing coinage to its booming territories was a factor in the emergence of territorial merchant token issues. Those stamped with the initials of a territory, such as A.T. for Arizona Territory or D.T. for Dakota Territory, are considered highly desirable. Post trader tokens, used by Indian traders as well as civilian merchants at military forts, are also hotly pursued. All 19th-century Western-themed tokens, including saloon, brothel, stagecoach, cattle and sheep ranch, ghost town, and fur-trading types, bring a premium over the average trade token of the Midwest or East. Unfortunately, many modern fantasy tokens on Wild West themes, sold as souvenirs at tourist sites, exist to confuse collectors.[17] (At least, a major reference on authentic saloon tokens is now available: Al Erickson's 2008 *Saloon Tokens of the United States*.)

Beginning in the 1870s, token manufacturers increased production by means of powered presses and stamping machines, and offered stock merchant styles in denominations of 2-1/2¢, 5¢, 10¢, 25¢, 50¢, and $1, with a blank space in the center for placement of the issuer's personalized data. The proprietor's initials or business name were then stamped in by means of a die insert. Many issues of the same metal, size, and design can only be differentiated by a cryptic set of letters or a surname. Collectors get a charge of satisfaction when they manage, through researching old business directories and census records, to attribute a "maverick" (an otherwise unidentifiable token) to a particular location. The Brunswick token, named after the Brunswick-Balke-Collender billiard-table manufacturer of Chicago that produced them most widely, caught fire in the 1870s and remained popular for decades. Tokens of this type, made from stock dies in dozens of varieties, advertised the names of taverns, hotels, billiards suppliers, and others likely to place their products in bars or restaurants, and the majority were "good for 1 drink." Generally, the merchant's name appeared on the obverse and an image of a pool table and the manufacturer's name appeared on the reverse. Jacob Strahle & Co. of San Francisco and Charles Pick & Co. of Chicago were other manufacturers of this type.

In the 1890s, aluminum took its place alongside other token materials. When it was first discovered at the beginning of the 19th century, this metal was more expensive than gold, but the development of a cheap, efficient smelting process in 1888 made it competitive with brass. Some token issuers mentioned their switch to aluminum with pride, like brewer A. Fitger & Co. of Duluth, Minnesota, whose 1893 token read "ALUMINUM / IS COMING TO THE FRONT / AND SO IS / A. FITGER & CO'S / CELEBRATED / LAGER BEER." In 1892 and 1893, many merchants had special dollar-size shop cards struck for the Chicago Columbian Exposition. Diesinkers went all-out with showy designs and splendid execution on these pieces.

In the meantime, shapes of tokens multiplied, with hexagonal, oval, star, cloverleaf, heart, square, and figural shapes making their appearance. Edges now were sometimes scalloped or star-pointed, and reeding of edges had disappeared entirely. Collectors navigating the oceans of available late-19th-century trade tokens will pay a premium for the ornate and beautiful designs that reached their apex in the 1880s and 1890s, over the plain, incuse-only or single-sided types that began to appear in ever larger numbers in the same period. Even simple pictorial tokens usually fetch better prices than those only bearing lettering. Unusual shapes and denominations may bring a premium, as may those struck in odd materials such as vulcanite or celluloid.

In November 1900, ex-silver miner Joseph Lesher of Victor, Colorado, opened a new mint to strike a silver $1 merchant-token series that has scored a very big hit with today's collectors; his rare pieces sell in the four- and five-figure range. Lesher, who owned a silver mine, wanted to increase the use of silver in commerce, and figured that minting silver money for local use was one way to facilitate this. Merchants who supported his views bought and circulated his octagonal "Lesher Referendum" dollars made from stock dies, adding their business names in the space provided. His handsome tokens were among the last of the handmade, custom-designed pieces that had their heyday in the 19th century.

THE 20TH CENTURY AND TODAY

By the turn of the 20th century, many token mints employed mechanized die engraving. Token issues multiplied along with the population of retailers and service providers demanding them. It can be a challenge to distinguish the mass-produced tokens of 1900 to 1920 from those of the late-19th century, because the same stock dies may have been used for decades of production.[18] One die-struck innovation commonly found in the early 20th century was the charge coin. This was the antecedent of today's credit card, and operated just like one. Patrons were issued a tag, often oval, rectangular, or some other off-round shape (and sometimes quite beautiful), holed for suspension from a key or watch chain. Their subscriber numbers would be engraved or punched onto this coin, which they showed whenever they made a purchase or bought a service at their favorite department store, taxi company, or clothier. The clerk or driver would then keep account of charges in order to bill the client monthly. These continued in popularity into the 1950s.

The tokens of the "Ingle System" of a Dayton, Ohio, manufacturer first appeared in 1909, and remained in use at general stores across the United States through 1928. Most issues of this series in values from 1¢ to $1 were dispensed to farm, mine, and factory workers from a special Ingle-made cash register on payday. They could only be spent at the stores that accepted them, and in many cases, the stores were named on the tokens.

The year 1919 brought a tough break for token producers, when passage of the Volstead Act launched Prohibition and killed demand for metal tavern and saloon tokens good for one drink. The scramble to come up with alternative tasks for idled presses brought an increase in the "good luck" and souvenir token types covered in Part II. During the Great Depression, retailers' demand for advertising tokens decreased along with their operating capital, but government agencies (such as the U.S. Civilian Conservation Corps) and states requiring sales tax tokens became new issuers. The metal shortages of World War II, and the passage of a 1944 federal law prohibiting tokens of the same size as any federal coin, further reduced metallic merchant-token production. Taverns switched to plastic drink tokens, general stores and supermarkets favored newspaper coupons and trading stamps, and many merchants looking for traditional token-based advertising switched to using wooden nickels (which had begun as a novelty in Tenino, Washington, during the Great Depression).

In 1974, elite jeweler Tiffany & Co. revived the "good for" idea with an elegant twist: they issued gift tokens (called "Tiffany Money") in sterling silver and vermeil in denominations of $25, $50, and $100, to be presented in a velvet drawstring pouch. Like many Tiffany products, each "coin" bore a four-digit security number registered to the owner-to-be, to deter counterfeiting or redemption of stolen coins. Brooks Brothers' clothiers sponsored a similar promotion in 1979. The occasional firm today issues merchant tokens as a novelty, but the practice is not followed widely enough to make them the everyday part of life they once were. Most metal token producers now rely extensively on their transportation, vending machine, and amusement token types to satisfy production quotas. One group of business people who can be counted on to continue production of advertising tokens is coin dealers. Their issues are populous enough to make up a whole collectible series.

In this chapter merchant tokens are listed by state, followed by mention of the best-known reference book for each state (if no specialized reference is listed, Russell Rulau's *Standard Catalog of U.S. Tokens, 1700–1900*, is recommended).

MERCHANT TOKENS, BY STATE

Alabama

Alaska

RULAU #	ISSUER	YEAR	METAL	COMMENTARY	F	EF	MS-63
ALABAMA							
Al-Bi-7	Dude Saloon	1880s	GS	Only seven specimens are known of this famous token	$400	$600	$1,000
	Profile Store	1900s	Br	Cotton mill store tokens came in eight denominations	—	45	—
ALASKA							
	Idaho Saloon	1898	WM	Landmark Skagway tavern tokens came in 50 and 25 cents, too	—	50	—
	Copper Block Buffet	1907	Ni/Gold	Lower denominations, in copper, have no gold nugget!	600	800	1,750

References: Roy J. Wood, *Alabama Trade Tokens*, 1995; Ron Benice, *Alaska Tokens*, El Cajon, CA, 1994.

Alaska (continued)

Arizona

RULAU #	ISSUER	YEAR	METAL	COMMENTARY	F	EF	MS-63
ALASKA (continued)							
	Fairbanks Chamber of Commerce	1959	Gilt Bz	A promotional statehood commemorative "dollar"	—	$2	$3
ARIZONA							
Wil 2	The Curio	1893	Alum	James Benham's Curio: tourist shop and Indian museum	$200	600	—
Wcx 7	Willcox Hotel	1899	Br	The bust is Admiral Dewey, not proprietor Otto Moore	600	2,500	—
	Del Monte	1910s	Br	Tavern good-for of a ghost town vacated in the 1950s	—	15	30
	Wolfville Western Days	1933	Cop	A "so-called dollar" of a Tucscon community event	—	8	20
	Eagle Eye Rare Coins	2000	Cop	Tucson dealer employs coin design on promotional piece	—	—	2

References: Ron Benice, *Alaska Tokens*, El Cajon, CA, 1994; Hal Birt, *Arizona Tokens*, 1994.

Merchant Tokens 29

Arkansas

California

RULAU #	ISSUER	YEAR	METAL	COMMENTARY	F	EF	MS-63
ARKANSAS							
	J.E. Morgan (4)	1890s	Cop	Morgan was a Ouachita County wholesaler	—	$25	—
	J.E. Morgan (40)	1890s	Br	Denominations in multiples of 4 for the company store	—	25	—
CALIFORNIA							
Calif 3	Berenhart, Jacoby & Co.	1851	Br	Goods arrived by ship as seen on this store card	$150	400	$800
	Barry & Patten	1868	Br	Shell card of a "Great Tonic" patent medicine	—	500	750
Sfo-55	Pitts'g Alum. Co.	1898	Alum	Admiral Dewey and aluminum: two sensations of 1898	50	125	300
Sfo-17	Art Saloon	1899	Bz	The wooden statue can still be seen at Ripley's San Francisco museum	50	100	250
	Barrister Cigars	1899	WM	Dewey's likeness was also used to sell cigars	—	25	60
	Dawson's Book Shop	1988	Cop	Los Angeles bookstore token was a novelty in 1988	—	—	2

References: Tom Robinson, *Arkansas Merchant Tokens*, 1986; Charles V. Kappen, *California Tokens*, 1986.

Colorado

RULAU #	ISSUER	YEAR	METAL	COMMENTARY	F	EF	MS-63
COLORADO							
Den 1	The Bull's Head	1891	Alum	Touting the benefits of aluminum	$250	$850	—
Dur 7	John Kellenberger	1890s	Alum	A city landmark on a liquor/tobacco good-for	350	1,000	—
Ldv 7	Pioneer Saloon	1890s	Alum	The monogram is PAG, but the identity is unknown	300	750	—
	Miss Olga	1900s	Gilt Br	Shell card of a Denver bawdy house, with madam's portrait	200	500	$750
	Lesher / Sam Cohen	1901	Silv	Under Pike's Peak, scene of famous silver strike	3,000	5,000	9,000
	Lesher / George Mullen*	1901	Silv	Made of .950 fine silver	2,000	3,500	7,000
Ldv 9	The Saratoga	1901	Alum	Saloons aplenty appeared in Leadville during the silver boom	20	30	—

Reference: Stuart Pritchard, *Guide to Colorado Merchant Tokens*, 2004.
* Voted No. 18 in *100 Greatest American Medals and Tokens* (Jaeger/Bowers).

Merchant Tokens

Connecticut

RULAU #	ISSUER	YEAR	METAL	COMMENTARY	F	EF	MS-63
CONNECTICUT							
Conn 1	Higley*	1737	Cop	Three-pence, from Dr. Samuel Higley's own copper mine	$60,000	$150,000	—
Conn 27a	Waterbury House	1820s	Br	Unique six-cent denomination from New Haven	1,500	3,500	—
	Rogers & Bro.	1860s	Silv	The trademark of the famed sterling manufacturer	—	100	$150
	Wheeler & Wilson's	1860s	Br	Bridgeport manufacturer issued a rare ferrotype storecard	—	750	1,250
	Hartford Livestock Insurance	1867	Br	Handsome shell card of Hartford insurer	—	350	500
	Fuller's Hair Restorative	1868	Br	Shell card of Waterbury's miracle cure for baldness	—	500	750
	Holmes, Booth & Haydens	1870s	Svd Br	Waterbury firm operated 1853–1922	—	250	400
	O.S. Platt	1887	Bz	Bridgeport metalworker likely made his own dies	—	150	—

Reference: Howard Knickerbocker, *New England Merchant Tokens*, knic.com/tokens
* Voted No. 7 in *100 Greatest American Medals and Tokens* (Jaeger/Bowers). Planchet quality within grade is an important factor in the value of colonial tokens.

Connecticut *(continued)*

Delaware

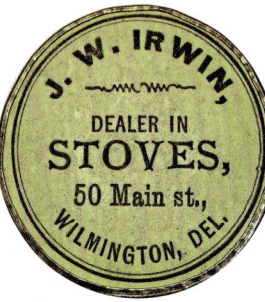

RULAU #	ISSUER	YEAR	METAL	COMMENTARY	F	EF	MS-63
CONNECTICUT *(continued)*							
	John Ridolph	1890s	Alum	Yalies likely hung out at this New Haven pool hall	$300	$500	—
	New England Brewing Co.	1908	Bz	Uniface spinner of a Hartford brewer (1897–1922)	—	30	$50
	Hartford State Bank	1908	Silv	Anniversary promotion by Whitehead and Hoag	3	4	5
DELAWARE							
	J.W. Irwin	1868	Br	Shell card of a Wilmington stove dealer	—	500	750
Mfd 2	Central Hotel	1890s	Br	A crudely made good-for, nonetheless rare	100	110	—
Wil 20	F.F. Slocomb	1900	Alum	Advertising piece made by Quint of Philadelphia	—	125	200
	Colonial Stamp & Coin	1976	Bz	Bicentennial-year store card of R. and A. Pugliese	—	—	2

References: Howard Knickerbocker, *New England Merchant Tokens*, knic.com/tokens; William T. Miller, *Delaware Merchant Tokens*, 1988.

Merchant Tokens

District of Columbia

Florida

Georgia

RULAU #	ISSUER	YEAR	METAL	COMMENTARY	F	EF	MS-63
DISTRICT OF COLUMBIA							
DC-Wa 23	Schwarzenberg's	1910s	Br	Orchestrion: a large automatic music machine	—	$100	$125
FLORIDA							
Fla 3	Governor Zespedes	1789	Silv	St. Augustine; Carlos IV proclamation medalet was a cast	$200,000*	—	—
	Doty & Stowe, Jacksonville	1901	Alum	Token featured Pohalski's Cubana Cigars	—	200	300
	H.C. Sullivan	1920s	Alum	Company store at Frostproof, in the heart of citrus country	—	35	—
	Murray Biscuit Co.	1976	Bz	National cookie maker with a plant in Miami	—	—	2
	David Alexander	1985	Silv	Metallic business card handed out at Christmas	—	—	5
GEORGIA							
	Bolshaw & Silva	1868	Br	Purveying wares for Savannah cooking and dining	—	400	600

References: David E. Schenckman, *Merchant Trade Tokens of Washington, D.C.*, 1982; C.R. Clark, *Florida Trade Tokens*, 1980; R.D. and J.D. Partin, *Georgia Trade Tokens*, 1990.
* Seldom seen on the market. This price was realized in the John J. Ford collection sale, Part XIII, Lot 660.

Georgia *(continued)*

Hawaii

Idaho

Illinois

RULAU #	ISSUER	YEAR	METAL	COMMENTARY	F	EF	MS-63
GEORGIA *(continued)*							
	Treat Orchard Company	1930s	Alum	Good at the Treat Mountain general store in Esom Hill	—	$25	—
	Atlanta Milling Co.	1940s	Fiber	An incentive to buy Capitola Flour: a movie pass	$10	20	$30
HAWAII							
	John T. Waterhouse	1860	Pew	Hawaiian king on this dry-goods importer's token	1,500	5,000	—
	Thomas Hobron Railroad	1879	Bz	Redeemable at a Kahului general store (Maui)	450	650	1,500
	Jim Dodd, Pantheon Saloon	1890s	Br	Enterprise Brewing was founded in San Francisco	200	400	750
IDAHO							
Id IC 3	Miner's Brewery / Bakery	1865	Cop	Possibly Idaho's earliest token	800	1,500	2,500
ILLINOIS							
Ill 8	Burbank & Shaw	1845	Cop	This Chicago pair issued several other copper token types	25	65	300
Ill 100	Clock face	1846	Bz	An anepigraphic token for a watchmaker	100	200	—

References: R.D. and J.D. Partin, *Georgia Trade Tokens*, 1990; Donald Medcalf and Ronald Russell, *Hawaiian Money*, 1978; R.S. Yeoman (ed. Kenneth Bressett), *A Guide Book of United States Coins*, annual. Frank R. Schell, *Idaho Trade Tokens, 1865–1972*, 1972; Ore Vacketta, *Trade Tokens of Illinois*, 1983.

Merchant Tokens

Illinois (continued)

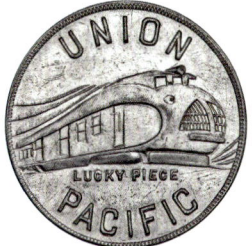

Indiana

RULAU #	ISSUER	YEAR	METAL	COMMENTARY	F	EF	MS-63
ILLINOIS *(continued)*							
Il-Ch 66	North Western Dental Infirmary	1880s	GS	The work was free because dentistry students performed it	$25	$60	$90
	Pullman Car & Mfg. Corp.	1933	Alum	Aluminum train cars at Century of Progress Expo	1	2	4
INDIANA							
	Burkhart's Saloon	1870s	Br	Cincinnati's Murdock made this Brookville good-for	125	200	—
	John T. Rademaker	1870s	Br	Another Murdock issue, for a Peru saloon	150	250	—
	Julius Schmidt, Madison	1870s	Br	Brunswick "Monarch" lion-leg pool table of 1875	200	250	—
Sey 2	J.A. Goodale	1870s	Br	A half smile = a shot of whiskey in Seymour	100	150	160
In-Ip 9	Whitney Sewing Machines	1874	WM	Hawking the product at the Indianapolis State Fair	5	15	30
	Wm. Hisgen's Billiards	1878	Silv	Half-dime denomination seldom seen in good-fors	75	175	275
	Henry Tucker	1890s	Alum	Buy a whip now, get a 50-cent discount next time	30	50	100
Evv-4	F.W. Cook Brewing	1890s	Alum	This Evansville brewer continued through 1917	40	60	90

References: Ore Vacketta, *Trade Tokens of Illinois*, 1983; Lloyd Wagaman, *Indiana Trade Tokens*, 1981.

Iowa

Kansas

Kentucky

RULAU #	ISSUER	YEAR	METAL	COMMENTARY	F	EF	MS-63
IOWA							
	Hickey Brothers Store	1905	Alum	There were four more Hickey cigar stores around Iowa	—	$5	$10
	Equitable of Iowa	1969	Alum (red)	Celebrating a company picnic held in Missouri	—	—	1
KANSAS							
KS DC 2	Culver & Webster	1881	GS	Stock Exchange Saloon used a Brunswick die	$500	2,000	—
	Coleman Lamp & Stove Co.	1939	Br	Wichita company's token for the Golden Gate Exposition	—	5	10
	Coronado Cuarto Centennial	1941	WM	Worth 5 cents at celebrations of Spanish exploration	1	1	1
	First National Bank	1961	Bz	Promotion for a Wichita Savings Bank	—	2	3
KENTUCKY							
Ky 33	H.E. Thomas & Co.	1832	WM	Handsome store card struck in England	3,000	10,000	20,000
	Majestic Café, Lexington	1870s	WM	A typical good-for of the "Horse Capital"	10	20	25

References: Jack Glass and Gawain O'Connor, *Iowa Trade Tokens*, 1999; William J. Waken, *Kansas Trade Tokens*, 1990.

Kentucky *(continued)*

Louisiana

Maine

RULAU #	ISSUER	YEAR	METAL	COMMENTARY	F	EF	MS-63
KENTUCKY *(continued)*							
	I.W. Harper's Bourbon	1904	Br	Proclaiming a gold-medal win in St. Louis	$3	$5	$6
	F.T. Burke, Ingle System	1909	Alum	$1; other Ingle denominations were 5, 10, 25, and 50 cents	3	4	5
	City Hall Café, Dayton	1910s	C-N	The triangular shape stands out from the crowd	2	3	4
LOUISIANA							
	J.H. Durruty	1840s	Br	Notched corners on this unique bakery check	—	5,000	—
La 2	Albert & Tricou	1853	Br	Paul Tricou's hats cost $3 in 1840s New Orleans	100	250	600
La 42	Robert Pitkin	1858	Br	Clothier's storefront on this Scovill-struck token	10	20	50
La 38	L.W. Lyons	1858	Br	Lyons's department store had it all	10	20	50
MAINE							
Me 3B	W.R. Field	1850	WM	Dining-room check is struck and countermarked	100	150	250
Me Yo 1	F. Quebe, York	1870s	WM	Quebe's activity in York is unknown today	—	750	1,500

Reference: Louis Crawford and Glyn Farber, *Louisiana Trade Tokens*, 1996.

Maine *(continued)*

Maryland

Massachusetts

RULAU #	ISSUER	YEAR	METAL	COMMENTARY	F	EF	MS-63
MAINE *(continued)*							
Me Fa 1	Chester Greenwood	1877	Br	Greenwood gave the world the earmuff	$10	$20	$50
	Golden Rule	1890s	Alum	A Machiasport confectioner—and paint dealer!	150	250	250
	"Babe" Binette	2002	Cop	A coin dealer's $1 good-for	—	—	2
MARYLAND							
Md 78	Keach	1847	GS	P.R. Keach manufactured and sold mineral water	35	100	300
Md Ba L36	Germania Maennerchor	1870s	Cop	Clubhouse token of a Baltimore German men's choir	6	10	20
	American Beer / Orioles	1954	WM	Orioles pocket calendar—never miss a game!	3	15	20
MASSACHUSETTS							
Mass 84	Horace Porter	1826	Svd Br	The "Britannia" advertised is akin to pewter	60	150	350
Mass 136	E.W. Strange	1860s	Steel	Advertising a Taunton letter-cutting trade	—	1,250	—
Mass 35	George Fera	1860	WM	A Merriam check for a Boston caterer/confectioner	150	250	450

Reference: David E. Schenkman, *Maryland Merchant Tokens*, 1998.

Massachusetts *(continued)*

RULAU #	ISSUER	YEAR	METAL	COMMENTARY	F	EF	MS-63
MASSACHUSETTS *(continued)*							
Mass 115	Apollo Gardens	1865	Cop	Rare Merriam muling; an unusual six-cent value	—	—	$1,000
Ma-Sp 37	J.A. Bolen	1865	Cop	Diesinker James Bolen's self-portrait; only 15 struck	—	$350	500
Ma-Sp 61	Moore Brothers	1865	Cop	Bolen used a British Conder token as a planchet	—	—	1,000
	Exchange Luncheon	1876	Br	Intact shell cards bearing a 1776 date are quite rare	—	350	600
Ma-Bo 94A	H.M. Richards	1878	Iron	Attleboro die maker's nickel-plated counter check	—	500	—
	Putnam's Clothing Warehouse	1880s	HR	Hard-rubber tokens sometimes came in red	—	30	60
	Geo. T. McLauthlin	1887	Br	These tokens came tied to bundles of elevator cable	—	100	—
Bos 90	L. Polcri	1890s	Br	Lorenzo Polcri's self-portrait good-for	—	75	—

Massachusetts *(continued)*

Michigan

Minnesota

RULAU #	ISSUER	YEAR	METAL	COMMENTARY	F	EF	MS-63
MASSACHUSETTS *(continued)*							
	Eagle Cotton Gin	1898	Cop	A Dewey-faced token to promote cotton gins	$75	$100	$150
Bos 14	Crosby's Restaurant	1900	Br	Whitehead and Hoag made this showy souvenir	5	10	20
	Brockton National Bank	1921	Br	Issued for the Brockton centennial	—	7	10
	Stuart Levine	2000	Br	Dealer's token based on Oregon Territory gold piece	—	—	3
MICHIGAN							
Mi-De 2A	Brown Brothers	1880s	Br	Cigars made in Detroit; tokens good everywhere	—	5	10
	Marack & Lehman	1910s	Br	Used to feed a cigar machine in Kent	—	5	7
	Chrysler Cars	1934	Br	Airflow design seen at Century of Progress Exposition	—	4	8
	General Motors	1954	Bz	GM's 50 millionth car was a 1955 Chevrolet Bel Air two-door hardtop	—	2	5
MINNESOTA							
	Wendell's	1928	Gilt Br	50th-anniversary token; this Minneapolis mint is still in operation today	—	—	3

Reference: Paul Cunningham, *Michigan Trade Tokens*, 1988.

Merchant Tokens 41

Mississippi

Missouri

Montana

RULAU #	ISSUER	YEAR	METAL	COMMENTARY	F	EF	MS-63
MISSISSIPPI							
	Casey's	1910s	Alum	A general store token for the Simpson County seat	$5	$10	$15
MISSOURI							
Mo-40	M.A. Abrahams	1852	Br	Santa Fe Trail outfitter; Independence and Westport	20	150	500
	Excelsior Manufacturing	1870s	Gilt / Svd Br	Bicolor shell card of a stove- and kettle-maker	—	300	400
	Inernational Nickel Company	1904	Nick	Likely struck on the grounds of the St. Louis Exposition	5	10	30
	Otto Oddehon	1946	Br	Oddehon commissioned many medals and tokens	—	—	6
MONTANA							
Mt Bu 11	Schmidt & Gamer	1876	GS	Centennial was the largest brewery in the northwest	1,250	2,500	—
Mt MC 3	King & Ward	1880s	Br	Miles City is on the Yellowstone at Fort Keogh	1,500	2,500	—

References: George Chatham, *Brozenes & Doodlum—Private Money in Mississippi*, 1999; George F. Gould, *Merchant Tokens of Montana, 1888–1939*, 2003.

Montana (continued)

Nebraska

Nevada

RULAU #	ISSUER	YEAR	METAL	COMMENTARY	F	EF	MS-63
MONTANA *(continued)*							
Ana 1	Montana Hotel	1896	Cop	Copper mining was the lifeblood of Anaconda	—	$100	$250
	Butte Concert Hall	1900s	Nick	Turn-of-the-century music hall with a saloon	$35	50	52
NEBRASKA							
Ne Om 9	Mills & McAlister	1860s	WM	"N.T." means this token predates statehood in 1867	2,000	6,500	8,500
	H. Brash	1868	Br	Shell card of an Omaha clothier with a rude surname	—	400	600
	Western Heritage Museum	1980s	Br	Home of Byron Reed's famed numismatic collection	—	—	5
NEVADA							
	Nevada Hotel	1870s	Br	The town of Candelaria sprang up around a rich silver mine	750	1,500	—
Nv-Hw 10	E. Van Alstine	1886	Br	Hawthorne was a Carson & Colorado railroad depot	600	1,500	—
Win 3	Lafayette Hotel	1896	Alum	Proprietor expressed his views on the hot issue of the day	250	700	—

References: George F. Gould, *Merchant Tokens of Montana, 1888–1939*, 2003; George Hosek, *Nebraska Merchant Trade Tokens, Town Rarity List*, 2000.

Merchant Tokens

Nevada *(continued)*

New Hampshire

RULAU #	ISSUER	YEAR	METAL	COMMENTARY	F	EF	MS-63
NEVADA *(continued)*							
	Louis Dutertre	1910s	Br	Dutertre ran the post office, livery, and the Hot Springs Hotel	$75	$200	—
	Redondo Saloon	1900s	Alum	First a gold-boom town, then a ghost town, now a town again	400	1,250	—
	Cosmopolitan Saloon	1900s	Br	In 1910 the Colorado flooded, wiping out half of Caliente	200	750	—
	Jack Givens	1910	Alum	"Fight of the Century": Johnson whups Great White Hope	—	500	$1,250
	C.M. Coddington / Wieland's	1910s	Alum	Advertising Wieland's, brewed in San Francisco	350	750	—
	C.M. Coddington / Sierra	1910s	Br	Sierra beer was brewed in Reno from 1903–1918	150	400	—
	Gardnerville Corner Saloon	1920s	Br	Drink token of a Carson Valley agricultural town	—	50	75
NEW HAMPSHIRE							
	M.B. Clough	1868	Br	Shell card was worth 10¢ in Concord	—	500	750
Man 12	Star Stamp Co.	1896	Alum	Star made semi-centennial pieces for several merchants	—	125	200
Man 2	Dumas Bros.	1896	Gilt Br	Gilt brass was the color choice for the Dumas Bros.	10	20	35

New Hampshire *(continued)*

New Jersey

RULAU #	ISSUER	YEAR	METAL	COMMENTARY	F	EF	MS-63
NEW HAMPSHIRE *(continued)*							
Man 4	Kimball the Clothier	1896	Gilt Br	Custom obverses could be simple or complex, as desired	$10	$20	$35
	W.P. Young	1902	Alum	The reverse shows this Portsmouth dealer's specialties	—	—	300
	G.S. Rollins	1910s	Alum	This type of good-for typical for New England in the 1910s	200	300	310
	Clark's Trading Post	1990s	Nick	The landmark is gone, but not forgotten in exonumia	—	1	2
NEW JERSEY							
NJ 16	S.A. Whitney	1852	Br	Whitney took over the famed 1779 glassworks in 1842	10	25	75
	Whitehead & Hoag	1898	Br	Dewey-faced store card of the prolific Newark medal maker	100	200	250
	Motor Car Co. of New Jersey	1909	Bz	The dealership liked Lincoln, but the car was a Cadillac	—	100	124
	V. Ricker's Saloon	1910s	Alum	A typical Camden saloon good-for of the era, but rare!	350	600	—
	Hamilton Trust Co.	1919	Alum	Gift tokens of Paterson bank became a cash deposit	—	5	—
	The Elusive Spondulix	2000s	C-N	The elusive term is 19th-century slang—for *money!*	—	—	15

New Mexico

New York

RULAU #	ISSUER	YEAR	METAL	COMMENTARY	F	EF	MS-63
NEW MEXICO							
NM Aq 12	W.E. Talbott	1883	GS	Good for wholesale tobacco and spirits too	$350	$750	—
NM Mg 3	Allen House	1880s	Br	Scalloped edge enhances this Socorro County good-for	400	750	$1,000
	Valdez Saloon	1890s	Br	Las Cruces tavern token dated by its maker, L.H. Moise	350	750	—
	Battle Ax Saloon	1890s	Br	Tennessee-born Oglesby lived until 1938	500	1,500	—
Tao 3	C.B. Ruggles	1890s	Bz	In the 1910 Taos census, Ruggles had wife and two kids	2,000	3,500	—
NEW YORK							
NY 877	Talbot, Allum & Lee*	1794	Cop	India traders issued many thousands of English-made pieces	150	400	750
NY 924	Richard Trested	1823	Br	Store card of New York City's earliest token maker	3,000	8,000	15,000
NY 632	Parthenon Museum	1825	Bz	The Peale family also had museums in Philadelphia and Baltimore	100	300	750
NY-654A	Rathbone & Fitch	1825	Svd Br	Castle Garden: a War of 1812 fort, then a restaurant	2,000	3,500	7,000

* Voted No. 36 in *100 Greatest American Medals and Tokens* (Jaeger/Bowers).

New York (continued)

RULAU #	ISSUER	YEAR	METAL	COMMENTARY	F	EF	MS-63
NEW YORK (continued)							
NY 137	David C. Buchan	1828	Br	Popular early chairmaker's card	$100	$200	$550
NY 663	Risley & McCollum	1840s	Br	These circus showmen toured the United States and abroad	65	150	325
NY 415A	Ladies' Restaurant	1850s	Br	Early dining establishments separated the sexes	300	400	500
NY 224	Doremus & Nixon	1850	Cop	Scovill created many tokens for this firm, 1820s–1850s	10	20	75
NY 209	J. Smith Dodge	1850s	Br	Prominent city dentist; also an American Institute manager	60	90	150
NY-966	Wm. P. Woodcock	1858	Cop	George H. Lovett engraved this butcher's namesake bird	40	85	200
NY 426	J.N.T. Levick**	1860	Br	Banker/numismatist displays a passion for tobacco	—	125	300
NY 358	Charles D. Horter	1860	WM	Diesinker depicts his own storefront on the reverse	—	100	150
	Pastor's Combination Troupe	1867	Br	Pastor had a New York opera house and traveling minstrels, too	—	350	500

** Voted No. 63 in *100 Greatest American Medals and Tokens.*

New York (continued)

RULAU #	ISSUER	YEAR	METAL	COMMENTARY	F	EF	MS-63
NEW YORK *(continued)*							
	Christoffel and Booth	1868	Br	Unusual device seen on the token was patented in 1867	—	$400	$500
	Mica Manufacturing Co.	1868	Br	Shell cards had clear mica faces to protect the printed inserts	—	500	750
	Buffalo Scale Works	1868	Br	Rare and desirable (especially in Buffalo) shell pictorial	—	400	600
	Bischoff Bank and Steamers	1870s	Br	German-Americans banked at Bischoff's, rode his steamers	—	250	400
	Edward Cogan, Brooklyn	1870s	Br	"Foine old" Brooklyn coin dealer was from Philadelphia	—	—	450
	Cooper Union Book Check	1870s	Br	Peter Cooper's free college tracked book returns with tokens	—	150	250
NY-NY 173	R.H. Macy & Co.	1876	Cop	Matthews made the soda fountain, Macy dispensed the soda	$20	75	125

New York *(continued)*

RULAU #	ISSUER	YEAR	METAL	COMMENTARY	F	EF	MS-63
NEW YORK *(continued)*							
NY-NY 292	Smith & Seward	1889	WM	Seward was final partner of well-known diesinker F.B. Smith	—	$150	$200
NY-NY 179	Manhattan Watch Co.	1880s	GS	Die-struck promotional sample with prices	$10	25	50
	Uncle Sam Hall	1890s	Br	Bowling was in vogue at this "amusement palace"	50	100	150
	Ehrich Bros.	1890s	WM	Kris Kringle: of interest across American numismatics	75	100	150
Nyk 3	Dunlop Tire Co.	1890s	Alum	Windy Aeolus says Dunlop tires enhance speed	—	10	20
Nyk 35	Eagle Engraving & Stamping Co.	1890s	Alum	A little-known work from the hand of Victor David Brenner	—	275	500
	Dr. Jaeger's Sanitary Woolens	1896	Ster	German M.D. believed only wool was safe next to the skin	—	125	200

Merchant Tokens 49

New York *(continued)*

North Carolina

North Dakota

RULAU #	ISSUER	YEAR	METAL	COMMENTARY	F	EF	MS-63
NEW YORK *(continued)*							
	Charles Hoefig, NYC	1898	Alum	Diecutter displays his talent at portraiture	—	—	$350
Syr 36	Syracuse Chilled Plow	1899	Gilt Br	Noting the company's gold-medal win at the 1900 Paris Exposition	$5	$15	25
	Madame Bonaparte	1900	Br	Touching shell-card memento of a bawdy-house visit	—	500	1,000
	Cavanaugh's Restaurant	1948	Br	Spin the token; the arrow decides who buys dinner	—	2	2
NORTH CAROLINA							
	U.S. National Bank, Aberdeen	1920s	Bz	A gift token enticed you to make a deposit	—	5	—
NORTH DAKOTA							
ND GF 2	O'Brien & O'Reilly	1884	GS	This Grand Forks tavern evidently had Irish roots	—	3,000	—
ND Lm 1	Roberts & Co.	1880s	Br	Any territorial ghost-town good-for is a great prize	—	3,750	—
ND St 1	Franklin Baer & Blatt	1886	Br	Octagonal Brunswick die for a Sturgis billiard parlor	—	900	—
	Hebron Co-operative Creamery	1945	WM	Milk token good for one quart	—	2	—

Reference: Peterson and Johnson, *North Dakota Merchant Tokens*, 1992.

Ohio

Oklahoma

RULAU #	ISSUER	YEAR	METAL	COMMENTARY	F	EF	MS-63
OHIO							
Ohio 19	E. & D. Kinsey	1851	Cop	Silverware maker exhibited at London's Crystal Palace	$15	$35	$85
	Murdock & Spencer	1868	Br	Civil War diesinkers moved on to shell cards after the war	—	250	350
	Joseph J. Sayre	1868	Br	Prolific token producer advertises his stencil work on a shell	—	350	500
Oh-Ci 210	Zanoni & Bacciocco	1870	Br	No doubt some of these were wagered in games of whist	10	15	30
Col 6	Columbus Buggy Co.	1892	Alum	Exhibiting the product on an exposition advertising giveaway	10	20	35
Cin 21	Cincinnati Pure Aluminum Company	1893	Alum	Their token was made of their product; an exposition giveaway	10	20	35
OKLAHOMA							
	Lee & Reynolds	1870s	Silv	These post traders served the Cheyenne nation with tokens	150	350	—
	B.B. Harris & Sons	1870s	Alum	A jeweler in the midst of Creek and Choctaw country	25	50	—

References: Gaylor Lipscomb, *Ohio Trade Tokens*, 1994; R.W. Chadwick, *The Oklahoma Token Catalog*, 2007.

Oklahoma (continued)

Oregon

RULAU #	ISSUER	YEAR	METAL	COMMENTARY	F	EF	MS-63
OKLAHOMA *(continued)*							
	Briscoe Brothers	1890s	Alum	Presumably the 5¢ value was not good at the undertaker	$250	$350	—
	Arcade Bar	1890s	Alum	Western Indian Territory became Oklahoma Territory, 1890; O.T. became a state, 1907	150	350	—
	Patterson & Reece	1890s	Br	Medford was the Grant County seat as of 1908	300	1,250	—
	New Phoenix	1920s	Br	A swastika was an ancient Indian symbol for good luck	5	20	$25
	Buttrey	1910s	Br	This Enid bakery also issued $1 tokens in aluminum	10	15	20
	Frankoma Premium Pottery	1940s	Alum	Both the tokens and the pottery are collectible today	—	2	—
	Rocket Skating Club	1950	Alum	Oklahoma City rink produced many national champions	—	2	—
OREGON							
Ore 1	North West Company*	1820	Br	Having the value of one dressed beaver pelt	7,000	40,000	—
Or Br-2	R.A. Sanders	1883	GS	A stock Strahle die for a drink by the pool table	750	1,750	—
	O.A. Giles	1928	Alum	Token of an Umatilla County grocery store	10	20	—

References: R.W. Chadwick, *The Oklahoma Token Catalog*, 2007; James Hemphill, *Oregon Trade Tokens*, 1992.
* Voted No. 12 in *100 Greatest American Medals and Tokens* (Jaeger/Bowers). The specimen shown is unholed; only three such are known. The valuation range covers both holed and unholed.

Pennsylvania

RULAU #	ISSUER	YEAR	METAL	COMMENTARY	F	EF	MS-63
PENNSYLVANIA							
Pa-430	Ricketts's Circus*	1793	Cop	George Washington attended, in Philadelphia, when he could	$5,000	$7,500	—
Pa 398	Peale's Museum**	1821	Cop	Gobrecht designed and the U.S. Mint struck this metal ticket	30	100	$300
Pa 19	A.D. Angue	1847	Br	Angue's cheap umbrellas were discontinued by 1848	10	20	50
	W.P. Hunker	1867	Br	Shell card of a Pittsburgh candy maker	—	350	500
	Armstrong Ice Cream Saloon	1868	Br	Printed side of a shell leaves plenty of room for details	—	750	1,000
	Maisons Fertile and Doree	1868	Gilt Br	Shell card good at two of W.H. Harrison's bawdy houses	—	500	750
	F. Rahter, Zingari Bitters	1868	Br	The medicinal component of bitters was alcohol	—	350	500

Reference: Herman M. Aqua, *Pennsylvania Merchant Tokens*, 2000 (covering mostly 20th-century types).
* Voted No. 23 in *100 Greatest American Medals and Tokens* (Jaeger/Bowers).
** Voted No. 55 in *100 Greatest American Medals and Tokens*.

Pennsylvania (continued)

RULAU #	ISSUER	YEAR	METAL	COMMENTARY	F	EF	MS-63
PENNSYLVANIA (continued)							
	Marvin's Crackers	1870s	Br/Mir	Shell had a useful mirrored side, to carry in pocket or purse	—	$75	$100
Pa-Ph 40	Dickeson's	1872	WM	Safe-maker hawked his product and favorite candidate	—	150	350
	Joseph Liebler	1876	Br	Shell cards dated 1776, struck for the nation's centennial	—	350	500
	Valentine Varnishes	1876	HR	Bicolor varnish-maker's token made for the carriage exhibition	—	40	75
Pa Ph 980	G. Kilbride	1876	WM	Philadelphia merchant tokens proliferated for the centennial exposition	$15	30	75
Pa Ph 760	Stilz & Son	1876	WM	Stock designs, like a Liberty Bell, for local advertisers	10	20	50
	Monarch Cycles	1893	Alum	Six Monarch bicycle models were not cheap: $40 to $100	15	50	75
Phl 27	Innes Festival	1896	Alum	Willow Grove Park hosted Innes, then Sousa, as maestros	10	35	50

Reference: Herman M. Aqua, *Pennsylvania Merchant Tokens*, 2000 (covering mostly 20th-century types).

Pennsylvania (continued)

Rhode Island

RULAU #	ISSUER	YEAR	METAL	COMMENTARY	F	EF	MS-63
PENNSYLVANIA (continued)							
	Heeren Bros. & Co.	1917	Alum	Pittsburgh jewelers in business since 1867; sold music boxes	—	$20	$40
RHODE ISLAND							
RI Pr 15	A.A. Plastridge	1850	WM	Eating-house check with an unknown purpose	$100	200	300
RI 6	S.S. Smith	1850s	WM	The numbers on Smith's checks corresponded to tables	75	150	250
RI Pr 8	George Finck	1876	Br	Washington's bust was a popular centennial design; this by Scovill	15	30	60
	Arnold Numismatic Co.	1890s	Alum	George C. Arnold was in Providence through the 1920s	3	8	12
	L. Kranz, Diesinker	1900s	Alum	Kranz shop card series bore various gods and goddesses	50	150	200
	Huntoon & Gorham	1900s	Alum	"Old Coon": In the cigar trade, peculiar brand names abounded	10	20	—
	Providence Institution for Savings	1936	Br	A token inducement to save during the Depression	—	2	—

Reference: Herman M. Aqua, *Pennsylvania Merchant Tokens*, 2000 (covering mostly 20th-century types).

Merchant Tokens

South Carolina

South Dakota

RULAU #	ISSUER	YEAR	METAL	COMMENTARY	F	EF	MS-63
SOUTH CAROLINA							
SC 5	W.W. Wilbur	1846	Br	Token doesn't mention the auctioneer's commodity: slaves	$75	$150	$400
	Saxon Mills Store	1900s	Br	Good at the company store of a Spartansburg cotton mill	—	75	—
	Jackson Co.	1900s	Br	Worth two bits at the cotton mill store in Piedmont	—	10	15
SOUTH DAKOTA							
	W.S. Fanshawe & Co.	1880s	Br	Fort Meade protected Black Hills miners from the Sioux	—	3,750	—
SD-Pi 1	Castle & Son	1880s	Br	Only two tokens are extant from this Pierre tavern	—	3,800	—
SD Ch 1	Atwater & Bargesser	1886	Br	This part of Dakota Territory became South Dakota in 1889	—	3,300	—
SD Dd-2	Cleveland Tin Mining	1890	Tin	Made of the least durable token material, therefore rare	575	850	900

References: Tony Chibbaro, *South Carolina Tokens*, 1990; Stephen Miedema, *A Guide to Collecting South Dakota Tokens and Exonumia*, 1999.

Tennessee

Texas

RULAU #	ISSUER	YEAR	METAL	COMMENTARY	F	EF	MS-63
TENNESSEE							
Tenn 59	H. & I. Kirkman	1828	Cop	Struck in England, and showing the merchant's wares	$500	$1,500	$4,000
	Larry Harmstad	1868	Br	The only known Tennessee shell card, from Memphis	—	1,000	1,500
TEXAS							
	Jose Antonio de la Garza*	1818	Cop	This "jola" had a value of 1/2 real in Spanish San Antonio	6,000	15,000	—
	Fort Macintosh Post Exchange	1870	HR	Fort at Laredo opened 1849; tokens in four denominations	—	2,000	4,250
	Fort Quitman Post Exchange	1871	Br	Moore & Sweet used shell cards at their trading post	—	750	1,500
Tx-Dn 2	Cow Boy's Saloon	1870s	GS	For thirsty cattle drivers at a Red River crossing	3,500	—	—
	Cattle Exchange	1870s	GS	From a time when Abilene had 8 saloons for 900 residents	—	3,000	—
	M.B. Tallant, Occidental	1870s	HR	Colorado City: a ranger camp and cattle town. Token: unique	—	3,000	—

Reference: Joe Copeland, *Trade Tokens of Tennessee*, 1998.
* Voted No. 96 in *100 Greatest American Medals and Tokens* (Jaeger/Bowers).

Texas *(continued)*

RULAU #	ISSUER	YEAR	METAL	COMMENTARY	F	EF	MS-63
TEXAS *(continued)*							
Tx-AH 1	The Harbor	1885	Br	Aransas Harbor, where the San Antonio Railroad met the sea	$400	$900	—
Tx-Lm 15	White Elephant	1880	GS	White Elephant: a popular saloon name in the southwest	750	2,000	—
Tx-Kr 4	The Ranch	1887	GS	Barlemann's saloon on the ground floor of the Weston Building	500	1,500	—
Tx-Au 4	Bismarck Saloon	1880s	GS	Ribbeck's place was the Austin hangout of writer O. Henry	400	750	$1,500
Tx-Bp 20	Osborn & Cartwright	1880s	GS	Bastrop: a Colorado River cattle center	500	1,200	—
Tx-Sa 115	Monroe Pratt	1890s	GS	Pratt's saloon was at 15 Soledad St. in 1891 city directory	150	350	—
Tx-Sn 9	Fred Schmidt	1890s	Br	Handsome pictorial of a west Texas livestock community	300	750	—
Smc 2	Faris & Williamson	1885	C-N	San Marcos: center for drayage from ranches to the coast	400	1,250	—

Texas (continued)

Utah

Vermont

Virginia

RULAU #	ISSUER	YEAR	METAL	COMMENTARY	F	EF	MS-63
TEXAS (continued)							
	Geo. Rist / Panhandle	1894	GS	Buffalo-bone fertilizer was big business in Panhandle City	$1,250	$3,500	—
	Winkler County Jubilee	1960	Gilt Br	Good for 50 cents in Kermit, the county seat	—	—	$5
	August's Pies	1962	Bz	August Moeller fried pies in 1937; his son Tim does today	—	2	—
UTAH							
	Spriggs & Crooks	1880s	Br	Now a ski resort, Park City was once a silver-mining center	15	35	—
	Pastime Club	1940s	Br	Salt Flats racers and Wendover airfield flyers were patrons	—	25	—
	All About Coins, Inc.	2000s	Alum	Advertising token of a Salt Lake City coin dealer	—	—	2
VERMONT							
	H.W. Dwinell	1900s	Alum	The active ingredient of most "nerve tonics" was alcohol	250	400	410
	Miss M.J. Drury	1910	Alum	Millie Drury also sold ice cream, notions, and toys	—	—	200
VIRGINIA							
Va 1	Gloucester Court House*	1714	Br	Famed as the first token made in the United States; 2 known	150,000	—	—
Va Ri-7	C. Lumsden & Son	1890	Alum	A jewelry store handout for visitors to the monument	25	50	90

Reference: David E. Schenkman, *Virginia Tokens*, 1980.
* Voted No. 33 in *100 Greatest American Medals and Tokens* (Jaeger/Bowers).

Merchant Tokens

Washington

West Virginia

Wisconsin

RULAU #	ISSUER	YEAR	METAL	COMMENTARY	F	EF	MS-63
WASHINGTON							
Wa-Ce 7	Obermann & Co.	1880s	GS	Centralia: layover on the Seattle-to-Portland stage trip	$2,000	$3,500	—
Wa-Dy 3	M.A. Cavanaugh	1880s	Br	Dayton is the home of Weinhard Brewery	1,500	3,000	—
	Seattle World's Fair	1962	Br	Exposition token was good for a dollar across the state	—	2	$5
WEST VIRGINIA							
WV Ma-10	J. Wisner & Son	1868	Br/Card	Guano: important international commodity since the 1850s	—	500	750
WISCONSIN							
Wi-Un 4	H. Shanfield	1890s	Bz	Good for a barrel of slop; now *that's* purchasing power	10	15	40
	Fisk's Tavern	1950s	Br	Tavern tokens of all kinds popular in this brewery state	10	20	—
	Numismatic News	1982	Alum	A $2 good-for issued to celebrate 30 years in print	—	—	1

Reference: Al Erickson, *Washington State Trade Tokens*, 1998.

Wyoming

RULAU #	ISSUER	YEAR	METAL	COMMENTARY	F	EF	MS-63
WYOMING							
	J.S. McCormick	1870s	Bz	Childs engraved this token for the Fort Laramie trading post	$550	$1,000	—
	C. A. Weidman & Co.	1870s	Br	Fort Russell at the Union & Pacific's Crow Creek crossing	1,500	2,500	$3,500
Wy-Cs 5	Sennate Billiard Parlor	1880s	GS	Wyoming was a territory until statehood came in 1890	2,000	5,000	—
	Powder River Ranch	1880s	Br	Ranch had a store, saloon, blacksmith, stable, and cabins	1,750	3,000	—
Nwc 2	C.J. Faehndrich & Co.	1890s	Br	Faehndrich moved to Deadwood, S.D., to sell autos in 1909	300	750	—
Thm 2	Erickson & Kinney	1900s	Br	The "therm" in Thermopolis is the world's largest hot spring	250	750	—

2

HARD TIMES TOKENS (1832–1844)

The term *Hard Times* describing the period 1832 to 1844 is something of a historical misnomer, because severe economic depression did not befall the nation until the Panic of 1837. For reasons explained below, a shortage of gold and silver coins in that year meant that copper cents and copper tokens the size of a cent were used to make all small purchases. Many of the tokens in circulation during and after the Panic of 1837 were political pieces referring to the 1832 and 1836 presidential elections, and the 1834 congressional elections. The actual hard times persisted through the presidencies of William H. Harrison (who died after only a month in office) and his successor, John Tyler.

Businessmen and merchants were attracted to using tokens because producers wholesaled them by the keg, charging 60¢ to 75¢ per hundred. Diesinkers' own costs ranged between 35¢ and 40¢ per hundred.[19] Large plants such as Scovill of Connecticut prospered, and new shops opened. Numismatists estimate that private mints of the era produced from 10 to 20 million tokens.[20] In 1889, numismatist Lyman Low cataloged Hard Times issues, assembling a total of 183 varieties. Token specialist Russell Rulau revamped the subject for his *Standard Catalog of Hard Times Tokens* in 1980, and subsequent editions of that book brought the number of included types above 500. Rulau's publications, and scores of books and articles by others, demonstrate the persistence of collector interest in the category and the remarkable depth of research to date. Rare pieces bring the highest prices of any United States tokens after those of the colonial period. In his 10th edition, Rulau lists four major groups:

1. Pieces referring to the Bank of the United States and the controversy surrounding it.
2. Those with inscriptions relating to political and satirical themes of the era.
3. Tokens with inscriptions and designs closely resembling regular federal cent coinage, but with some differences in order to evade the counterfeiting laws.
4. Examples bearing the advertisements of merchants.

He includes varieties made from die mulings of the above groups, as well as counterstamped coins.

A basic understanding of the era's politics is necessary to make sense of the strange satirical legends and designs on many of its tokens.[21] In brief, the issues creating the hottest controversy, and generating the majority of satirical tokens, were differences of opinion over U.S. banking and land sale policies, and whether the nation should endorse the concept of credit backed by paper currency.

Tennessee congressman Andrew Jackson was elected to his first term as president in 1828. Most important to his popularity were his military reputation as the "Hero of New Orleans" in the War of 1812, and his appeal to the common citizen as a rough-hewn Westerner, rather than a highly educated member of the upper class like his predecessors from Virginia and Massachusetts. During his first term, Jackson alienated many Southerners with his support of the protective Tariff of 1828, which imposed duties on raw materials favorable to the industrial North but damaging to the agricultural South. The state of South Carolina voted to nullify the tariff's provisions within its borders. Jackson took a strong stand against a state's right to nullify a federal law or to leave the Union, making a statement that appeared on many tokens: THE UNION MUST AND SHALL BE PRESERVED.

Jackson indicated his disagreement with the lending practices of the Second Bank of the United States with another remark later struck in metal: THE BANK MUST PERISH. His objection stemmed from the nation's experience of the Panic of 1819. To finance a boom in real-estate speculation after the War of 1812, the Second Bank (chartered in 1816) printed currency for land loans, totaling more than 10 times the amount of specie (gold and silver) held to back it up. When an economic recession occurred, citizens tried to redeem their paper for the nonexistent "hard money" and a string of banks, followed by private businesses, failed in rapid succession. Though many factors contributed to the recession, Jacksonians blamed the Second Bank and its paper money credit, and Jackson vowed to veto any attempt to extend or renew its charter. Advocates of national banking and credit picked Jackson's long-time foe, Kentuckian Henry Clay, to run against him in 1832.

Clay also wanted to preserve the Union, but was determined that Southern interests be accommodated. In a famous senatorial speech, he outlined his "AMERICAN SYSTEM," a term duly featured on tokens. This system would retain protective tariffs on imports to support industry, emphasize national banking to foster commerce, and provide federal funding for much-needed agricultural infrastructure (especially railroads and canals). The monies for such improvements would come from tariffs on the sale of federal land. Popular distaste for all tariffs combined with Jackson's beloved "Old Hickory" persona carried the 1832 election in Jackson's favor. In 1833, he began pulling federal deposits from the Second Bank of the United States, whose rechartering he had already vetoed, and placed them in various state banks. In the process, he made a bitter enemy of Second Bank president Nicholas Biddle.

Leading up to the congressional elections of 1834, working-class level opposition to paper money and banks began gathering steam. The May 12 issue of the New York newspaper *The Man* published a list of "mechanics and other working men" who pledged themselves to a platform of "Hickory, Homespun, and Hard Money." They opposed paper money, banking, and all licensed monopolies, and pledged to fight new bank charters and work toward the passage of a law "abolishing, gradually, all bills of banks now existing under twenty dollars." On the other side, staunch bank supporter and Whig party darling Daniel Webster portrayed Jackson as a greedy tyrant, and his backers as enemies of the Constitution. Whigs mocked Jackson on their tokens, depicting him as a thief coming out of a bank with moneybags in his hands, turning his words I TAKE THE RESPONSIBILITY into a sneer at his motives. On some tokens, Jackson was shown holding both a purse and a sword—a situation deemed by some to be inadvisable in a democracy. Other Whig tokens bore statements such as PERISH CREDIT PERISH COMMERCE; FLOURISH COMMERCE, FLOURISH INDUSTRY; and THE CONSTITUTION HURRAH.

The Whigs carried the elections of 1834, but Jacksonian fiscal policy seemed vindicated by its results. For the first time, the federal government was free of debt and actually boasted a surplus: public land sales were filling the nation's coffers. Nicholas Biddle, however, was not happy. To ensure his bank's survival, he rechartered it in Pennsylvania and exercised the last remaining vestige of its power, which was to call in all its loans, many of which had been made to Jackson's "pet" state banks for immense canal and railroad projects. Biddle insisted on specie or specie-backed bank notes as payment. As in

1819, adequate specie did not exist, and some banks failed while others issued even more worthless paper, some of it in fractional denominations (called *shinplasters*) to take the place of disappearing coins. Diesinkers, who of course advocated the use of hard money over paper, issued tokens with the legend, SUBSTITUTE FOR SHINPLASTERS.

Jackson's own treasury was filling up with unbacked paper, and to regain control of the situation, he issued his Specie Circular of July 1836, which decreed that only gold and silver coins could be used to purchase public lands. Land speculation did not slow as Jackson had predicted, but instead the specie went west with the land buyers. By 1837, Easterners fearing that banks could not redeem their outstanding currency hoarded the remaining specie, and sought to withdraw their bank deposits. Banks and businesses failed. Inflation drove prices of even food staples out of reach and, in New York and other cities, people rioted and looted.

The election of handpicked Jackson protégé Martin Van Buren in 1836 was almost a foregone conclusion. Some satirical tokens of 1837 made teasing reference to Van Buren's inaugural statement, calling Jackson his "illustrious predecessor." These showed a jackass. Others, supporting Daniel Webster, showed a healthy, fully rigged ship of state sailing along on "Webster credit currency," while on the reverse, they showed the ship wrecked with the legend "Van Buren metallic currency." Some tokens poked ire at Senator Thomas Hart Benton, coauthor of the Specie Circular and spokesman for hard money. Struck in copper, these "Mint Drop" tokens implied that Benton's insistence on a minted gold and silver coinage standard had led to the current degraded condition of all money.

Many tokens issued at the height of the Panic of 1837 and afterward were of the NOT ONE CENT variety. These resembled federal Liberty Head large cents of 1816 to 1857, but on the reverse they bore the legend MILLIONS FOR DEFENSE / NOT ONE CENT / FOR TRIBUTE. The phrase (NOT) ONE CENT was a protection against counterfeiting charges, and the added terms turned it into a quotation of Charles Cotesworth Pinckney in the 1797 "XYZ affair." (French diplomat Charles Maurice de Talleyrand, negotiating a treaty with the United States, had demanded a large bribe for himself. U.S. envoy Pinkney famously refused, saying, "No, no, not a sixpence!" His statement evolved into the popular patriotic saying, "Millions for defense, not one cent for tribute.")

Researching the meanings of Hard Times token designs adds to the fun of collecting them. As Q. David Bowers points out, "Completion is not a realistic goal in this series, and sometimes there are long periods between market appearances of rarities."[22] As to condition, Uncirculated examples do exist, but may be 19th-century restrikes. The quality of strike varies from type to type, but usually if one token of a given type is weakly struck, then all of them are, so this is not the most important cost factor—rarity is. An intimate knowledge of the series is critical to keeping costs down, because Hard Times tokens are possibly the most studied American token category, and the competition is sharp.

SATIRICAL ISSUES

HT NO.	YEAR	METAL	COMMENTARY	F	EF	MS-63
1	1832	Cop	A supportive campaign piece by Wright & Bale	$2,000	$7,500	$25,000
4	1832	Br	A great rarity of the series; only two pieces known	80,000	—	—

SATIRICAL ISSUES (continued)

HT NO.	YEAR	METAL	COMMENTARY	F	EF	MS-63
7	1833	Br	A supportive Jackson piece by Robert Lovett Sr.	$250	$750	$2,000
9	1834	Cop	Foes of Jackson ridiculed his much-touted military glory	15	50	300
14	1834	Br E.E.	After congressional elections, a new party reigned	225	750	1,750
15	1834	Cop R.E.	Identifying Whig ideals: liberty and the Constitution	1,250	2,500	5,500
16	1841	Cop P.E	Protectionist Webster favored banking and lending	10	40	250
19	1841	Cop	Would Van Buren's hard money wreck the ship of state?	175	500	1,500
22	1841	Cop	A lightning-free version of the HT-19 design	10	40	250
23	1841	Cop	Obverse imitating that of the scarce federal-issue large cent	50	225	600
24	1841	Cop	Pro-Webster piece supports agriculture and commerce	100	350	1,000
25	1834	Cop	Jackson's "plain democracy" called into question	15	75	350
26	1834	Br	Whig Seward eventually won in 1838, but not this time	125	500	2,000
30	1834	Br	Like Seward, Verplanck lost in 1834 to William Marcy	65	175	800

Satirical Issues (continued)

HT NO.	YEAR	METAL	COMMENTARY	F	EF	MS-63
32	1837	Cop	Mocking Van Buren's inaugural statements	$12	$45	$250
35	1837	Cop	"Not one cent"—because real cents were so scarce	40	275	900
44	1837	Cop	James Moffet's homely Miss Liberty is desirable today	35	250	1,500
46	1837	Cop	One of the most common Hard Times issues, in copper	10	35	250
52	1837	Cop	A further variation of the "Not One Cent" theme	12	50	275
65	1837	Cop	Scovill issue noting the fateful date the panic began	15	50	275
67	1837	Cop	November 1837: bankers sought resumption of specie payments	10	40	250
69	1837	Cop	Blaming Van Buren for the dire situation	10	40	250
70	1833	Cop	Commonplace issue of engraver Hulseman of Attleboro	10	35	225
73	1837	Cop	A half-cent denomination advertises genuine value	60	150	600
75	1840	Cop	Holed campaign issue made for the lapel, not for circulation	40	150	600

MERCHANT ISSUES

Note: This listing includes just one type per issuer; struck tokens only.

HT NO.	ISSUER	YEAR	METAL	COMMENTARY	F	EF	MS-63
104	Benedict & Burnham	1837	Cop	Company's metal products included tokens	$45	$150	$500
150	H.M. & E.I. Richards	1834	Cop	Owners admired Lafayette and made tokens	12	45	250
152	Robinson's Jones	1833	Cop	A facsimile gold medal for a token design	10	40	300
158	S.B. Schenk	1834	Cop	Touting a versatile planing machine	12	40	275
176	Francis L. Brigham	1833	Cop	Depicting a New Bedford "shopping center"	75	300	1,000
204	T. Duseaman	1837	Cop	Botched Belleville, New Jersey, issue used in Canada	25	125	600
216	Walsh's General Store	1835	Cop	Lansingburgh, New York, "plough penny"	12	45	350
219	Henry Anderson	1837	Cop	Largest boot store in the country	10	40	250
240	Centre Market	1837	Cop	Serving Grand Street in Manhattan	10	35	250
244	H. Crossman	1837	Cop	Reverse resembled the dime and quarter	20	65	350

MERCHANT ISSUES (continued)

HT NO.	ISSUER	YEAR	METAL	COMMENTARY	F	EF	MS-63
263	Feuchtwanger	1837	GS	Proposed substitute for a three-cent piece	$1,250	$3,000	$12,000
268	Feuchtwanger	1837	GS	One-cent piece also circulated as money	60	175	450
291	Merchant's Exchange	1837	Cop	Heart of New York City commerce for a generation	10	40	250
304	Phalon's Hair Cutting	1837	Cop	For a wealthy gentleman's haircut	25	85	350
305	Abraham Riker	1837	Cop	A shoemaker's store card	15	45	250
315	Smith's Clock Establishment	1837	Cop	170 years later, time still is money!	30	110	350
347	O. & P. Boutwell	1835	Cop	High rarity a feature of this Troy, New York, token	3,000	10,000	20,000
428	Ephraim Hathaway	1833	Cop	Elegant fireplace screen for a coal dealer	15	45	250
441	Beck's Public Baths*	1832	Cop	Matchless engraving art by C.C. Wright	250	900	4,000

* Voted No. 86 in *100 Greatest American Medals and Tokens* (Jaeger/Bowers).

3
CIVIL WAR TOKENS (1860–1865)

America's economy slowly recovered after the Panic of 1837, but veered off balance once again at the outbreak of the War Between the States in April 1861. The disruption of commerce between North and South and the material demands of war had powerful effects on how Americans handled money on both sides of the Mason-Dixon line. An early financial symptom of the conflict was a war budget that outstripped the contents of the federal Treasury. In February of 1862, Congress passed an act creating a new series of paper money called *Legal Tender Notes*, payable not in specie, but only in other notes. Knowing their government was operating on unbacked paper, and assuming the cost of all metals would rise, nervous citizens hoarded specie. Not only gold and silver but copper coins quickly disappeared from circulation, and later that year, the United States issued Fractional Currency notes in denominations of 5¢, 10¢, 25¢, and 50¢ to take their place.

Hoarding of coins was going on in the South as well, and commercial entities of all kinds issued paper scrip, fractional notes, bearer checks, and even cardboard tokens as small-money substitutes. Since the Confederacy had few diesinkers and never managed to mint its own circulating coinage, these substituted until war's end. (The "Wealth of the South" tokens, made in Cincinnati, were mainly pre-war issues.) In the North, where the experience of 1837 had taught people to distrust shinplasters, two different forms of small money also came into use: postage stamps and cent-sized copper tokens.

ENCASED POSTAGE STAMPS

Following the suggestion of newspaperman Horace Greeley, Northerners believed it patriotic to use postage stamps for money, since buying stamps supported the government. In August 1862, Congress passed an act allowing this practice. There were eight denominations less than a dollar: 1¢, 3¢, 5¢, 10¢, 12¢, 24¢, 30¢, and 90¢. Unfortunately, stamps did not hold up well after repeated hand-to-hand transfers. People pasted them on cardboard or put them in small envelopes to protect them as they circulated. About this time, Bostonian John Gault came up with a better encasement: an embossed metal frame with a clear mica window on its face. He made an agreement with Scovill in Connecticut to manufacture these, and marketed them to 31 merchants around the Northeast and Midwest.[23] He justified his 2¢-per-holder price tag by the return in value from the merchant advertising on the back. His encasements were short-lived. At the same time they came into use, the United States issued its first run of Postage Currency notes (based on postage stamp designs) and concurrent with its second run in 1863, the government ordered all other types of postage being used as money to be turned in.

Encased postage stamps are sought not only by exonumists, but also by stamp collectors and Civil War enthusiasts in general. This high demand for a category with only 225 or so known varieties fosters some healthy prices. The rarest types may have only one or two examples known. The major factors evaluated in grading are the condition of the postage stamp, how well it is centered in its holder, the condition of the encasement, and how well the stamp can be seen through the mica.

Civil War Tokens 69

HB NO.	EP NO.	DENOM.	ISSUER	F	EF	MS-63
HB-42	EP-173	30¢	Ayer's Sarsaparilla, Lowell, Massachussetts	$2,500	$5,000	$10,000
HB-65	EP-67	5¢	Brown's Bronchial Troches	450	700	1,500
HB-78	EP-163	24¢	Burnett's Cocaine, Kalliston, Boston	2,500	5,000	10,000
HB-117	EP-44	3¢	G.G. Evans, Philadelphia	1,200	2,250	4,000
HB-145	EP-80	5¢	L.C. Hopkins & Co., Cincinnati	2,500	6,500	11,000
HB-212	EP-55	3¢	Schapker & Bussing, Evansville, Indiana	700	1,250	2,000

TOKEN CURRENCY

Meanwhile, diesinkers were poised to take advantage of the coin shortage with issues of their own. In the fall of 1862, Cincinnati producers were the first to step up,[24] striking copper tokens in the roughly the same (19 to 20 mm) size as the copper-nickel Flying Eagle (1856–1858) and Indian Head (1859–1864) cents, on a slightly thinner planchet. The major difference, aside from thickness, was color: while the cupronickel federal cents had a yellowish tint, the bronze or pure copper war tokens had a redder hue, giving rise to their nickname, *copperheads*. By early 1863, New York diesinkers had joined the trade, quickly followed by their counterparts in Philadelphia, Boston, Waterbury, and elsewhere. In three years, they created more than 10,000 different token types, and struck an astonishing total estimated at 50 million pieces. Collectors typically separate these into two classes: *store cards* and *patriotic issues*. The merchant store card concept was no different than it had been in the past, except that the populations were far greater. But the design themes of anonymous/patriotic Civil War issues, unlike those of the Hard Times era, were more or less innocuous in political content. Perhaps diesinkers realized that a bitter, bloody internal conflict was not a good subject for satire.

A great many tokens simply mimicked the designs from circulating United States coins, with versions of the Indian head from the new small cent or a Liberty head. Some legends made direct allusion to the unfortunate need for replacement coinage, such as the ones reading MILITARY NECESITY [sic]. Others repeated the Hard Times joke, NOT ONE CENT. Some replaced ONE CENT with EXCHANGE. Diesinker William Bridgens created varieties for New York bearing the legends KNICKERBOCKER CURRENCY and TRADESMEN'S CURRENCY. Openly patriotic tokens were the specialty of Philadelphia diesinker William Key, who depicted a U.S. flag flying from a pole with the legend LONG MAY IT WAVE. The simple patriotic slogans, FREEDOM, ARMY AND NAVY, and UNION FOR EVER were repeatedly used. Some diesinkers used Abraham Lincoln portrait bust dies left over from the 1860 election campaign, and pressed into service stock portraits of George Washington and Benjamin Franklin.

The legality of the token coinage was questionable from the start. Both the government and the public suspected that merchants did not have the means to redeem their tokens on demand, especially if presented in quantity. And what about the millions of anonymous tokens that did not even name a specific business to cash them in? There was no federal law against the use of tokens in trade, but clearly the government never intended to have its own mint supplanted by private producers. On April 22, 1864, Congress enacted a law forbidding the manufacture of all tokens in denominations of 1¢ and 2¢, and authorized large quantities of new bronze one- and two-cent coins to fill the void (this was the first appearance of any two-cent U.S. coin). Citizens resumed their use of federal coins, and the war tokens disappeared.

The supply of Civil War tokens surviving today is large enough to keep them more affordable than those of many other 19th-century categories. But, demand is growing. Prices in the early 1970s ranged between $1 and $3 for common tokens, and lower for bulk buyers. Now common varieties, in any grade, are getting hard to find under $12. With their comprehensive 1975 catalogs *U.S. Civil War Store Cards* and *U.S. Civil War Patriotic Tokens*, updated occasionally by members of the Civil War Token Society, Melvin and George Fuld advanced knowledge of the category and stimulated a good deal of interest among numismatists. The average history buff, however, still had never heard of Civil War tokens; even renowned historian Bruce Catton was unfamiliar with this extensive material culture of his favorite epoch.[25] The Internet has changed everything—bringing in a seemingly endless supply of new collectors from all over the world. Recent hobby books have also picked up on (and promoted) increasing collector interest. The 2007 edition of the *Guide Book of United States Coins* (the "Red Book") tripled its previous year's coverage of Civil War tokens, and both store cards and patriotics were represented among the *100 Greatest American Medals and Tokens* (Jaeger/Bowers, 2007).

For practical purposes in this huge category, collectors must narrow their focus to a particular line. For example, you might concentrate on just the issues of a certain state, or just patriotic issues. You might exclude all issues struck after the Act of April 1864 (such as those relating to the 1864 election campaign). You might also exclude any war-era piece that does not measure 19 or 20 mm, so you are sure to be collecting cent replacements rather than tokens intended for other purposes. The most ambitious specialist might attempt to acquire one example of each Fuld-numbered die. Because stock dies were muled repeatedly in both store card and patriotic combinations, many of the 10,000-plus recorded types are merely recombinations of known dies. A basic dies-only collection would still number several thousand.

Civil War Tokens

Patriotic Tokens

FULD DIE COMBINATION	DESIGN TYPE	F	EF	MS-63
0001-0359b	French liberty head / Not One Cent	—	$50	$200
0002-0270b	French liberty head / Union Forever	$250	750	1,500
0006B-0308a	French liberty head / Army & Navy	10	20	40
0009-406a	French liberty head / Proclaim Liberty Thru Land	75	200	500
0009-431a	French liberty head / Value Me As You Please	60	150	400
0016-0353a	French liberty head / Cannon–drum–flag	12	25	65
0026-0418a	French liberty head / Peace Forever–handshake	12	25	65
0031-0275a	Coronet liberty head / Our Card	100	250	500
0036-0340a	No Slavery liberty head / Flags and shield	20	35	90
0037-0255b	Public Accomodation / Knickerbocker Currency	10	20	40
0037-0256a	Public Accomodation / Horrors of War	12	35	75
0037-0434a	Public Accomodation / United States Copper	10	20	40
0043-0387a	Leichtweis liberty head / Not One Cent	15	35	75
0050-0335a	Indian princess head/ Our Army	10	20	40
0050-0342Ae	Indian princess head / Union Forever	40	70	200
0054-0179a	Indian princess head / Equestrian Jackson statue	10	20	40
0055-0162a	Indian princess head / Our Army	10	25	60
0056-0229do	Indian princess head / Our Country	150	375	650

Note: This chart has no column for metal, because this information is coded as the last digit of the Fuld number. a = Cop, b = Br, c = Nick, d = C-N, e = WM, f = Silv, g = Lead, h = HR, i = Zinc j = GS, k = gilt, m = tin.

PATRIOTIC TOKENS (continued)

0056-0436b
0058-0439a 
0059-0385a 
0061-0198do 
0062-0367a 
0063-0443a 
0066-0370a 
0070-0281a 
0079-0351a 
0083-0264a 
0091-0119b 
0091-0435j 
0096-0129a 
0096-0144a 
0105-0229b 
0106-0432a 
0108-1201d 
0115-0115Ab 

FULD DIE COMBINATION	DESIGN TYPE	F	EF	MS-63
0056-0436b	Indian princess head / United Country	—	$125	$300
0058-0439a	Indian head / All-seeing eye–bow–hand	$25	60	150
0059-0385a	Indian head / Not One Cent	12	30	90
0061-0198do	Indian head / Eagle on shield	150	375	650
0062-0367a	Indian head / Not One Cent	10	20	40
0063-0443a	Indian head / New York	10	20	40
0066-0370a	Indian head / Not One Cent	10	20	40
0070-0281a	Indian head / Spread eagle	100	350	700
0079-0351a	Indian head / Drum–flag–cannons	10	20	40
0083-0264a	Indian head / Pay Bearer One Cent	30	70	200
0091-0119b	Indian head / Washington bust right	—	150	400
0091-0435j	Indian head / United We Stand–fasces	—	150	300
0096-0129a	Indian head / Lincoln bust right	—	350	750
0096-0144a	Indian head / Grant bust left	—	125	350
0105-0229b	Star / Washington bust right–Our Country	—	125	300
0106-0432a	Washington bust right / No Compromise With Traitors	—	125	300
0108-1201d	Washington bust right / Our Union	50	125	300
0115-0115Ab	George Washington bust right / Martha bust left	—	200	400

Note: This chart has no column for metal, because this information is coded as the last digit of the Fuld number. a = Cop, b = Br, c = Nick, d = C-N, e = WM, f = Silv, g = Lead, h = HR, i = Zinc j = GS, k = gilt, m = tin.

PATRIOTIC TOKENS (continued)

FULD DIE COMBINATION	DESIGN TYPE	F	EF	MS-63
0115-0530b	Washington bust right / Don't Tread on Me	$400	$850	$1,500
0117-0420a	Washington bust right / Drum–cannons–Exchange	10	22	50
0125-0160f	Lincoln bust left / Liberty for All	—	400	1,200
0125-0248a	Lincoln bust left / Chain–OK	100	200	450
0126-0294a	Lincoln bust left / Freedom	75	135	300
0127-0185a	Lincoln bust left / Live and Let Live	—	—	7,500
0134-0283d	Lincoln bust left / Eagle with anchor	—	—	500
0135-0440a	Jackson bust left / Now and for Ever	10	20	40
0137-0395a	Jackson bust left / This Medal Price One Cent	15	30	70
0138-0255a	McClellan bust left / Knickerbocker Currency	15	30	70
0141-0307a	McClellan bust left / Army & Navy	15	30	70
0144-0349b	Grant bust left / Cannons–flags–drums	—	100	250
0146-0472f	Rhode Island / East Boston	—	—	4,500
0147-0227b*	I Am Ready / The Union Must & Shall Be Preserved	150	400	750
0151-0430a	Franklin bust right / Penny Saved Is a Penny Earned	10	22	50
0153-0282e	Fur-cap Franklin left / Flying eagle	—	—	2,500

* The specimen shown is silver-plated brass.

PATRIOTIC TOKENS (continued)

FULD DIE COMBINATION	DESIGN TYPE	F	EF	MS-63
0154-0417a	Stephen Douglas bust left / America	$60	$150	$300
0167-0435d	Union shield–eagles / United We Stand–fasces	—	—	400
0168-0311a	Cannon with cannonballs / Army & Navy	15	35	75
0171-0428a	The Peacemaker–cannon / C.L.R.	650	1,500	2,750
0172-0429A	Crossed cannons / Military Necessity	50	110	250
0174-0272a	Equestrian Washington statue / Union for Ever	10	20	400
0188-0435d	Industry–beehive / United We Stand–fasces	—	—	350
0189-0399a	Union–crossed flags / Radiant six-point star	10	20	40
0190-0432f	Liberty cap–rays / No Compromise With Traitors	—	—	15,000
0191-0443a	Pro Bono Publico / New York	10	20	400
0203-0412a	Flag of Our Union / DIX	10	20	40
0239-0422a	Our Little Monitor / 1863–wreath	30	55	130
0254-0255a	Money Makes Mare Go / Knickerbocker Currency	10	20	45
0260-0447d	Constitution / Concession Before Secession	125	250	600
0433-0434b	Union for Ever / United States Copper	—	125	300
0481-0482a	Hope–anchor / Dogs treeing bird	—	150	500

Civil War Tokens 75

PATRIOTIC TOKENS (continued)

0481-0486b

0511-0514a

FULD DIE COMBINATION	DESIGN TYPE	F	EF	MS-63
0481-0486b	Hope–anchor–shield / Vermont militiaman	—	$150	$500
0511-0514a	Wealth of the South / Palmetto–No Submission to the North**	$350	550	1,100

** Voted No. 64 in *100 Greatest American Medals and Tokens* (Jaeger/Bowers).

STORE CARDS, BY STATE
Alabama

AL-425A-6b

Connecticut

CT-35A-1a

CT-560A-1a

Iowa

IA-150A-1a

IA-570A-1a

FULD NO.	REVERSE NO.	ISSUER	F	EF	MS-63
ALABAMA					
AL-425A-6b	1047	White & Swann, Huntsville	$2,500	$4,000	$6,000
CONNECTICUT					
CT-35A-1a	1002	E.W. Atwood, book dealer, Bridgeport	12	22	50
CT-560A-1a	x	New York Store, millinery, Waterbury	60	135	300
IOWA					
IA-150A-1a	x	Reynolds & Co., New York Store, Cedar Rapids	400	700	1,500
IA-570A-1a	1368	Gage, Lyall & Keeler, grocers, Lyons	300	600	1,200

Note: A two-letter state code has been added to the Fuld store-card numbers to identify each token as follows: State code, hyphen; numerical city code and upper-case letter for each merchant in that city, hyphen; digit for each different reverse employed, with a lowercase letter at the end to identify the metal. a = Cop, b = Br, c = Nick, d = C-N, e = WM, f = Silv, g = Lead, h = HR, i = Zinc, j = GS, k = gilt, m = tin. When a lowercase "o" appears at the end of the Fuld number, it indicates an overstrike. Reverse numbers are per Fuld. A lowercase "c" in this column indicates a custom-made reverse die.

Illinois

IL-45A-1b
IL-150BD-1a 
IL-150I-4a 
IL-150R-1a 
IL-150Y-1a 
IL-660A-2a 
IL-680A-1a 
IL-755D-1a 
IL-775C-1a 
IL-795A-1a 

Indiana

IN-185A-2a
IN-190A-1b 
IN-290D-1d 
IN-290E-5d 
IN-460N-1a 
IN-460V-1a 

FULD NO.	REVERSE NO.	ISSUER	F	EF	MS-63
ILLINOIS					
IL-45A-1b	x	George B. Ames, druggist, Belvidere	$12	$25	$75
IL-150BD-1a	x	P. Stumps, firemen's hat dealer, Chicago	400	750	1,500
IL-150I-4a	1356	A. Candler, watch and clockmaker, Chicago	25	50	125
IL-150R-1a	1080	A.W. Escherich, engraver, Chicago	30	60	250
IL-150Y-1a	1286	F. Gall, New York Meat Market, Chicago	35	70	200
IL-660A-2a	1338	A. & H. Alschuler, Ottawa	30	60	150
IL-680A-1a	1195	Dean Slade, dry goods, Palatine	40	80	200
IL-755D-1a	1107	William Knapp, well driller, Rockford	30	60	200
IL-775C-1a	1316	A.G. Greenman, druggist, Sandwich	45	90	250
IL-795A-1a	1172	J.C. Yager, trunkmaker, Springfield	—	—	900
INDIANA					
IN-185A-2a	1295	Jacob Groyer, grocer, Como	45	100	250
IN-190A-1b	1127	Samuel Beck, hide and pelt dealer, Corunna	50	125	300
IN-290D-1d	1299	A.D. Brandiff, stove dealer, Fort Wayne	—	400	1,250
IN-290E-5d	1323	W.H. Brooks Jr., wallpaperer, Fort Wayne	—	400	1,250
IN-460N-1a	c	R.R. Parker, clothier, Indianapolis	60	125	300
IN-460V-1a	1351	Tyler's Bee Hive, dry goods, Indianapolis	40	100	200

Civil War Tokens 77

Indiana *(continued)*

IN-500S-1a

IN-630A-5b

IN-740B-4a

IN-890A-1a

Kansas

KS-550A-1a

Kentucky

FULD NO.	REVERSE NO.	ISSUER	F	EF	MS-63
INDIANA *(continued)*					
IN-500S-1a	1318	Joseph Thew, shoemaker, Kendallville	$60	$125	$300
IN-630A-5b	1328	H.D. Higgins, optician, Mishawaka	100	175	450
IN-740B-4a	1331	J.S. Queeby, dry goods, Peru	20	40	100
IN-890A-1a	c	Union Steam Bakery, Terre Haute	275	500	1,000
KANSAS					
KS-550A-1a	1085	A. Cohen, gents' clothing, Leavenworth	1,500	3,500	6,000
KENTUCKY					
KY-150C-1a	1278	J. Dolman, stockings, Covington	65	135	300
KY-370A-1e	c	W.S. Johnson, soda check, Henderson	2,000	3,000	4,500
KY-480B-3a	c	J.W. Lee, baker/confectioner, Lexington	150	225	600
KY-510A-2b	c	George Bruchlacher, tavern, Louisville	350	550	1,200
KY-510B-1a	c	H. Preissler, soda water, Louisville	650	900	2,000

Massachusetts

MA-115A-1a   MA-115B-1a   MA-115D-2b

MA-115EA-1a   MA-115G-1a   MA-260A-1f

MA-320A-1a   MA-970A-1b

Maryland

MD-60B-1b   MD-60D-1b

MD-60N-1b   MD-560A-1b

Maine

ME-100A-2a

FULD NO.	REVERSE NO.	ISSUER	F	EF	MS-63
MASSACHUSETTS					
MA-115A-1a	c	Comers Commercial College, Boston	$150	$250	$750
MA-115B-1a	1413	Dunn & Co.'s Oyster House, Boston	30	75	200
MA-115D-2b	1284	Joseph Merriam & Co., engraver, Boston*	2,000	3,000	6,500
MA-115EA-1a	1371	Pulmonales cough remedy	20	45	90
MA-115G-1a	c	G.F. Tuttle's Restaurant, Boston	125	225	450
MA-260A-1f	c	E.P. Francis City Hotel, Fall River	—	650	1,750
MA-320A-1a	1120	Bay State Horse Power, Harvard	80	200	500
MA-970A-1b	c	Charles Lang, Die Sinker, Worcester	100	225	500
MARYLAND					
MD-60B-1b	1001	Shakespeare Club, Baltimore	350	600	1,750
MD-60D-1b	1352A	G. Bauernschmidt, tavern, Baltimore	300	450	1,000
MD-60N-1b	c	P.H. Odenwald, tavern, Baltimore	300	400	1,000
MD-560A-1b	c	G.R. Bowman, confectioner, Hagerstown	1,750	3,750	5,500
MAINE					
ME-100A-2a	1200	R.S. Torrey, Maine State Bee Hive, Bangor	100	175	250

* Voted No. 83 in *100 Greatest American Medals and Tokens* (Jaeger/Bowers).

Michigan

FULD NO.	REVERSE NO.	ISSUER	F	EF	MS-63
MICHIGAN					
MI-3-A1a	c	Smith Brothers, dry goods, Addison	$30	$65	$200
MI-40A2do	1015	Philip Bach, dry goods, Ann Arbor	—	300	650
MI-225N2a	c	Campbell, Linn & Co., dry goods, Detroit	12	22	50
MI-280E1a	c	A. Schmitz, iron dealer, East Saginaw	30	75	250
MI-300E1b	1340	A. Mester, marble works, Eaton Rapids	350	650	1,350
MI-300F1a	c	Stirling, dry goods, teas, Eaton Rapids	25	60	125
MI-320A1b	c	Giles Bishop, grocer and druggist, Flint	30	50	125
MI-370D1b	1305	Goodrich & Gay, hardware, Grand Rapids	12	22	75
MI-370F1a	c	C. Kusterer, brewer, Grand Rapids	125	200	500
MI-495A1a	c	James Kennedy, exchange agent, Ionia	12	25	60
MI-525D2a	1348	W. Jaxon, grocer, Jackson	12	25	75
MI-770C1a	c	A. Parker, druggist, Pontiac	—	200	500
MINNESOTA					
MN-680A-2a	1272	A.W.E., Red Wing	2,500	4,000	7,500
MN-720A-3a	1168	F.W. Andrews, dry goods, Rochester	500	750	1,500
MN-760A-1a	c	D.C. Greenleaf, watchmaker, St. Paul	400	500	750
MN-980A-1b	1310	C. Benson, druggist, Winona	400	750	1,500

Missouri

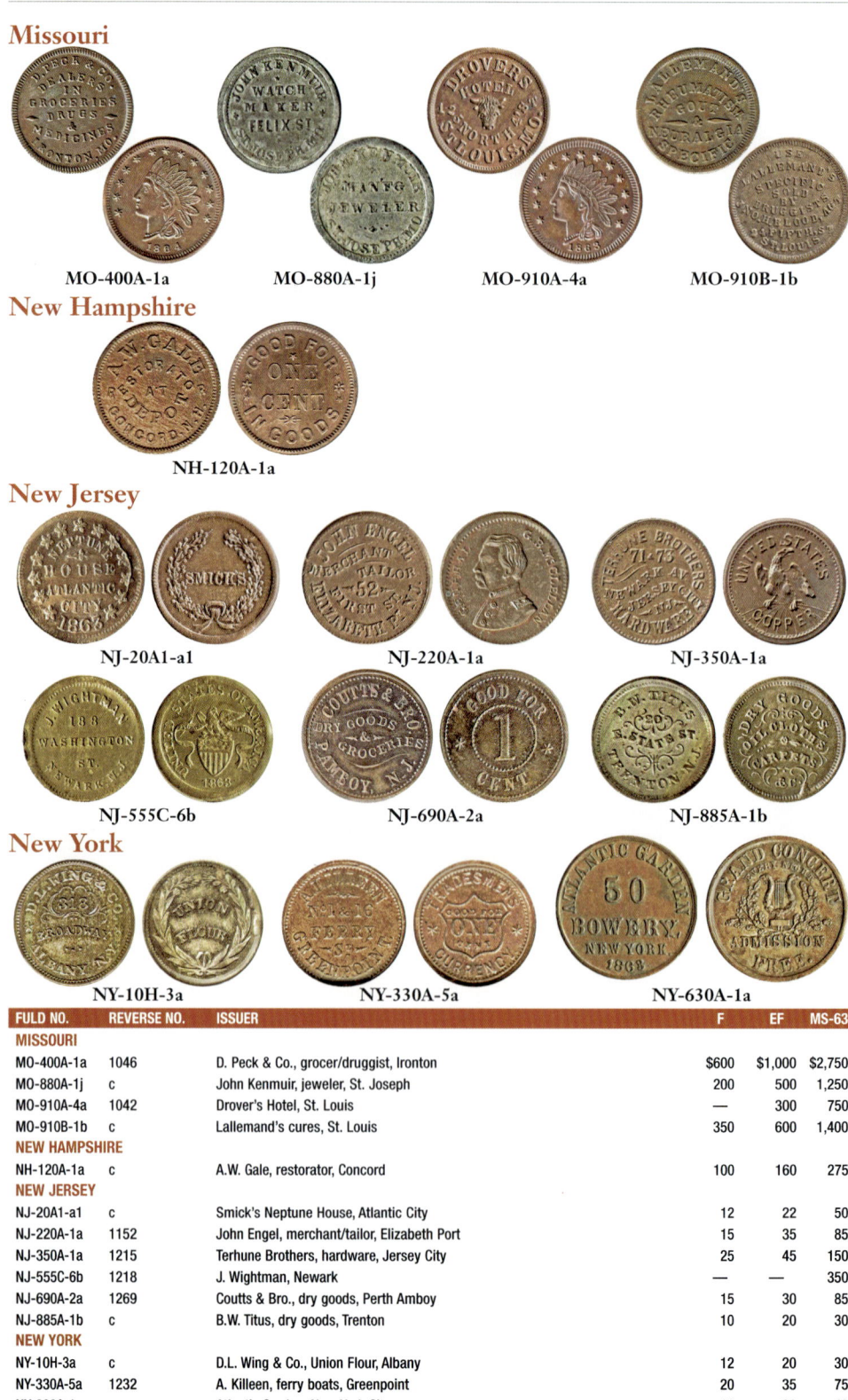

MO-400A-1a   MO-880A-1j   MO-910A-4a   MO-910B-1b

New Hampshire

NH-120A-1a

New Jersey

NJ-20A1-a1   NJ-220A-1a   NJ-350A-1a

NJ-555C-6b   NJ-690A-2a   NJ-885A-1b

New York

NY-10H-3a   NY-330A-5a   NY-630A-1a

FULD NO.	REVERSE NO.	ISSUER	F	EF	MS-63
MISSOURI					
MO-400A-1a	1046	D. Peck & Co., grocer/druggist, Ironton	$600	$1,000	$2,750
MO-880A-1j	c	John Kenmuir, jeweler, St. Joseph	200	500	1,250
MO-910A-4a	1042	Drover's Hotel, St. Louis	—	300	750
MO-910B-1b	c	Lallemand's cures, St. Louis	350	600	1,400
NEW HAMPSHIRE					
NH-120A-1a	c	A.W. Gale, restorator, Concord	100	160	275
NEW JERSEY					
NJ-20A1-a1	c	Smick's Neptune House, Atlantic City	12	22	50
NJ-220A-1a	1152	John Engel, merchant/tailor, Elizabeth Port	15	35	85
NJ-350A-1a	1215	Terhune Brothers, hardware, Jersey City	25	45	150
NJ-555C-6b	1218	J. Wightman, Newark	—	—	350
NJ-690A-2a	1269	Coutts & Bro., dry goods, Perth Amboy	15	30	85
NJ-885A-1b	c	B.W. Titus, dry goods, Trenton	10	20	30
NEW YORK					
NY-10H-3a	c	D.L. Wing & Co., Union Flour, Albany	12	20	30
NY-330A-5a	1232	A. Killeen, ferry boats, Greenpoint	20	35	75
NY-630A-1a	c	Atlantic Garden, New York City	10	20	40

New York (continued)

FULD NO.	REVERSE NO.	ISSUER	F	EF	MS-63
NEW YORK (continued)					
NY-630D-1b	c	H.J. Bang Restaurant, New York City	—	$50	$125
NY-630F-1a	c	V. Benner & Bendinger, liquors, New York City	12	25	55
NY-630H-1a	c	J.L. Bode, birdstuffer, New York City	15	30	65
NY-630Z-1a	c	F.R. Friese, undertaker, New York City	20	40	90
NY-630AK-2a	1163	Hussey's Special Message Post, New York City	20	45	125
NY-630AQ-1a	c	Gustavus Lindenmueller, tavern, New York City	10	20	45
NY-630AR-1do	c	Charles A. Luhr's Pike Slip, New York City	—	300	650
NY-630BA-1a	c	G.M. Mittnacht's Eagle Safe, New York City	12	20	45
NY-630BC-1a	c	Henry C. Montz, Orpheus Hall, New York City	15	30	75
NY-630BH-1a	1293	Christian Rauh, confectioner, New York City	12	25	55
NY-630BQ-1a	c	Ph. J. Seiter's Market, New York City	10	25	65
NY-630BU-2a	c	S. Steinfeld, liquor seller, New York City	10	20	45
NY-630CC-04a	1353	Washington Market, New York City	15	30	75

New York (continued)

NY-695A-2a NY-845A-1a NY-890C-1h

Ohio

OH-74A-7i OH-100B-4a OH-160Da-1a OH-165AK-6b

OH-165BJ-16a OH-165CJ-10a OH-165CN-1e OH-165CV-3a

OH-165DEa-1e OH-165DL-4a OH-165DV-8d OH-165DY-9a

FULD NO.	REVERSE NO.	ISSUER	F	EF	MS-63
NEW YORK (continued)					
NY-695A-2a	c	M.L. Marshall, sporting goods and rare coin, Oswego	$20	$45	$95
NY-845A-1a	c	D. Skidmore's Hotel, Seneca Falls	150	300	550
NY-890C-1h	c	Fred A. Plum, India Rubber Depot, Troy	80	150	250
OHIO					
OH-74A-7i	1042	D.E. Stearns, grindstones/hardware, Berea	—	—	450
OH-100B-4a	1346	E.G. Selby & Co., hardware, Bryan	20	45	100
OH-160Da-1a	1295	J. Kirchenschlager, tavern, Chillicothe	100	225	450
OH-165AK-6b	1283	Downing, sheet music, coins, Cincinnati	750	1,500	3,000
OH-165BJ-16a	1026	Carl Haas, Cincinnati	25	50	$125
OH-165CJ-10a	1331	Warren Kennedy News Depot, Cincinnati	18	30	75
OH-165CN-1e	c	B. Kittredge & Co., gun dealer, Cincinnati	—	—	750
OH-165CV-3a	1242	H. Kreber, grocer, Cincinnati	—	200	600
OH-165DEa-1e	c	J.O. Loewe, Cincinnati	500	900	1,500
OH-165DL-4a	1290	McClenahan & Co., grocer, Cincinnati	18	35	85
OH-165DV-8d	1279	J.T. Moore, fruit dealer, Cincinnati	—	—	1,500
OH-165DY-9a	1283	Jas. Murdock Jr., die sinker, Cincinnati	—	750	2,000

Ohio (continued)

Pennsylvania

FULD NO.	REVERSE NO.	ISSUER	F	EF	MS-63
OHIO (continued)					
OH-165FM-4a	1298	Wm. Senour, hotel proprietor, Cincinnati	$150	$250	$550
OH-165FX-11a	1160	John Stanton, diesinker, Cincinnati	—	275	650
OH-165GC-10a	1288	Van Wunder, meat market, Cincinnati	80	135	250
OH-270A-6a	1337	D. Farnham & Co., dry goods, Edgerton	45	85	200
OH-340A-1a	1333	D. & W. Riblet, Galion	2	25	60
OH-520A-2a	1088	A.E. Griffin, dentist, Marion	135	225	500
OH-765B-4a	1344	D.R. Jennings, surgeon, dentist, Ravenna	150	300	575
OH-995B-1a	c	H.G.O. Cary's cough cure, Zanesville	20	35	90
PENNSYLVANIA					
PA-13C-2A	c	National Planing Mill, Allegheny City	20	35	80
PA-464A-1a	1006	Petersen's, jeweler, Honesdale	20	40	100
PA-525A-1a	1148	S.H. Zahm, coin dealer, Lancaster	80	150	300
PA-615A-1a	c	G.C. Porter, dry goods, clothier, Meadville	12	25	50
PA-750A-1b	c	Adams, Ton Hall, Philadelphia	10	20	50
PA-750C-2a	c	Amon Bakery, Philadelphia	20	50	110
PA-750J-1a	c	R. Flanagan's Punch, Philadelphia	20	22	50
PA-750JA-1a	c	Fox's Casino, Philadelphia	18	30	75

Pennsylvania (continued)

PA-750M-3a
PA-750O-2b 
PA-750P-1a 

PA-765C-1a
PA-765J-1a 

Rhode Island

RI-700A-3j
RI-700B-2f 
RI-700C-6a 

RI-700D-1a
RI-700F-1a 
RI-700G-2f 

Tennessee

TN-180A-5a
TN-430B-05a
TN-600A-6b
TN-600A-9b

FULD NO.	REVERSE NO.	ISSUER	F	EF	MS-63
PENNSYLVANIA (continued)					
PA-750M-3a	1379	North Military Hall, Philadelphia	$10	$22	$45
PA-750O-2b	c	H. Mulligan, watchmaker, Philadelphia	65	150	300
PA-750P-1a	c	F.P. Rogers, dairy equipment, Philadelphia	50	100	225
PA-765C-1a	c	Buffum's Mineral Water, Pittsburgh	12	25	75
PA-765J-1a	c	A. Ludewig, tobacconist, Pittsburgh	20	45	125
RHODE ISLAND					
RI-700A-3j	1374	Arcade House, Providence	—	200	500
RI-700B-2f	c	Frank L. Gay, bookseller, Providence	—	—	5,000
RI-700C-6a	1429	Charnley, Providence	—	—	6,000
RI-700D-1a	1285	H. Dobson, Providence	—	—	7,000
RI-700F-1a	1294	Le Fevre, Pro Empire Saloon, Providence	75	150	400
RI-700G-2f	1159	City Fruit Store, Providence	—	—	1,500
TENNESSEE					
TN-180A-5a	1168	N.O. Underwood, Dedham	850	1,750	3,000
TN-430B-05a	c	Chamberlain Bros., Arctic Soda Water, Knoxville	1,000	1,500	3,500
TN-600A-6b	1423	Cossitt Hill & Co., Memphis	600	800	1,500
TN-600A-9b	1426	Cossitt Hill & Co., Memphis	600	800	1,500

Civil War Tokens

Tennessee *(continued)*

TN-600C-4a

TN-690C-4a

TN-690E-6a

Virginia

VA-580A-1e

Wisconsin

WI-45A-1a

WI-220E-3a

WI-250D-1a

WI-330A-1a

WI-340B-1a

WI-360A-1a

WI-410G-2a

WI-510A-1a

WI-510B-1a

WI-510C-1do

WI-510E-1a

WI-510I-1a

FULD NO.	REVERSE NO.	ISSUER	F	EF	MS-63
TENNESSEE *(continued)*					
TN-600C-4a	1401	B.E. Hammar & Co., wagoneer, Memphis	$500	$750	$1,500
TN-690C-4a	1394	D.L. Lapsley & Co., Nashville	2,000	3,000	5,000
TN-690E-6a	1047	Walker & Napier, Nashville	2,000	3,000	5,000
VIRGINIA					
VA-580A-1e	1284	Pfeiffer & Co., Norfolk	450	650	1,500
WISCONSIN					
WI-45A-1a	1145	Peck & Orvis, druggists, Baraboo	—	—	750
WI-220E-3a	1220	F. Fritz, grocer, Fond du Lac	—	—	450
WI-250D-1a	1089	Philipp Klaus, notions/toy dealer, Green Bay	30	65	150
WI-330A-1a	c	N.A. Brown's Cream Ale, Kenosha	250	400	750
WI-340B-1a	1194	T. Hoffman, brewer, Kilbourn City	125	225	500
WI-360A-1a	1280	Mons. Anderson, dry goods, La Crosse	45	100	225
WI-410G-2a	c	J. Rodermund, Madison Brewery, Madison	200	450	1,000
WI-510A-1a	c	E. Aschermann, tobacconist, Milwaukee	30	60	150
WI-510B-1a	c	Wisconsin Brewery, Milwaukee	45	100	300
WI-510C-1do	c	Philip Best, Empire Brewery, Milwaukee	—	400	750
WI-510E-1a	c	V. Blatz, City Brewery, Milwaukee	30	50	125
WI-510I-1a	c	D.J. Doornink, grocer, Milwaukee	30	50	150

Wisconsin *(continued)*

WI-510L-3a WI-510M-1a WI-510R-1a

WI-510U-1a WI-510AB-1a WI-510AG-1a1

WI-590A-1a WI-920H-4a

West Virginia

WV-100B-2b WV-220A-6a WV-260A-1b

WV-890B-3a WV-890D-4a WV-890F-2a

FULD NO.	REVERSE NO.	ISSUER	F	EF	MS-63
WISCONSIN *(continued)*					
WI-510L-3a	c	Wm. Frankfurth, hardware, Milwaukee	$100	200	$400
WI-510M-1a	c	Goes & Falk, Bavaria Brewery, Milwaukee	35	65	125
WI-510R-1a	c	C. Hermann stoneware factory, Milwaukee	30	60	150
WI-510U-1a	c	A. Kleinsteuber, mechanic, Milwaukee	40	80	250
WI-510AB-1a	c	Friedrich Miller, Plankroad Brewery, Milwaukee	25	50	110
WI-510AG-1a1	c	J. Pritzlaff & Co., hardware, Milwaukee	25	55	150
WI-590A-1a	1174	Mrs. J. Tate, milliner, Oconomowoc	6,500	10,000	15,000
WI-920H-4a	1341	Chas. Goeldner, harness maker, Watertown	70	100	225
WEST VIRGINIA					
WV-100B-2b	c	(Unknown merchant), Snow Hill	1,750	3,000	4,500
WV-220A-6a	c	Bassett's, hoop skirts, Glen Easton	225	350	750
WV-260A-1b	1391	Kelly's Store, Hartford City	400	700	1,500
WV-890B-3a	1169	John Eckhart, hosiery, Wheeling	60	135	350
WV-890D-4a	1322	R.C. Graves, news and books, Wheeling	60	135	350
WV-890F-2a	1225	J.W.C. Smith, leather goods, Wheeling	70	165	400

Sutlers' Tokens

Highly prized are the Civil War sutler tokens, issued by civilians who followed Union and Confederate troops around as they camped and decamped, with wagons full of goods to supply the soldiers' needs. Sutlers carried items such as books, writing paper, patent medicines, and warm socks. Because they often charged outrageous prices for these common materials, troops did not like to patronize them, and after the war, when the armies moved west to protect the territories and manage "Indian troubles," private post traders took over the military trade. In the 1890s, these civilian-run posts were replaced with government-operated post exchanges. A good reference for sutler issues is David Schenkman's *Civil War Sutler Tokens and Cardboard Scrip* (1983).

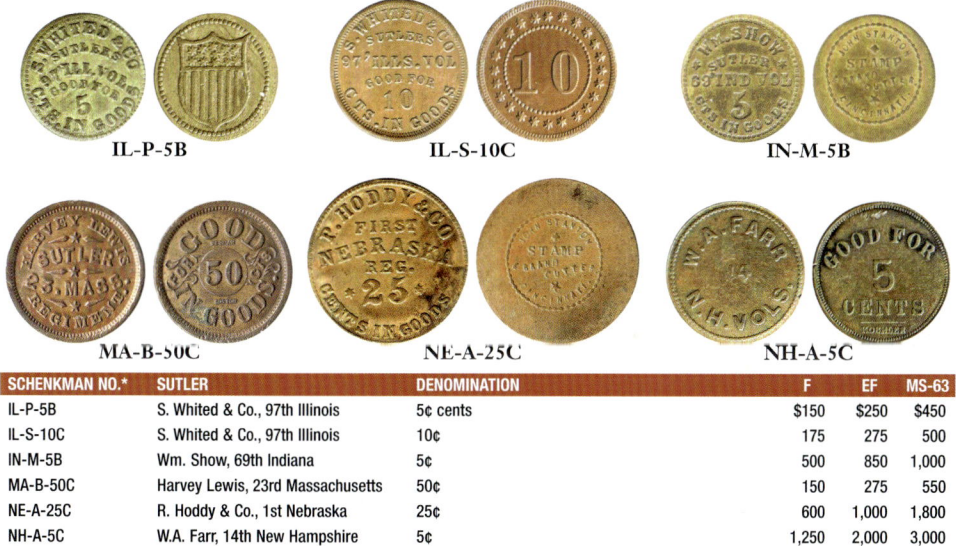

SCHENKMAN NO.*	SUTLER	DENOMINATION	F	EF	MS-63
IL-P-5B	S. Whited & Co., 97th Illinois	5¢ cents	$150	$250	$450
IL-S-10C	S. Whited & Co., 97th Illinois	10¢	175	275	500
IN-M-5B	Wm. Show, 69th Indiana	5¢	500	850	1,000
MA-B-50C	Harvey Lewis, 23rd Massachusetts	50¢	150	275	550
NE-A-25C	R. Hoddy & Co., 1st Nebraska	25¢	600	1,000	1,800
NH-A-5C	W.A. Farr, 14th New Hampshire	5¢	1,250	2,000	3,000

* In the Schenkman numbering system, the suffix "C" = copper, "B" = brass.

4

COMPANY STORE AND COMMISSARY TOKENS

The booming demand for fuel, building, and agricultural products in rapidly industrializing America gave rise to a new form of token-based currency, fostered by the captains of industry to manage the spending habits of their enormous workforces. Tokens may have first been issued as payment for labor in 1840, when the Hard Times coin shortage prompted the Bergen Iron Works of Lakewood, New Jersey, to issue copper tokens for employees to spend at its company store. By the end of the 19th century, from coalfield to forest, from factory to farm, "the company" credited workers with tokens and scrip, and there was only one place the credit was good: at the company store.

> You load sixteen tons, and what do you get?
> Another day older and deeper in debt.
> Saint Peter don't you call me 'cause I can't go
> I owe my soul to the company store.

Songwriter Merle Travis was recalling the experience of his father—a Muhlenberg County, Kentucky, coal miner—when he composed those lyrics, immortalized by Tennessee Ernie Ford for Capitol Records in 1955.[26] A West Virginia woman told of her family's frustration with shopping at the company store:

> How I remember the mixed feelings we had about coal company scrip. If you went down to the company store to purchase groceries, you "drew" scrip. If you needed dry goods you charged them—and those charges along with whatever scrip you drew were taken out of Dad's pay on payday. Many times my father picked up an empty envelope trying to feed 12 children and clothe them...You had to decide between two evils: drawing scrip and having no cash on hand—or not drawing scrip so that Dad could draw a payday, by trying to stretch the groceries at home—canned food in the meantime. Usually, our family, due to its size, lost the scrip battle.[27]

MINING-COMPANY TOKENS

American mining companies began issuing paper scrip and tokens by necessity, in areas deep in the mountains and far from stores and banks. It wasn't until the late-19th century that the practice became widespread, even in well-settled regions. The majority of the 10,000-plus coal token varieties originated in the bituminous fields of West Virginia and Kentucky. At the height of American coal production in the 1920s, tokens could be found in aluminum, brass, and copper, but during World War II's metal shortages, fiber replaced these metals. Collectors of token, paper, and cardboard scrip find them cataloged together in Donald O. Edkins' 1983 work, *Edkins' Catalog of United States Coal Company Store Scrip* (volumes I and II). Tokens usually carried the company name, a token denomination, and the punched-in number of the particular mine or the initial of

Company Store and Commissary Tokens

the town where the company store was located. Companies mining ores other than coal issued tokens as well: the Nevadaville, Colorado, tokens of the Hubert silver mine are an example. Ore haulers were paid by the "cord," that is, a 7- to 10-ton wagonload of ore, and two of the Hubert issues are marked 1/3 CORD and 1/4 CORD.

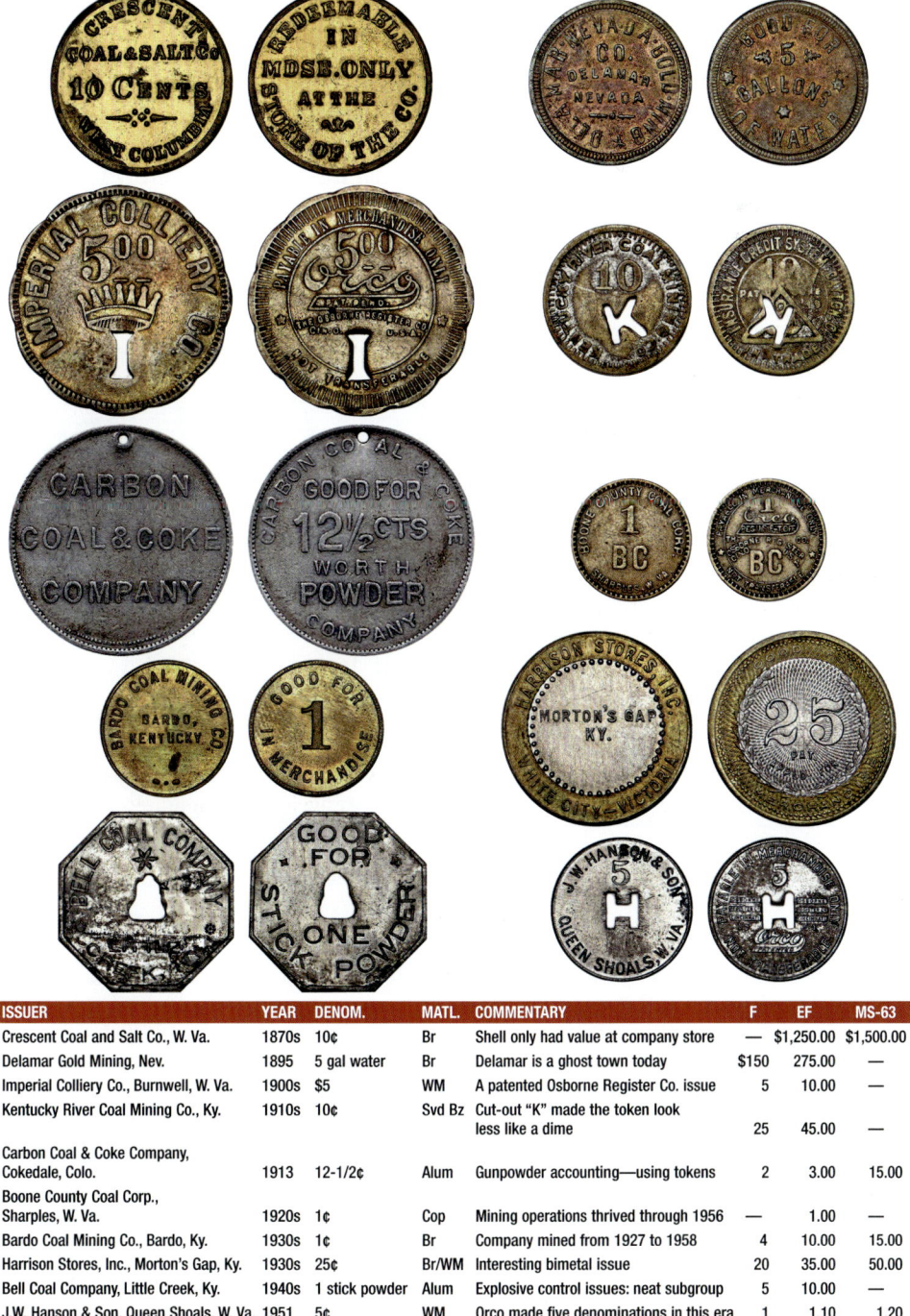

ISSUER	YEAR	DENOM.	MATL.	COMMENTARY	F	EF	MS-63
Crescent Coal and Salt Co., W. Va.	1870s	10¢	Br	Shell only had value at company store	—	$1,250.00	$1,500.00
Delamar Gold Mining, Nev.	1895	5 gal water	Br	Delamar is a ghost town today	$150	275.00	—
Imperial Colliery Co., Burnwell, W. Va.	1900s	$5	WM	A patented Osborne Register Co. issue	5	10.00	—
Kentucky River Coal Mining Co., Ky.	1910s	10¢	Svd Bz	Cut-out "K" made the token look less like a dime	25	45.00	—
Carbon Coal & Coke Company, Cokedale, Colo.	1913	12-1/2¢	Alum	Gunpowder accounting—using tokens	2	3.00	15.00
Boone County Coal Corp., Sharples, W. Va.	1920s	1¢	Cop	Mining operations thrived through 1956	—	1.00	—
Bardo Coal Mining Co., Bardo, Ky.	1930s	1¢	Br	Company mined from 1927 to 1958	4	10.00	15.00
Harrison Stores, Inc., Morton's Gap, Ky.	1930s	25¢	Br/WM	Interesting bimetal issue	20	35.00	50.00
Bell Coal Company, Little Creek, Ky.	1940s	1 stick powder	Alum	Explosive control issues: neat subgroup	5	10.00	—
J.W. Hanson & Son, Queen Shoals, W. Va.	1951	5¢	WM	Orco made five denominations in this era	1	1.10	1.20

Lumber-Company Tokens

America's lumber industry issued scrip and tokens, too—not just to lumberjacks who felled trees, but to everyone associated with the forest-products industry: the haulers who brought logs out of the forest, the sawmill and lumberyard workers—even the tanners who used hemlock bark in the tanning process, and turpentine makers who used pine sap in their spirit stills.[28] The lumber companies followed the trees, depleting first the hardwood forests of New England and the mid-Atlantic states, and then the Southern pines, including those of Texas and Florida. Michigan, Wisconsin, and Minnesota experienced heavy turn-of-the-20th-century timbering, until the loggers forged westward to the forests of northern California, Oregon, and Washington. For this reason, lumber-company tokens can be found across the country. They looked much like the coal-company tokens and came in denominations of 1¢, 5¢, 25¢, 50¢, and $1, with a few rare $10 and $20 issues. Collectors of both mining and lumber company scrip (including tokens) unite in the National Scrip Collectors' Association, which publishes the newsletter *Scrip Talk*.

DESCRIPTION	YEAR	DENOM.	MATL.	COMMENTARY	F	EF	MS-63
Pacific Lumber, Scotia Co., Cal.	1910s	$1	Alum	Redwood logging giant is still in business	$5	$10	$15
Paul's Valley Lumber, Okla.	1920s	5¢	Alum	Wilburn cut trees from Tennessee to Oklahoma to Mississippi	25	35	50
Suttle-Patton Lumber Co., Felix, Ala.	1920s	50¢	Alum	The town of Felix is now part of Suttle	3	3	10

Farm and Factory Checks

Large agricultural concerns also compensated their workers in tokens. Anne Arundel County, Maryland, used the system extensively, beginning with the tokens of strawberry grower John A Hancock in 1853. Hancock's check was as simple as could be: he stamped his initials on a thin round disc of galvanized iron. It was an ideal way to tally output per acre, as well as to keep wages commensurate with the volume of work: one pint of strawberries (or one bushel of peanuts, one pail of milk, or one shorn sheep) would be worth one token to the worker, who could redeem it for pay either at the end of the day or at the end of the week. Work checks were not always redeemable for cash, but might be good for merchandise at local general stores (either the farmer's own company stores, or independently owned stores serving multiple farms). The storeowners paid farmers for produce with the same currency; thus everyone in a given area kept track of inventory by the same method. Pickers were often seasonal workers living in on-farm barracks just for the period of harvest, so this system encouraged them to leave all their wages behind when they

Company Store and Commissary Tokens

departed. In the 20th century, the name of the plantation or farm issuer would be printed on the aluminum or brass token, usually in a ring around the product unit, such as 1 PINT.

The check system worked just as well in factories. Seafood, fruit, and vegetable cannery tokens; meatpacking plant tokens; silk-mill tokens; and others make the category a broad and interesting one.

ISSUER	YEAR	DENOM.	MATL.	COMMENTARY	F	EF	MS-63
Howell Works, Garden, N.J.	1835	1¢	Cop	(HT-200) First work checks were Hard Times issues	$150	$450	$2,000
Bergen Iron Works, N.J.	1840	1 cent	Br	(HT-205) In what is now called Lakewood	75	125	500
Jos. J. Sayre, Cincinnati, Ohio	1860s	1 box berries	Br	Berry check by prolific Civil War diesinker	500	2,500	4,250
Wailuku Plantation, Maui, Hawaii	1871	12-1/2¢	Bz	Part of the Hawaiian coinage series	750	1,500	—
E. New Market Packing Co., Md.	1900s	1 bushel tomatoes	Br	Cannery token of distinctive shape	3	5	—
Victor Sais, Casa Colorada, N.M.	1901	5 shorn sheep	WM	With hand shears, 5 sheep = one half hour	350	1,250	2,000
Derrickson & Martin, Dover, Del.	1910s	tomato check	Br	Extensive use of picker checks	—	100	105
M. Records Sons' Co., Forest, Del.	1910s	snip 10¢	Alum	The task was named, valued on the token	—	150	155
M. Records Sons' Co., Forest, Del.	1910s	bean picking	Alum	Picking was worth less than snipping	—	150	155
M. Records Sons' Co., Forest, Del.	1910s	1 bucket tomatoes	Alum	Rate for tomatoes was higher than for beans	—	150	155
Duenweg State Bank, Duenweg, Mo.	1920s	1 tray (6 qt)	Alum	Take your tokens to the bank for exchange	—	1	—

COMMISSARY TOKENS

Other organizations that issued their own tokens for on-site redemption were military bases, prisons, and private academies. For military personnel, tokens were a convenience, assuring them access to quality American-made products at special canteen prices, wherever in the world they might be posted. For prisons, tokens provided good security for handling and accounting the wages of prisoners, and the principle was similarly applied at residential schools.

20TH-CENTURY MILITARY COMMISSARY TOKENS

Military clubs such as the Airmen's Club, Officer's Club, or NCO Club issued tokens on posts and bases as a form of credit. Personnel could charge a certain amount of tokens for food and drink purchases, against the next paycheck, with a credit scale based on rank. Paper military chits were issued for the same purpose. Both tokens and chits might be issued at the same location, but usually it was one or the other. In Japan, Korea, and Vietnam, all military personnel received military payment certificates (MPC) instead of cash on payday, to thwart black-market activity. These certificates covered fractional denominations as well as whole-dollar amounts. Here, club tokens were used to operate pool tables, jukeboxes, and slot machines. (Caution: Vietnam-era tokens were made of base metal plated in brass. Some with the brass coating removed have been marketed as new varieties!) In Afghanistan and Iraq, naval ships and military bases issued tokens or cardboard POGs[29] for similar purposes, as did some veterans' facilities and "old soldier's homes" in the United States. This broad category includes issues from 1) permanent military bases in United States territories and on foreign soil, and 2) temporary bases established in combat zones around the world.[30] A good set of references for these issues is Paul Cunningham's *Military Tokens of the United States, Vol. 1, Domestic Issues* (1995), and *Vol. II, Overseas Issues* (1998). He lists not only 20th-century but also earlier issues.

ISSUER	YEAR	DENOM.	MATL.	COMMENTARY	F	EF	MS-63
Fort Mansfield Post Exchange, R.I.	1900s	5¢		Scarce issue unlisted in Cunningham	$350	$600	—
Lowry AFB, NCO Open Mess, Denver, Colo.	1940s	50¢	Bz	Received as part of a paycheck	—	3	—
USMC Camp Jay Books, Danang, Vietnam	1960s	25¢	Br	FLC = Force Logistics Command	—	6	$8
Nha Trang Air Base NCO Club, Vietnam	1960s	10¢	Br	South Vietnam shared this base with the USAF	—	6	8
U.S. Army HACOM, Saigon, Vietnam	1960s	unk	Br	HACOM = Headquarters Area Command	—	6	8
Danang Air Base, Vietnam	1960s	10¢	Br	Home of the USAF Tactical Air Command	—	6	8

20TH-CENTURY MILITARY COMMISSARY TOKENS (continued)

ISSUER	YEAR	DENOM.	MATL.	COMMENTARY	F	EF	MS-63
I Corps Air Defense Vietnam	1960s	5¢	Br	Serving the entire area bordering North Vietnam	—	$6	$8
Langley AFB, NCO Club, Va.	1976	none	Bz	A Bicentennial souvenir issue	—	—	2

PRISON COMMISSARY TOKENS

Prison tokens are generally very simple, and their interest lies not in their designs but in their issuers—the many different kinds of American penal institutions. Federal and state penitentiaries, county and city jails, juvenile reformatories, work camps, and even POW camps and mental hospitals issued tokens. The practice may have begun with the "Junior Republics" of the 1890s. These residential facilities for impoverished wayward boys paid tokens to the boys in exchange for work to teach them self-sufficiency and the self-discipline of operating on a budget.

The prison-token category is cataloged by Jerry Zara in *Prison Tokens and Medals of the United States* (1992).

ISSUER, LOCATION	DENOM.	MATL.	COMMENTARY	F	EF	MS-63
Arkansas Department of Corrections, statewide	10¢	Alum	Generic token for use in many facilities	$5	$7	$10
Glenwood State Hospital School, Iowa	1¢	Br	Children's mental institution work check	5	10	15
Hutchinson Correctional Facility, Kan.	unk	Br	Having no value outside prison walls	2	3	5
Kinross State Prison, Kincheloe, Mich.	25¢	Br	These came in denominations through $5	1	2	3

5

AMUSEMENT TOKENS

Collecting amusement tokens can be as much fun as playing the machines that once accepted them! This affordable category covers tokens designed to be paid into amusement machines, beginning in the 1890s with the introduction of coin-operated slot machines and continuing to the present. (Dollar- and half-dollar-sized metal gaming tokens minted for casino slot machines in the 1960s, and modern casino chips of all kinds, form their own specialty, discussed in chapter 6.) The standard reference is *Video Arcade, Pinball, Slot Machine, and Other Amusement Tokens of North America*, by Stephen P. Alpert and Kenneth E. Smith, published by the Amusement Token Collectors Association in 1984. Alpert's synopsis of the subject in *Tokens and Medals* (1992) is quoted extensively here.

GAMBLING-MACHINE TOKENS

Beginning in the 1890s, slot machines proliferated in taverns, cigar stores, restaurants, game rooms, and amusement emporiums. In places where gambling was prohibited, they paid out in tokens rather than coins. Similar devices called *trade stimulators* appeared around the same time. These came in standing floor-size models as well as countertop size. Their object was to get customers to buy more of a certain product. They featured games of chance, such as wheels of fortune and rows of spinning picture reels, which at the drop of a coin or pull of a handle might match three pictures of a kind. How did this stimulate trade? Patrons paid for their cigars, beers, etc., by putting coins in the machine. They had a chance to win a free cigar or beer, but the only way to win one was to buy one, and of course, the odds were in the merchant's favor.

Slot-machine and trade-stimulator tokens bore the name of the amusement companies that manufactured them, or the name of the machine they were designed to fit, or some phrase such as NOT REDEEMABLE, FOR AMUSEMENT ONLY, or NO CASH VALUE. This satisfied local ordinances, and if a particular merchant chose to redeem the tokens for money, it was an under-the-table affair. Many tokens bore serial numbers, each number corresponding to a specific machine or business, and all tokens corresponded in size to circulating U.S. coins. Nickel-sized varieties are the most common through the early 20th century, but cent-sized, dime-sized, and quarter-sized tokens were also issued. A console-type gambling machine featuring a mechanical horse derby became popular in the 1930s, and its tokens depicted horses or horseshoes. Tokens for cigarette-pack trade stimulators might read GOOD FOR 1 PACK CIGARETTES.

DESCRIPTION	YEAR	DENOMINATION	MATERIAL	COMMENTARY	F	EF	MS-63
Gopher Sales Co., Faribault, Minn.	1890s	1 free play	Br	Generic token for many machines	—	$1	—
Caille-Scheimer Co. "Puck"	1899	Not shown	Br	A musical slot machine	$20	40	$75

GAMBLING-MACHINE TOKENS *(continued)*

DESCRIPTION	YEAR	DENOMINATION	MATERIAL	COMMENTARY	F	EF	MS-63
Automatic Cashier and Discount Machine	1905	5¢	Alum	A game of chance and music, too	$10	$15	$16
The Pile Driver countertop machine	1933	1 free play	Br	Product of Automatic Games Co.	—	1	2

ARCADE TOKENS

Around 1900, America saw the birth of the penny arcade, and many tokens from this era are the size of a cent. Patrons tried their aim at shooting galleries, rang bells with the blow of a mallet, plucked up prizes with mechanical crane arms, played skee-ball and other games of skill, and even viewed short peep-show films, all for a token. The name of the traveling carnival, amusement park, or peep show, or perhaps the name of the amusement company that manufactured the machines, appeared on these tokens.

Pinball machines were a development of the 1930s, and if these accepted tokens rather than coins, they often bore the name of the game manufacturer. The late 1970s saw the introduction of arcade franchises such as Chuck E. Cheese, a kids' pizza-and-game parlor. Children bringing home a token or two as a souvenir of their visit could expand their collection by visiting as many arcades and amusement parks as possible. Chuck E. Cheese tokens interest collectors because their issues bear dates, and some include the franchise location as well. At today's shopping-mall video-game parlors, players pay in tokens and are paid out in cardboard tickets, redeemable only in candy or toys. Video-arcade tokens are the size of a quarter dollar or slightly smaller, and are not stamped with any denomination, so operators may adjust pricing at will. They are rapidly disappearing as machine manufacturers switch to computerized, card-operated machines.

DESCRIPTION	YEAR	DENOMINATION	MATL.	COMMENTARY	F	EF	MS-63
Toledo Amusement Exchange, Ohio	1900s	No cash value	Cop	For all machines at a penny arcade	—	$1	—
Baltimore Fair Grounds	1900s	1¢	Cop	For use in the penny arcades	—	1	—
Bacigalupi's Penny Arcade, San Francisco	1903	1¢	Br	Arcade lost in 1906 earthquake	$40	75	—
Mills Edisonia (Chicago, Cincinnati, St. Louis)	1904	1¢	Br	Bought gum, nuts, cigars, games	5	10	$15
Silver King Novelty Co., Indianapolis	1920s	Not shown	Alum	For trade stimulators and slots	—	1	—
American Sales Co.	1920s	Not shown	Ni	Designed to fit company machines	—	1	—
Aladdin's Palace	1960s	Not shown	Br	Aladdin's arcades were in Europe, too	—	1	—

ARCADE TOKENS (continued)

DESCRIPTION	YEAR	DENOMINATION	MATERIAL	COMMENTARY	F	EF	MS-63
Fantasy Isle, Fond du Lac, Wisconsin	1980s	Not shown	Br	The walls were modeled as a cave	—	$1	—
Four Lucky Sisters from Italy	1980s	25 points	Alum	On the Boardwalk in Atlantic City	—	1	—
Putt-Putt Golf & Games	1982	Not shown	Br	A nationwide arcade chain's token	—	—	$1
Chuck E. Cheese	1988	25¢	Br	Arcade's tokens may bear dates	—	1	—

MUSIC-MACHINE TOKENS

Music-machine tokens recall the era before recorded music, when people lived in silence unless they attended a live performance, sang, or played an instrument. In our music-saturated 21st century it is hard to imagine their thrill at dropping a token into an automatic music machine, to fill the air with happy sound. In his 2001 work *The Golden Age of Automatic Musical Instruments*, Arthur Reblitz illustrates hundreds of fabulous devices such as the Wurlitzer automatic harp, the mechanical PianOrchestra, the Mandolin Quartette, and the huge salon orchestrions, automatic banjos, player pianos, and band organs, as well as wheeled street organs that enlivened public places and brought a goldmine to their owners. Between 1890 and 1920, playing most of these devices cost but a nickel, or a nickel-sized token. Token-operated phonographs and, later, jukeboxes have carried on the tradition. Most tokens carried the name of the manufacturer of the music machine, or the name of the machine itself, with the phrase GOOD FOR ONE TUNE. The standard reference for this category is Q. David Bowers's monograph, *A Tune for a Token: A Catalog of Tokens and Medals Relating to Automatic Musical Instruments, 1850–1930*.

ISSUER	YEAR	DENOMINATION	MATERIAL	COMMENTARY	F	EF	MS-63
Berry's Barber Shop, St. Joseph, Mo.	1900s	5¢ music	Br	Get a haircut and hear a tune	$25	$50	$51
Bohemian Beer Garden, Willard, Ohio	1900s	5¢ music	Br	Probably fed a mechanical piano	35	50	51
Colley Novelty Co., Allegheny, Penn.	1900s	1 tune	Br	Company outside of Pittsburgh	8	20	21
The Big Onion	1900s	5¢ piano	Br	"Drop me in the piano"	25	40	41

Music-Machine Tokens *(continued)*

ISSUER	YEAR	DENOMINATION	MATERIAL	COMMENTARY	F	EF	MS-63
Fountain Café, Cincinnati, Ohio	1900s	5¢ music	Br	Mechanical music popular in Ohio	$35	$50	$51
Chicago Talking Machine Co.	1904	1 tune	Ni	Operated Busy Bee phonograph	—	2	3
Yale Wonder Clock	1905	5¢	Nick	Yale was in Burlington, Vermont	5	15	—
Palm Garden Pianolin	1906	5¢	Cop	Cabinet piano with violin tones	20	35	50
Mandolin Quartette (by Wurlitzer)	1907	1 tune	Br	Hammers hit strings, piano style	25	35	36
Putman & Merick, Covington, Ky.	1910s	5¢ piano	Br	Good for a drink as well!	—	50	51
Wm. Wagner "The Club"	1910s	5¢ banjo	Br	Automatic banjo, Marysville, California	25	50	51
Marquette Music Co.	1915	1 tune	Br	Marquette was based in Detroit	—	25	26

6

GAMING CHIPS AND TOKENS

Money substitutes used in gambling have been with us a long time. Around 1000 A.D., Scandinavians carved them from bone and antler. Three centuries later, Chinese craftsmen carved them from bone and mother of pearl. From these origins developed later metal pieces, including those used in the United States.

PLAY MONEY AND GAME COUNTERS

Die-struck metal gaming tokens, called *jetons* in French and *spiel marken* in German, made their appearance in 16th-century Europe. The Kettle diesinking firm of Birmingham, England, exported imitations of U.S. $2.50 and $5 coins (dated 1803) for use as game counters, and through the 19th century Ludwig Lauer of Nuremburg, Germany, was a major supplier of U.S. spiel marken.

In the first half of the 19th century in New England and the mid-Atlantic states, gambling opportunities for the adventurous simply did not exist. In the genteel South, wagers on village horse races and private card games were tolerated, but commercial gaming parlors were nowhere to be found. The rough-and-ready Mississippi valley on the Western frontier, however, was made to order for gambling. By 1830 busy casinos crowded New Orleans, and through 1860 flashy riverboat gamblers ruled the waterway from the Gulf states to St. Louis. There is no evidence that anything but hard cash was at stake in these early games on land and water.

The discovery of gold at Sutter's Mill on January 24, 1848, opened California to the risk-takers, and San Francisco quickly eclipsed New Orleans as the heart of U.S. gambling. As settlement spread outward with miners looking for new strikes, gaming establishments proliferated across the West. Players wagered gold and silver coins—and even gold dust and nuggets—at the tables, but die-struck spiel marken began to be seen in quantity in the early 1850s as well. Most were struck in brass and imitated the designs of federal circulating half eagle ($5), eagle ($10), and double eagle ($20) gold coins.

San Francisco card sellers Thurnauer & Zinn dealt in spiel marken made by Lauer. Playing-card dealer Theodor Bollenhagen of New York packed a Lauer spiel marke inside every deck of cards he sold. New York importers Strasburger & Nuhn also dealt in Lauer marken. Some of these had made-to-order merchant imprints, while others bore portraits of popular personalities such as George Washington, Abraham Lincoln, Jenny Lind, and Tom Thumb. (These were used not only at the poker and blackjack tables of the West, but also in parlor games of whist and euchre across the country.) Chinese gaming houses in San Francisco and Oakland used round brass tokens with square holes cut in the center, bearing Chinese characters and looking like Chinese coins.[31]

By the end of the century, use of die-struck gaming tokens had virtually ceased. Clay-composition poker chips, introduced in the 1880s, were easier to handle and stack. Furthermore, the ruthless activities of certain professional gamblers, or *sharps*, who bilked countless greenhorns of their savings, plus a few national lottery-related scandals and horse-racing frauds, aroused Victorian sensibilities against all gambling. One by one, states outlawed not only table gambling but also race wagering, lotteries, and even bingo.

Gaming Chips and Tokens

ISSUER/DESCRIPTION	YEAR	MATL.	COMMENTARY	F	VF	MS-63
California Token with flag and sidewheeler	1849	Br	For use on Gold Rush gaming tables	$100	$250	$800
Jenny Lind jeton by Ludwig Lauer	1850	Br	The Swedish Songbird's visit generated scores of issues	8	10	25
Theodor Bollenhagen (Coronet Liberty, $20 size)	1850s	Br	One free token inside each pack of cards	15	40	125
Compositions Spiel Marke, Liberty	1850s	Bz	A very common Ludwig Lauer issue	3	5	10
Compositions Spiel Marke, Washington	1850s	Bz	Collected as part of the Washington series	3	7	15
Weil & Levi, San Francisco (importers) $10 size	1860s	Br	Counters came in $5, $10, and $20 sizes	—	750	1,250

BOARD-GAME MONEY

People turned to parlor games for entertainment. Since the 1870s, board games included a variety of coin-shaped game counters that had no value in real money. These were not always struck in metal; some were of turned wood or lithographed cardboard, and aluminum and plastic prevailed in the 20th century. In 1878 McLoughlin Bros. of New York marketed a board game called "Monopolist," featuring metal counters marked as $1 coins. The box read, "On this board the great struggle between Capital and Labor can be fought out to the satisfaction of all parties, and if the players are successful, they can break the Monopolist and become Monopolists themselves." It was stamped with images of scientists, farmers, merchants, and mechanics, whose speculative pitfalls were RUIN / FAILURE / BANKRUPTCY / DISHONOR / UNLUCKY VENTURE / IMPAIRED CAPITAL / EMBARRASSMENT / LOSS OF CREDIT.

Other 19th-century games known to feature play money were:[32]

> United States Educational Toy Money (Milton Bradley, 1877)[33]
> The Cash Boy (Selchow & Righter, 1885, for boys)
> The Good Old Game of Corner Grocery (Parker Brothers, 1887)
> The Game of Store (J.H. Singer, 1890, for girls)
> The Game of What D'Ye Buy (McLoughlin Bros., 1890)
> Cash: Honesty is the Best Policy (J.H. Singer, 1890)
> The Game of Playing Department Store (McLoughlin Bros., 1898)

Board-Game Money *(continued)*

ISSUER	DESCRIPTION	DENOM.	YEAR	MATL.	COMMENTARY	F	EF	MS-63
Milton Bradley	U.S. Educational toy money	10¢	1878	Sd Card	Set came in a box with a game board	$2	$3	$5
Milton Bradley	U.S. Educational toy money	50¢	1878	Sd Card	Game included a full set of U.S. coin denominations	2	3	5
	Two bits play coin / two horses' heads	25¢	1900s	Alum	From an unknown 20th-century game	—	1	—
American Chicle Co., Mazuma	Buffalo Bill	10¢	1930s	Alum	Coins came inside packs of chewing gum	—	3	5

Casino Chips

The Great Depression was the catalyst for the return of casino gambling in America. In hopes of stimulating a desperate economy, Nevada introduced state-supervised gambling in 1931, giving birth to a collecting category that has seen remarkable gains in popularity in recent decades: casino chips. The issues of Nevada alone present a wide field, and since 1989, Mississippi riverboat-casino chip varieties have been issued by more than 100 floating casinos berthed in six states (Iowa, Illinois, Mississippi, Louisiana, Indiana, and Missouri). American Indian–operated franchises now exist in many states, and there are also issues of coastal day and weekend cruise liners to collect. Collector Robert Eisenstadt cautions beginners about how to define casino chips:

> There is a world of difference between a "casino chip" and a "poker chip." Poker chips usually had on them just a picture (animal, boat, flag, design, etc.), no denomination, and came in different colors. They were made through the inspiration of any chip manufacturer (no authorization was needed), and hundreds of thousands may have been sold over the years throughout the country in retail stores and by mail order, mainly for private games. Consequently they are generally (but not always) common and inexpensive. Casino chips typically have on them the names of the casino, city, and state, the casino logo, and a dollar amount. They were ordered in limited quantities by a commercial gambling establishment for gambling at table games at that place; that is, authorized and made for a particular casino. They are treated like money by the casinos and are often destroyed after they are retired, in which case the old ones that reach collectors today were bought or won at the tables years ago and taken home. Consequently, casino chips are often rare and valuable, particularly the higher-denomination ones.[34]

"Chip Professor" Michael Knapp notes that each of these colorful discs made of clay composition or plastic evokes the ambience of a particular casino, and that

> casinos that have been in existence for some time have had a number of different styles, designs, and types of chips [because] chips eventually wear out and must be replaced. Sometimes marketing drives the decision to issue new chips: a casino changes its logo or its advertising campaign. . . . Chips are almost always changed when the ownership of a casino changes. In Nevada, chips may be "demonetized," or rendered non-negotiable, at any time. The casino is required to publish a notice in newspapers of general circulation, specifying a redemption period for all existing chips in public hands, and notifying the public of the date after which those chips will no longer be accepted. After the redemption period is over, the old chips are obsolete, and are of value only to collectors.[35]

Desirable, obsolete chips can be expensive, but according to Knapp, most beginners get started by buying new chips at face value at casinos. For example, in Atlantic City "there are 12 casinos now, and each casino uses chips in different denominations, colors, and designs: $1, $2.50, $5, $25, $100, and even higher. Just collecting the $5 and under denominations from each casino would produce a complete collection of current chips, 36 of them, at a cost of $102." From there, collectors may begin on another geographical area, such as Las Vegas or Reno, and may even move on to non–U.S. casinos or cruise-line issues. Or they could acquire the chips of the legendary casinos of yesteryear, such as the Sands (Las Vegas, 1942–1996), the Flamingo (Las Vegas, 1946–1970), and the Overland Hotel (Reno, 1933–1948, 1957–1977). Dozens of collector/dealer Internet sites give access to chips from the Mississippi gambling boats, the Indian-reservation casinos, the small-town casinos of Nevada, the card rooms of California and Texas, and even the illegal Prohibition-era casino boats run by mobsters along the coasts. The major collectors' organization is the Casino Chip and Gaming Token Collectors' Club, which maintains a library of standard chip references and publishes a quarterly magazine, *Casino Chip and Token News*. A standard reference on Nevada issues is *Nevada Gaming Checks and Chips*, by Howard and Kregg Herz.

CASINO	YEAR	DENOMINATION	CONSTRUCTION / COMMENTARY	F	EF	MS-63
Harrah's, Reno / Lake Tahoe, Nev.	1970s	$1	Composition; brass slug core	$2	$4	—
Dolphin Cruise Line, Miami, Fla.	1980s	$5	CHIPCO Pro-Tech construction	1	2	—
Kewadin Casino, Sault Ste. Marie, Mich.	1980s	50¢	CHIPCO house chip	1	2	—

Casino Chips (continued)

CASINO	YEAR	DENOMINATION	CONSTRUCTION / COMMENTARY	F	EF	MS-63
Imperial Empress, Fort Lauderdale, Fla.	1980s	$25	CHIPCO ship chip	$1	$2	—
Swinomish Northern Lights, Anacortes, Wash.	1980s	$1	Molded composition; plastic center inlay	2	3	—
Palm Hotel and Casino, San Juan, Puerto Rico	1990s	$25	Composition; metal center inlay	3	5	—
El Capitan, Hawthorne, Nev.	1990s	1 (NCV)*	Stamped composition; promotional piece	—	—	$1
Surfside Casino Day Cruise, Freeport, Tex.	1990s	$5	High color; bold graphics from CHIPCO	1	2	—
Kickapoo Casino, McCloud, Okla.	1990s	$5	Versatile CHIPCO designs popular	1	2	—
Seminole Hard Rock Casino, Tampa, Fla.	2004	25¢	Special two-sided grand opening issue	2	4	—
Bugsy's Hideaway, Las Vegas, Nev. (nonexistent)	2008	$5	Fantasy casinos created for poker sets	—	—	1

* NCV = No Cash Value. The "beginner" chips illustrated here were purchased from an exonumia dealer's "junk box" for the prices indicated.

Casino Tokens

As discussed in chapter 12, slot machines premiered in the 1890s, and though they featured gambling, most paid out in metal tokens having no value in real money. It was not until 1965 that metal tokens intended to have the same value as coins began to be minted for casinos, after a sequence of economic events plunged the gambling business into a state of emergency. In 1964, the price of silver surged to a high of $1.29 per ounce, causing the U.S. Mint to announce that it would no longer strike dimes and quarters in silver, and that the silver fineness of half dollars would be reduced. People began to hoard 90%-silver Morgan and Peace dollars, which had been used since the 1930s in Nevada's slot machines.

Casinos had good stocks of them in their vaults, but they were disappearing from the tables in alarming numbers, so the state gaming commission beseeched Congress to authorize minting of gaming tokens to take their place. When the go-ahead came, casinos hired private mints to make their tokens, starting with Pennsylvania's Franklin Mint.

Franklin Mint founder Joseph Segel remembers the 1965 ceremony where he presented Reno casino magnate Bill Harrah with a special platinum Proof strike of the first token designed just for Nevada gaming. It was a big moment for Segel, whose mint, prior to this, had only created medal series for mail-order sale to collectors (see chapter 13). Said Segel, "Harrah's sent a number of security people to oversee operations. We had no real reputation at that point; we'd only been in operation one year. They had people stationed at every point in the minting process, to make sure we did things on the up-and-up. When orders began coming in from all the other casinos, we expected them each to send their own security overseers. They didn't!" The typical token run for a casino was from 5,000 to 250,000 circulation strikes, up to 500 Proofs in individual coin holders, 2,500 prooflike sets for Franklin Mint stockholders, and up to 500 silver Proof sets for presentation purposes.

Each casino was legally bound to redeem only its own tokens, but patrons moved from casino to casino, mixing the tokens of competing casinos together. Casino owners then had to exchange the tokens among themselves. Eventually, each casino was given its own edge-reeding pattern, so dealers could readily feel and remove a foreign token during stacking. In 1971 the federal government, just before its issue of the Eisenhower dollar, withdrew permission for casinos to mint private tokens. In 1979, when the U.S. Mint introduced its Susan B. Anthony dollar in a reduced diameter, tokens were once again permitted, so slot-machine coin acceptors would not have to be refitted to the new smaller size. At this point, several new token producers got into the act. Of all metal casino tokens, however, the most valuable to collectors are the high-quality Franklin Mint issues of 1965 to 1969. Harrah's platinum presentation piece was the highlight of a 2005 eBay sale that garnered a whopping $1 million winning bid for a full collection of chips and tokens.

CASINO	YEAR	DENOMINATION	MATERIAL	F	EF	MS-63
(Proof) Cactus Pete's, Jackpot, Nev.	1968	$1	C-N	—	—	$10
(Proof) Pussycat a' Go Go, Las Vegas, Nev.	1968	$1	C-N	—	—	10

Casino Tokens *(continued)*

CASINO	YEAR	DENOMINATION	MATERIAL	F	EF	MS-63
(Proof) Horseshoe Club, Reno, Nev.	1968	$2.50	Bz	—	—	$15
Caesar's Palace, Las Vegas, Nev.	1969	$1	C-N	—	$5	—
Sands Hotel and Casino, Atlantic City, N.J.	1982	$1	C-N	—	5	—
Gold Strike Inn, Boulder City, Nev.	1985	$1	C-N	—	5	—
Playboy Hotel and Casino, Atlantic City, N.J.	1987	$1	C-N	—	10	—
Showboat Hotel, Casino, and Bowling Center, Atlantic City, N.J.	1987	$1	C-N	—	5	—

"Buy the Book Before the Coin!"

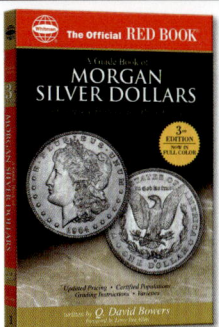

A Guide Book of Morgan Silver Dollars, 3rd ed.

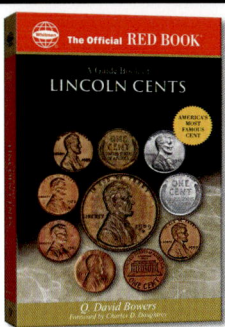

A Guide Book of Lincoln Cents

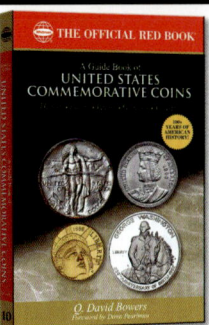

A Guide Book of United States Commemorative Coins

Whitman Publishing offers books for every collector.

The best way to enjoy your hobby (and profit from your investment) is to learn as much as possible, from recognized experts in the field. Whether you collect classic U.S. coins, world coins, ancients, medals, tokens, or paper money, Whitman Publishing has the perfect book to add to your library. The guide books pictured here are from the Bowers Series. The entire Whitman catalog is online at whitmanbooks.com.

Other books in the Bowers Series include:
- *A Guide Book of Double Eagle Gold Coins*
- *A Guide Book of United States Type Coins, 2nd ed.*
- *A Guide Book of Modern United States Proof Coin Sets*
- *A Guide Book of Shield and Liberty Head Nickels*
- *A Guide Book of Flying Eagle and Indian Head Cents*
- *A Guide Book of Washington and State Quarters*
- *A Guide Book of Buffalo and Jefferson Nickels*
- *A Guide Book of United States Tokens and Medals*

The entire Whitman library is available at www.whitman**books**.com
Alao available at local bookstores, hobby retailers, or wherever books are sold.

To place your order, please call toll free: 1-800-546-2995
customerservice@whitmanbooks.com

7

TRANSPORTATION TOKENS

After the United States fought its war for independence, the new nation's survival hinged not only on military power and statecraft, but also on transportation. As settlers opened new territories they built networks of roads, canals, and rails to carry their rich provincial resources to market, while urban populations required public transportation for productivity. Often, the price of passage was a token. Through the 19th century, tokens bought rides on horse-drawn stages, omnibuses, streetcars, and hacks, and steam-powered cable cars, electric streetcars, funicular railways, subways, taxis, and buses.[36] A *vecturist* is someone who collects and studies these travel-related issues. The diverse category is composed not only of "tickets to ride" but also "tickets to pass," because vehicle owners needed tokens to pay for the plank roads, canal locks, tunnels, and turnpikes they traveled. Some tokens served as checks for services: to stable a team of horses at a livery, to buy an automatic car wash, or to rent a space in a parking garage. Bridge and ferry tokens form their own subcategories, as do depot-to-hotel checks or *depotels*. Collectors exchange research and arrange meetings through the American Vecturist Association (inaugurated in 1948), which publishes a journal called *The Fare Box*.

Today, anyone who has paid a fare with a token probably recalls it as a metal object, and might be surprised to learn that many 19th-century transportation tokens were made of celluloid or vulcanite (hardened rubber). In fact, half of all hard-rubber tokens manufactured in the United States were for transportation uses. Vulcanite was not cast in a mold, as were celluloid and plastic; rather, it was struck between dies in the manner of metal—with the difference that the dies were heated. Metal tokens were generally of brass, copper, copper-nickel alloy, or aluminum. The 19th century was the heyday of beautiful pictorial tokens, desirable to collectors for their engraved renditions of the vehicles of a bygone era. After the 1914 development of the registering fare box, which counted each token as it was fed in by passenger, the use of metal tokens proliferated, and mass production and standardization of types precluded most pictorial issues. Then arose the familiar perforated transit token bearing the initial of the city or system that employed it, in a diameter slightly smaller than a dime (less than 18 mm). A cut-out letter in the middle of the token made it distinguishable at a glance from coins and other tokens.

STAGE, OMNIBUS, AND HACK TOKENS

The brass Gibbs U.S.M. stage tokens of 1831 are our earliest known American passenger tokens. John Gibbs, the Hard Times–era diesinker, operated his mint in Belleville, New Jersey. Beginning in 1829 he also ran a stage service from Belleville to New York City by way of Newark. Since 1806 (if not earlier) the stage had traveled a well-made plank road from the Hudson River ferry terminal to Newark, and Gibbs added the four-mile leg from Newark to Belleville. According to an English tourist who made the trip, it was no picnic:

> Here [at Paulus Hook on the Hudson River] we got into a vehicle called a Stage Coach and rode to Newark eight miles. . . . They have

no elegance of form nor is their construction adapted to the ease and convenience of passengers, they generally contain four seats placed before each other, each one with good crowding is made to hold three persons, the driver occupies one place in front, while much of the baggage is stowed within to the great inconvenience of the passengers, whose attention is often wholly taken up in keeping from breaking their skins, in some of the rugged roads I think their bones even must be in danger.[37]

Horse-drawn omnibuses were the urban version of the stagecoach, and just as uncomfortable, with two long benches facing each other across an aisle running front to back. The first American omnibus lines to issue tokens were the Roxbury and Maverick Coach lines of Boston, in 1837. Many New York omnibus tokens were holed, so they could be placed on a long string kept by the driver.

Horse-drawn hacks, operated by individuals as well as by hack companies, transported passengers through many cities and towns—well into the 20th century—until motorized taxis replaced them. Some hack lines offered service between certain hotels and train depots. Many hotels issued tokens free to guests, good for one passage to the station.

Horsecar Tokens

By 1831 in New York City, plans were already in motion to run omnibuses on rails, which not only leveled the ride, but also extended the useful life of the horses. The first "horsecar" entered service along 4th Avenue in 1832 for the New York and Harlaem Railroad, and the firm of Bale & Smith supplied fare tokens for this line in 1835. These tokens were octagonal, but according to John Coffee, round tokens evolved later on, as an easier way for the conductor to collect fares:

> The car was entered from the rear, and the passenger placed his [coin of] fare in a long trough which was raised at the rear, so that the coin would roll down the trough and fall into a fare box beside the driver. Passengers who had purchased reduced-rate tickets had to hand them forward, an awkward arrangement in a crowded car.... [M]any [horsecar tokens] are inscribed 'Ticket' on the reverse.[38]

The L & P Street railway of Louisville, Kentucky, which got under way in 1844, is considered the country's earliest full horsecar rail system. It issued its first tokens sometime in the 1850s. In 1872, a catastrophic equine influenza epidemic took the lives of 20,000 horses in the United States. In August of that year, animals were dying at a rate of 200 per day in the cities, bringing horsecar lines to a complete standstill. Teams of men pulled the cars until the epidemic subsided and adequate numbers of replacement horses could be imported and trained, but many horsecar companies never recovered from their losses. By 1917, most had gone out of business or converted to steam- or electric-powered systems.

Cable-Car and Electric Streetcar Tokens

The first steam-powered cable-car line was installed in San Francisco in 1873, and by 1890 many American cities had gladly exchanged the manure, flies, feeding, and stabling expense of horses for the noisy rattle of the traction systems. Now the cars were pulled by long cables of braided iron and hemp, resting on pulleys between the tracks, and powered by huge steam engines in centralized cable houses. Each car had a gripman who gripped or loosened the continuously moving cable with a long-handled lever, to change speed or stop. There were dangers inherent in the system: the cable ran at a constant speed of nine miles per hour, and if one trolley rear-ended another, a chain-reaction pileup could result. Gripmen knew that if they applied the brakes in the middle of a curve, the cars would become stranded, so they did not slow down or make any concession for other vehicles or pedestrians at curves.[39] If the cable snapped anywhere on the line, every car came to a halt.

On the streets of Richmond, Virginia, and Scranton, Pennsylvania, in the 1880s, electric-powered streetcars proved their superiority to cable cars, and eventually supplanted them around the country (with the exception of San Francisco, which still maintains its cable system). Some streetcar lines were known as "traction companies." Because they sold the electric power they generated for other purposes besides urban transit, the term ELECTRIC COMPANY is seen on many streetcar tokens. Streetcars enabled the birth of the American suburb: the establishment of commuter lines meant that city workers no longer needed to be city dwellers. Electric street railways endured through the 1940s, until high operating costs, as well as competition from buses and private automobiles, effected their demise in most areas.

SUBWAY AND BUS TOKENS

Boston's Green Line was the first subway in the United States, opened in 1897 to help alleviate the terrible traffic congestion of the streets. In 1904 and 1907, New York and Philadelphia followed suit. Laurel Canyon, California, near Los Angeles, was the site of the first motorized public bus, called a *trackless trolley* or *trolley bus* by its owners. The first true city buses or *jitneys* hit the streets of Los Angeles in 1914. According to Coffee, "the attraction of the jitney was not just that the fare was lower than that charged on streetcars . . . it was that few people at that time had ever ridden in an automobile . . . so when the jitney came along just in front of the trolley . . . people would climb aboard."

Whether in large cities or small towns across the country, early transit systems were all privately owned, and their tokens were designed according to the tastes of their operators. By the 1970s, the high costs of fuel and maintenance, as well as low ridership, drove most of the private operators out of business. Public transportation authorities supported by state or municipal taxes took over. Afterward, a single token issued by a transit authority might cover a standardized rate for any ride on a bus, a subway, or even a harbor ferry, and tokens generally just named the city or the issuing authority.

FERRY TOKENS

There are about 130 varieties of U.S. ferry tokens, making them a small but popular transportation category, among which the 12 known pictorial issues are the most valuable. Scores of town names containing the words *Landing* or *Ferry* recall the huge numbers of sail- and steam-powered, stern- and side-wheeled, poled or paddled ferries that offered passage across U.S. rivers, harbors, bays, and lakes before bridges and tunnels took over their role. Most ferry operators accepted coins for fares, but where traffic was high and the company was well established, tokens were issued. Passenger ferries are experiencing a 21st-century renaissance, with hydrofoils, catamarans, hovercrafts, and water taxis seen in many waterside cities, though few of these now require a token fare.

Tokens for Passage

The best way to finance construction and maintenance of transportation infrastructure has traditionally been to charge a toll for its use. Since the days of the first Lancaster County, Pennsylvania, toll road of 1806, tokens have been issued for turnpikes, parkways, bridges, tunnels, and canals, to avoid wayfarers fumbling for the correct amount of money as they passed through. The lover of historic bridges may find great appeal in the bridge token category. There is humor there as well: consider the "One Foot Passage" token of Pennsylvania's Parker's Landing bridge, which pictures a one-legged man! The study of tokens of passage recalls a fascinating geographic patchwork of travel, linking sea to sea, bustling cities to vast, open spaces, and citizens to one another.

COFFEE NO.*	ISSUER	YEAR	METAL	TYPE	F	EF	MS-63
NY 630 A	Gibbs U.S.M. Stage	1831	Br	Stage	$2,000	$6,000	—
NY 630 DA	New-York & Harlaem Railroad Company**	1830s	GS	Horsecar	350	650	$3,000
Mass 115 C	Eastern Railroad	1836	Br	Locomotive	—	1,000	2,000
Mass 115 A	Roxbury Coaches	1837	GS	Omnibus	100	300	900
Mass 115 B	Maverick Coach	1837	GS	Omnibus	200	300	1,000
PA 526 IA	Marietta–Maytown Turnpike Co.	1847	Br	Turnpike	20	25	40
NY 630 M	Third Avenue Railroad	1850s	Lead	Horsecar	350	500	1,500
NY 630x	James T. Ware	1850s	Cop	Hack, dray	100	200	350
NY 630 Lb	Tyson & Co. Telegraph Line	1851	Br	Omnibus	50	75	300
PA 750 A	Reed St. Ferry–Navy Yard Route	1858	Br	Ferry	75	125	250

* This chart employs reference numbers of Atwood and Coffee.
** Voted No. 85 in *100 Greatest American Medals and Tokens* (Jaeger/Bowers).

COFFEE NO.*	ISSUER	YEAR	METAL	TYPE	F	EF	MS-63
PA 750 N	Hestonville, Mantua & Fairmount Passenger Railroad	1859	HR	Horsecar	—	$60	$100
MT 320 A	Baker Street Ferry	1860	Br	Ferry	$400	750	—
OH 60 A	Bellaire Ferry	1863	Cop	Ferry	150	300	600
MI 225x	Ward's Lake Superior Line	1863	Cop	Steamer	150	300	600
	B. Altman & Co. department store	1860s	Cell	Carriage check	—	250	255
	USS *Vanderbilt*	1868	Br shell	Steamer	—	200	350
MI 470 B	Portage Lake Bridge	1870s	HR	Bridge	16	20	30
CA 575 Aa	Oakland, Brooklyn & Fruitvale Railroad	1871	Bz	Horsecar	8	20	50
TX 360A	Galveston City Railroad	1880s	WM	Horsecar	200	250	400
NB 700A	Omaha Horse Railway Co.	1885	HR	Horsecar	50	100	150

* This chart employs reference numbers of Atwood and Coffee.

Transportation Tokens

COFFEE NO.*	ISSUER	YEAR	METAL	TYPE	F	EF	MS-63
IN 280 A	Evansville Street Railway Co.	1890s	WM	Horsecar	$60	$80	$200
IL 150 B	Chicago Street Carette	1890s	Alum	Streetcar	250	450	500
PA 405 A	The Gettysburg Electric Railway Co.	1893	Br	Cablecar	60	75	125
ND 600 B	J.L. Smith Hack, Bus & Transfer Line	1910s	Alum	Depotel	175	200	300
CO 260Bb	Denver Tramway City Lines	1917	WM	Streetcar	—	3	5
GA 580 A	Macon Railway & Light Co.	1918	Bz	Streetcar	10	11	12
La 670 C	New Orleans Railway & Light Co.	1919	Coated WM	Streetcar	12	15	16
UT 750F	ULATCO / Salt Lake City Lines	1926	WM	Streetcar	—	1	—
MI 225 F	Detroit & Canada Tunnel Co.	1930	WM	Tunnel	—	1	—
MS 660	Natchez & Vidalia Ferry	1930s	WM	Ferry	50	60	70
WA 780 T	Seattle Transit	1939	WM	Trolley	—	1	—
KA 40 E	Nestler Taxi Co.	1940s	Fib	Taxi	7	12	15
NB 580 A	McCook Air Base	1944	WM	Bus	—	5	—
Ala 750F	Sylacauga City Lines	1945	Alum	Bus	15	20	25
MI 775 B	Blue Water Ferry Co., Inc. (Port Huron)	1946	Bz	Ferry	—	3	—

* This chart employs reference numbers of Atwood and Coffee.

COFFEE NO.*	ISSUER	YEAR	METAL	TYPE	F	EF	MS-63
Cal 445B	Long Beach Lines (Queen Mary)	1948	WM	Bus	—	$3	—
Haw 240E	Honolulu Rapid Transit Company, Ltd. (Hula girl)	1951	Bz	Bus	—	1	—
KY 480S	Lexington Railway System	1954	WM	Bus	—	1	—
NH 710 A	New Hampshire Public Works and Highways	1956	WM	Turnpike	—	1	—
FL 930A	Treasure Island Causeway	1961	WM	Causeway	—	1	—
IL 760P	Rock Island Centennial Bridge	1963	Br	Bridge	—	1	—
CO 690D	Manitou Incline Railway	1984	Alum	Incline railway	—	—	$3

* This chart employs reference numbers of Atwood and Coffee.

8
GOVERNMENT-SPONSORED TOKENS

The 20th century was no different from the 19th in that its wars and economic emergencies prompted the issuance of tokens, and some of these were issued by government agencies. During the Great Depression, banks closed, agricultural prices and manufacturing wages fell, and by 1932, more than 13 million workers, with 30 million dependents, were unemployed. In his New Deal for recovery, President Franklin Roosevelt devised a number of federal programs, and some of these issued tokens.

CIVILIAN CONSERVATION CORPS TOKENS

The Civilian Conservation Corps (CCC), inaugurated in 1933, combined the need to occupy the unemployed, most of whom resided in the East, with an initiative to reforest the country after a century of logging. The U.S. Army managed the relocation of thousands of young men to rural work camps around the country, where they resided as they planted an estimated three billion trees. Some of the larger CCC work camps established canteens that issued tokens—not much different from the lumber-company tokens, except that the CCC tokens were for planting trees instead of chopping them down.

COMPANY	LOCATION	DENOMINATION	METAL	F	EF	MS-63
321	Kinzua, Penn.	5¢	Br	$150	$175	$178
531	Temecula, Calif.	1 haircut	Br	200	205	—
1763	Cawker City, Kan.	25¢	Br	100	105	—
651	Long Lake, Wisc.	5¢	Br	200	205	—
3774	Mt. Vernon, Mo.	2-1/2¢	Br	75	125	150
1774	Rochester, Minn.	10¢	Br	15	20	30

Alaska Rural Rehabilitation Corporation Tokens

By 1934, hordes of drought-stricken Midwestern farm families had left the "Dust Bowl" and were wandering, impoverished, from state to state looking for work. Meanwhile, Alaska's fertile Matanuska Valley, with its immense capacity for supplying produce to a starving America, lay fallow. In 1935 the federal Alaska Rural Rehabilitation Corporation addressed both these problems. It transported 200 Dust Bowl families and their necessary support services north to establish a farm colony, which became today's city of Palmer, Alaska. Each adult colonist was issued $30 in bingles (an Alaskan term generally used for tokens), with $5 for each child, to be redeemed at an on-site trading post. One-cent through $1 bingles were of aluminum, while $5 and $10 pieces were of brass, in the same sizes as the corresponding U.S. coins, except for the octagonal one-cent piece. For its 50th anniversary, the town of Palmer struck reproduction bingles from the original dies, adding the reverse legend 50th ANNIVERSARY 1935–1985.[40] These tokens are covered annually in the *Guide Book of United States Coins*.

BREEN NO.	DENOMINATION	METAL	F	EF	MS-63
8020	1¢	Alum	—	$75	$125
8021	5¢	Alum	—	75	125
8022	10¢	Alum	—	75	125
8023	25¢	Alum	—	100	200
8024	50¢	Alum	—	100	200
8025	$1	Alum	—	125	225
8026	$5	Br	—	150	275
8027	$10	Br	—	200	350

State Sales-Tax and Emergency-Relief-Tax Tokens

The Great Depression was the catalyst for many states to institute general taxes on sales. Many of their assessed tax rates resulted in "extra" amounts being paid on small purchases, due to rounding up of fractional amounts smaller than 1¢. Shoppers resented paying these extra fractions, and the chamber of commerce of Kewanee, Illinois, was the first to come up with fractional-cent tokens to be distributed and accepted by city merchants as change. The idea caught on, and other municipalities began issuing local "provisional" sales-tax tokens or paper *tax scrip*. Realizing this unofficial currency should be curbed, 12 state governments decided to issue official state sales-tax tokens: Alabama, Arizona, Colorado, Illinois, Kansas, Louisiana, Mississippi, Missouri, New Mexico, Oklahoma, Utah, and Washington.

In 1933, Governor H.H. Blood of Utah created a State Emergency Commission "to assist farmers, stockmen, and others to raise the existing ruinously low commodity price level, and to employ productively the able-bodied unemployed citizens of Utah." To fund its efforts, he imposed an emergency-relief tax, and tokens reading EMERGENCY RELIEF FUND were adopted to pay fractions of cents. Aluminum tokens in 1-mill and 5-mill denominations, struck by the Osborne Register Co. of Cincinnati, were popularly known as *Blood money*.[41] Derogatory names were used for sales-tax tokens in other states: in Alabama, they were "Bibbies," after instituting governor Bibb Graves, and in Kansas, "Huxies," after governor Walter Huxman. In Missouri, where the first token issues were stamped on cardboard planchets prepared for use as milk-bottle stoppers, they were sneered at as "dairy money" and "milktops."

By 1937 the Utah emergency-relief tax had become the state sales tax, and afterward the tokens were stamped UTAH SALES TAX TOKEN. In Louisiana, a sales tax on luxuries was enacted in 1936, for the benefit of the state hospital board and public welfare. Tax tokens were struck with the legends LUXURY TAX and PUBLIC WELFARE TAX. In Oklahoma, the emergency tax was applied to support the elderly, with tokens stamped FOR OLD AGE ASSISTANCE. In New Mexico, the tax funded the school system, and tokens were marked EMERGENCY SCHOOL TAX.

Most states made a concerted effort to ensure their tokens did not look like coins: some were made of colored fiber; others were holed at the center. The use of sales-tax tokens ended when the Great Depression was replaced with wartime prosperity. Many states specified a time period during which they could be redeemed for cash, but it is estimated that fewer than 40% of the total populations were turned in. The major collectors' group for this category is the American Tax Token Society, based in Asheville, North Carolina, and the most complete reference book is M.K. Malehorn's 1994 *United States Sales Tax Tokens & Stamps*.

STATE	ISSUER OR PURPOSE	MATERIAL	DENOMINATION	F	EF	MS-63
AL	Department of Revenue Sales Tax	Pl	5 mills	—	$1	—
AZ	Tax Commission	Cop	5 mills	$1	3	$6
CO	Retail Token	Fiber	2 mills	—	1	—
KS	Sales Tax Token	WM	2 mills	—	1	—
LA	Luxury Tax Token	Alum	1 mill	—	1	—

STATE	ISSUER OR PURPOSE	MATERIAL	DENOMINATION	F	EF	MS-63
MO	Retailer's Receipt	Card	1 mill	—	$1	—
MO	Sales Tax Token	Pl	5 mills	—	1	—
OK	Old Age Assistance	Fiber	1 mill	—	1	—
UT	Sales Tax Token	Pl	2 mills	—	1	—
WA	Tax Commission	Fiber	1 mill	—	1	—

OPA Ration Tokens

America's entrance into World War II and the resulting need for armament put pressure on the availability of raw materials. Conservation of metals became necessary, and producers of all kinds of tokens switched from metal to fiber, vulcanite, cardboard, wood, and plastic. Commodities such as coffee, sugar, meat, and gasoline were also in short supply. To ensure the availability of adequate supplies for overseas troops, the U.S. Office of Price Administration (OPA) instituted a nationwide rationing program, and by February 1944 it was issuing related tokens. Families were allotted books of ration tickets filled with the number of ration points adequate for the household's need. They paid for their goods with U.S. paper money and received U.S. coins in change as usual, but at the same time, they turned in their ration stamps, and received tokens in change.[42]

The vulcanized-fiber OPA tokens were slightly smaller than a dime and came in two colors: red for meat, fish, dairy products, and cooking oils; and blue for canned and processed foods. By 1945, 1.75 billion red and 1 billion blue tokens had been struck at Ohio's Osborne Register Co. Each token was worth one ration point, and had a pair of letters stamped on its face. These letter pairs in 54 different combinations (30 on red, 24 on blue) helped identify and track shipments for security purposes. The significantly rare variety of the series, on a red token, has the letter pair MV.[43]

For their significant role during a dramatic time in U.S. history, OPA ration tokens, as a class, were voted No. 81 in *100 Greatest American Medals and Tokens* (Jaeger/Bowers).

COLOR	LETTER PAIR	MATERIAL	F	EF	MS-63
Red point	V/C	Fiber	—	$1	—
Red point	U/V	Fiber	—	1	—
Blue point	U/U	Fiber	—	1	—
Blue point	T/T	Fiber	—	1	—

INTERNMENT-CAMP TOKENS

Another token issue of World War II was struck in 1942 for the internment camp at Crystal City, Texas. Crystal City was the largest of 27 internment camps designed to hold Japanese, Germans, and Italians who were not technically military prisoners, but were considered "dangerous enemy aliens," through the course of the war. Few of these people were charged with actual treasonous activity, so they were called "detainees" rather than "prisoners of war." Crystal City held more than 3,300 detainees—and their families too—because "relocation" of the aliens included the seizure of their homes, property, and bank accounts. It was deemed unsafe for detainees to have access to U.S. currency, so a scrip-and-token system was devised. Detainees were assigned housing and food allowances based on family size, and given work tasks appropriate to their ages and abilities. Their token wages were redeemable at two canteens and a general store on the grounds of the fenced-in camp.

These tokens issued by the Immigration and Naturalization Service (INS) came in cent, nickel, quarter, and dollar sizes, and were used through 1948. They are fairly scarce; circulated examples sell for $30 to $60.

FOOD-STAMP CHANGE TOKENS

Some of the emergency programs of the Great Depression evolved into what is now known as the welfare state. Abuses of the food-stamp program (instituted in 1939) were the cause of one more government-imposed token issue: food-stamp change tokens. Families whose annual income met the federal definition of poverty were issued monthly coupon books of stamps that could be spent at supermarkets for strictly defined foodstuffs and necessities. Change for high-denomination food stamps was given out in lower-denomination food stamps, but change of less than $1 was made in U.S. coins. Recipients sometimes spent these coins on ineligible items such as tobacco and alcohol, and in 1961 the government declared it illegal to pay out food-stamp change in U.S. currency.

Stores had to find a new way to give out small change, or be barred from accepting food-stamp customers. More than 3,000 markets issued paper scrip for the purpose, but most ordered plastic tokens in different colors for all the U.S. coin denominations, placing the value on one side and their logo or name on the other. The multiplicity of food-stamp tokens issued through 1978 is just beginning to be cataloged, state by state. The U.S. Department of Agriculture rendered food-stamp tokens unnecessary in 1979, when it once again allowed food-stamp customers to receive coins in change. The ongoing problem of food stamps being swapped for cash or ineligible items was finally solved in

2004, when stamps were eliminated in favor of swipeable debit cards. Now there is nothing to swap and no need to make change, since amounts spent are deducted from the balance left on the card.

STATE	ISSUER	DENOMINATION	MATERIAL	F	EF	MS-63
NY	Red Apple Supermarkets	1¢	Alum	—	$1	—
NY	Red Apple Supermarkets	5¢	Alum	—	1	—
WA	Nevins Post Office Grocery	5¢	Pl	—	1	—
WA	Nevins Post Office Grocery	10¢	Pl	—	1	—

Part II
SOUVENIR AND COMMEMORATIVE MEDALS AND TOKENS

Commemorative exonumia celebrating historic events generally fall into two types: the grand, elaborate, expensive table medals commissioned as *official* mementoes; and souvenir medals and tokens, concocted independently as *commercial* mementoes. Examples of each type may be found issued *contemporary* to the commemorated event, or *subsequent* to it. As a rule, contemporary pieces are the most desirable, because their historical interest and limited quantities combine to raise their values.

The symbolic content of the obverse and reverse of official medals was chosen with great care, and the best artists and mints were selected to execute them. Commercial types have been issued for sale or to be given away as advertising souvenirs during major events, or for no other reason than to record the subject's historical interest. Historical subjects struck in metal have been popular with American collectors ever since the commemorative medal craze of 1858 to 1861, sparked by New York City coin dealer and American Numismatic Society founder Augustus B. Sage. Interest in the genre has waxed and waned a few times since then, but historical souvenirs and commemoratives continue to be struck in the 21st century, and this huge category offers many arenas for specialized collecting.

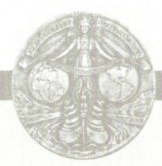

9

CONTEMPORARY MEDALS AND TOKENS

Die-struck historical relics of America have been created ever since Europe's great powers started colonizing the New World. From the era of discovery, through the establishment of Britain's colonies and their war for independence to the present day, commemorative medals and tokens have captured the events of the day in durable form.

Pre-Federal Medals

Numismatist Charles Wyllys Betts once said, "It is safer to quote a medal than a historian." In the 1880s, the Betts family cataloged 623 wonderful "historical documents in metal" pertaining to the American colonies prior to their declaration of independence in 1776. It was a full six decades after Columbus's voyage of discovery before any European monarch troubled to order a medal acknowledging the existence of the Americas: the first was a 1556 piece struck to commemorate the accession of Philip II to the Spanish throne, which expressed his title as PHILIPPVS HISPANIAR ET NOVI ORBIS OCCID-VIREX: "King of Spain and the New Western World." The Old World only gradually came to understand the monumental import of the discoveries reported by Vespucci, Cortez, Pizarro, Cabot, Hudson, and their kind, and these explorers were not commemorated on medals in their lifetimes.[44] Once European nations realized the incredible mineral, agricultural, and territorial wealth available in the West, they vied vigorously for supremacy there. The themes of the Betts medals reflect the Spanish, Dutch, French, and British view of the Americas as pieces of empire for the taking.

Betts cataloged the pre-federal medals chronologically, dividing them into periods of discovery (1556–1631); colonization (1632–1737); intercolonial wars (1745–1763); the Peace of Paris to the Revolution (1763–1775); and the Revolutionary War (1775–1782). These included the European Indian peace medals, and a curious group of satirical pieces known as the John Law medals (dealing with the failed banking scheme of the Scotsman's Compagnie d'Occident, which came to be known as the *Mississippi Bubble*). Also included were the Vernon medals, today known to number 270 different types, celebrating the exploits of British admiral Edward Vernon, who captured the Spanish fort at Portobello (in Panama) in 1739. Portobello was a major shipping station for Spain's New World treasure cargos, and many Vernon medals featured the legend THE SPANISH PRIDE HUMBLED. Two multiple-issue groups from Spain—the proclamation medals of Ferdinand VI (1746–1747) and Charles III (1760–1761)—were struck to announce Spanish dominion over territories from Buenos Aires to Florida. A 1631 medal of Holland showing a bust of Frederic Henry, prince of Orange, had a Dutch lion pulling down one of a pair of pillars on the reverse. Its legend translated to "He has extended his bounds beyond the columns of Hercules." The French, too, struck medals to proclaim their foothold in the West. One 1756 medal of French Canada read SEDEM NON ANIMUM MUTANT, or "They change their home but not their hearts."

After Britain finally surrendered control over its 13 American colonies and signed the preliminary articles of peace in November 1782, all the countries that hoped to establish good North American trading relations struck medals acknowledging the United States as an independent nation. On Benjamin Franklin's order, America's very first commemorative medal was struck in France for the same purpose. The obverse of the 1783 Libertas Americana medal, with its year date 1776 and bust of the flowing-haired goddess Liberty, became the model for the Liberty Cap, Head Facing Left, design of the U.S. half cent of 1793, as well as dozens of commemorative coins, medals, and tokens struck since then.

BETTS NO.	YEAR	COMMEMORATING	ARTIST / MINT	METAL	F	EF	MS-63
3	1559	Philip II of Spain. First mention of the New World.	G. Poggini / Spain	Silv	$12,000	$13,500	$15,000
33	1631	Prince Frederic Henry; Dutch expansion to the west	Unknown/Holland	Silv	13,000	14,500	16,000
35	1650s	Cecil Calvert, Lord Baltimore; Maryland settlement	Unknown	Silv	40,000	45,000	50,000
97	1702	Queen Anne and the British victory at Vigo	J. Croker / England	Gold	16,000	17,000	18,000

Pre-Federal Medals (continued)

BETTS NO.	YEAR	COMMEMORATING	ARTIST / MINT	METAL	F	EF	MS-63
114	1720	John Law's speculation on the riches of Louisiana	Strassberg	Tin	$2,500	$3,000	$3,500
170	1737	Georgia colony founder James Oglethorpe	J. Tanner / England	Silv	15,000	25,000	35,000
305	1739	Vernon's humbling of Spanish pride—with six ships only!	England	Bz	125	450	1,250
393	1756	French colonizing Canada under Louis XV	R. Filius / France	Silv	600	1,500	3,500
401	1757	Peace. Quaker Indian peace medal struck in Philadelphia	Duffield/Richardson	Silv	35,000	75,000	150,000
410	1758	British takeover of French Louisbourg	T. Pingo / England	Gold	—	35,000	60,000

Pre-Federal Medals *(continued)*

BETTS NO.	YEAR	COMMEMORATING	ARTIST / MINT	METAL	F	EF	MS-63
454	1760	Proclaiming Charles III Spanish king of Florida	Spain / Mexico City	Silv	$200,000	—	—
556	1777	Revolutionary War battle at Germantown	J. Milton / England	Bz	15,000	$40,000	—
563	1779	British Admiral Howe's victory at Rhode Island*	Unknown	Br	1,250	2,500	$6,000
603	1782	Holland's recognition of her "free sister"	Holtzhey/Holland	Silv	150	400	1,000
615	1783	Libertas Americana; proclaiming independence**	A. Dupre / France	Cop	2,500	6,000	18,000

* Voted No. 50 in *100 Greatest American Medals and Tokens* (Jaeger/Bowers).
** Voted No. 1 in *100 Greatest American Medals and Tokens*.

National Medals

Because the new republic had no mint of its own and no engravers of suitable talent, our first national medals—a group of 17 authorized by the revolutionary government in 1776—were struck at the Paris Mint in the 1780s. Called the *Comitia Americana* medals,[45] they honored America's first military heroes, the likes of George Washington, Horatio Gates, Anthony Wayne, and Daniel Morgan. Every court in Europe had its "king's cabinet" of medals, and in 1787 Thomas Jefferson arranged that one of each Comitia Americana medal be given to each sovereign, as well as to each of the major European learning academies. These diplomatic presentations helped gain respect for the new nation as a power capable of upholding long-established political traditions.

The U.S. Mint opened in 1792, and began producing the nation's official medals in 1801. At first, private artists sank the dies on commission, but by the mid-19th century, Mint staff performed all engraving and striking. In 1861 there were 64 national die pairs in the Mint's possession. Among them were the Indian peace medals and presidential medals (see part III); military and naval medals awarded during the War of 1812, the Mexican War (1846–1848), and the Civil War (1861–1865); and the special lifesaving and heroism awards ordered by Congress (see part V). Dies for the Comitia Americana medals were still in France, and the Paris Mint would not relinquish them. For restriking purposes, the U.S. Mint made copy dies, using original medals as models. In the 1870s, J.F. Loubat, author of *The Medallic History of the United States 1776–1876*, was able to locate two more die sets. One pair, for Commodore Edward Preble's 1804 naval medal for his victory at Tripoli, was being used as paperweights on the desk of Rear Admiral Joseph Smith! The other, for Cornelius Vanderbilt's 1862 congressional medal, lay in the cellar of a New York City bank. Good historical descriptions and images of 19th-century mint medals can be found in R.W. Julian's 1977 work, *Medals of the U.S. Mint: the First Hundred Years, 1792–1892*.

It was in the 1860s that the Mint commenced recording events in its own history with medals. Assay Commission medals were presented annually to members of the commission, and Mint director and superintendent medals were struck for occupants of those posts. Beginning in the 1890s, each new secretary of the Treasury received a specially designed medal. Commercial restrikes of all of these, plus the national medals listed above, were called *list medals* because every year the Mint published a list of which ones were available for purchase. The Mint still sells bronze replicas of its medals to the public, and the list of available pieces can now be found on its Web site, usmint.gov.

From the 1870s through the 1910s, restrikes of certain U.S. Mint medals were surreptitiously made by members of the staff, and sold "out the back door" through several Philadelphia medals dealers, William Idler and John Haseltine being the most prominent. For the most part, these were *not* the national medals, but rather those produced on the order of private citizens, employing the facilities of the Mint's medals deparment.[46] The practice of the Mint taking commercial orders for medals ended in 1910, and commercial medal production ceased altogether in the 1940s.

In the 20th century, Mint engravers designed special congressional medals for specific recipients, such as George Morgan's 1909 plaquette honoring Orville and Wilbur Wright for their successful powered flight and Gilroy Roberts's 1955 medal to Dr. Jonas Salk for his development of a successful polio vaccine.

Contemporary Medals and Tokens

Actual size 65 mm

JULIAN NO.	DATE	COMMEMORATING	ARTIST	METAL	F	EF	MS-63
MI-1	1776	George Washington; evacuation of Boston*	DuVivier	Bz	$1,500	$3,500	$8,000
MI-2	1777	Horatio Gates; victory at Saratoga**	Gatteaux	Bz	4,000	5,000	6,000
NA-1	1778	John Paul Jones; victory off Scotland***	Dupre	Bz	5,000	6,000	7,000

* Voted No. 2 in *100 Greatest American Medals and Tokens* (Jaeger/Bowers).
** Voted No. 56 in *100 Greatest American Medals and Tokens*.
*** Voted No. 35 in *100 Greatest American Medals and Tokens*.

NATIONAL MEDALS *(continued)*

Actual size 64 mm

Actual size 65 mm

Actual size 65 mm

JULIAN NO.	DATE	COMMEMORATING	ARTIST	METAL	F	EF	MS-63
NA-3	1804	Edward Preble; victory off Tripoli	Reich	Bz	—	$1,000	$2,000
NA-9	1812	Stephen Decatur; naval victories	Furst	Silv	$10,000	20,000	40,000
MI-12	1835	George Croghan; victory at Sandusky	Furst	Cop	—	325	900

NATIONAL MEDALS *(continued)*

Actual size 90 mm

Actual size 105 mm

JULIAN NO.	DATE	COMMEMORATING	ARTIST	METAL	F	EF	MS-63
MI-24	1848	Zachary Taylor; victory at Buena Vista	Wright	Gold	—	—	$500,000†
MI-29	1863	Ulysses S. Grant; Civil War victories	Paquet	Silv	—	—	30,000
AC-19	1879	Annual assay of coinage	Barber	Bz	—	$300	550

† In November 2006 this unique gold specimen—Taylor's own awarded example—sold for $460,000 through Stack's Rare Coins. Contemporary bronze specimens are more readily available to collectors.

NATIONAL MEDALS *(continued)*

Actual size 76 mm

Actual size 81x56 mm

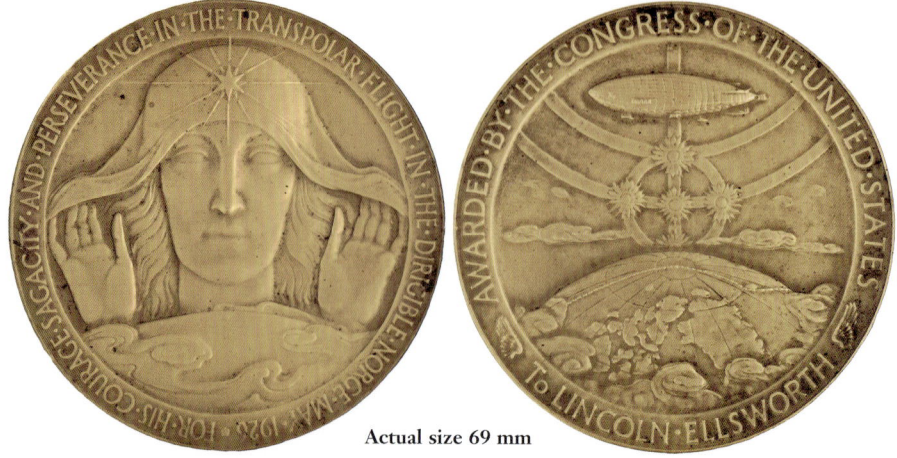

Actual size 69 mm

JULIAN NO.	DATE	COMMEMORATING	ARTIST	METAL	F	EF	MS-63
MT-17	1889	Mint Superintendent Oliver Bosbyshell	Morgan	WM	—	—	$250
	1909	Wright Brothers; flight at Kitty Hawk	Morgan	Bz	—	$25	60
	1926	Lincoln Ellsworth; transpolar flight	Sinnock/Pietz	Gilt Bz	—	—	200

NATIONAL MEDALS *(continued)*

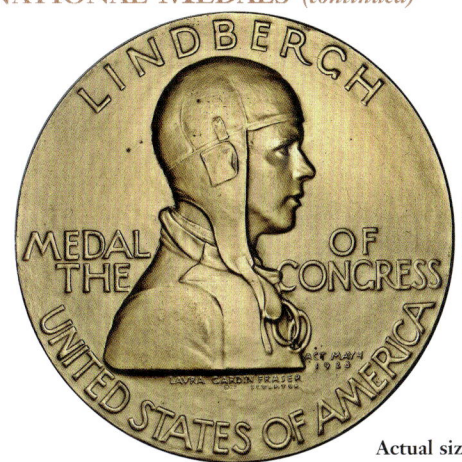 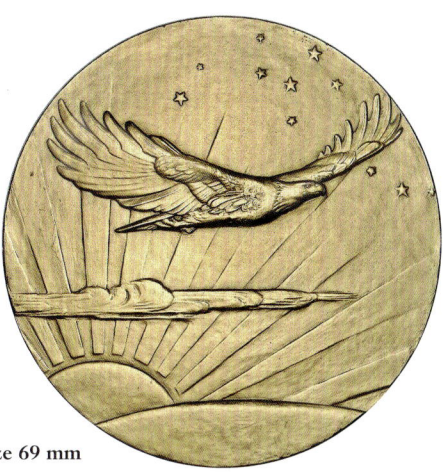

Actual size 69 mm

Actual size 76 mm

 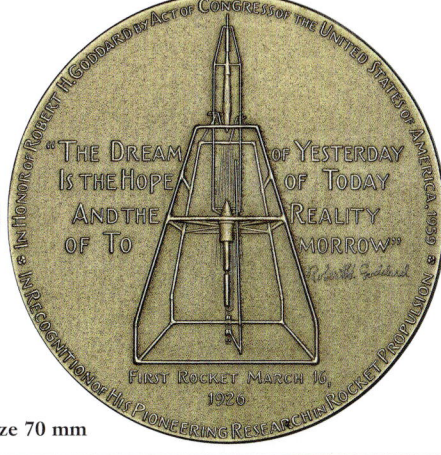

Actual size 70 mm

JULIAN NO.	DATE	COMMEMORATING	ARTIST	METAL	F	EF	MS-63
	1928	Charles Lindbergh; transatlantic flight	L.G. Fraser	Bz	—	$40	$80
	1955	Jonas Salk; development of polio vaccine	Roberts	Bz	—	—	25
	1959	Robert Goddard; rocket propulsion	Von Hebel	Bz	—	—	20

Major-Event Medals

The commemoratives issued by the City of New York to celebrate the opening of the Erie Canal and honor its founders are typical of *major-event* medals. A special art committee ordered the production of 81 mm medallions engraved and struck in England by Sir Edward Thomason in 1825, and 44 mm presentation medals engraved by Charles C. Wright and struck by goldsmith Maltby Pelletreau in New York in 1826. Both featured a design by committee chairman Archibald Robertson. Richard Trested applied the lettering to the dies on the Wright medals, and woodworker Duncan Phyfe made the presentation boxes out of curled maple, birdseye, and red cedar harvested on an island in Lake Erie and brought to New York on the first canal boat, the *Seneca Chief*. Fifty-one gold strikes were presented to President John Quincy Adams, General Andrew Jackson, Governor DeWitt Clinton, the mayor, city council members, and important invited guests. Other dignitaries and organizers received silver and pewter strikes. It was the beginning of a long tradition of official medals celebrating public works, from the Croton Aqueduct to the transcontinental railroad to the Panama Canal. Top-of-the-line producers such as Tiffany & Co., Medallic Art Company, Whitehead & Hoag, and the Robbins Company were responsible for many official commemoratives. Usually official medals were presented in handmade cases for display on tables, hence the name *table medals*.

Wealthy corporations, state and local organizations, and clubs acknowledged their important happenings with medals too, sometimes placing their orders with local jewelers, who subcontracted them out to private diesinkers. Some issues can be termed *relic medals*, because they were made of a material from the commemorated event, such as the 1895 Tiffany medal for the 150th anniversary of the siege of Fortress Louisbourg. The General Society of Colonial Wars arranged for these to be made of brass from cannons recovered by divers from the wreck of the French frigate *Le Célèbre*, destroyed during its battle with the British at Louisbourg. Designs followed the tastes of the times: compare the Beaux Arts styling of Tiffany & Co.'s 1902 medal commemorating the opening of the New York Chamber of Commerce building, to the 1933 Art Deco medal by Norman Bel Geddes, celebrating the 25th Anniversary of the General Motors Corporation (illustrated).

Numismatic organizations have been especially fond of marking major occasions with medals. The Archer Huntington Medal of the American Numismatic Society, designed by Emil Fuchs for its 50th anniversary in 1908, and the 125th-anniversary medal designed by Marcel Jovine in 1983, both feature images of coin presses and minting processes. Eugene Daub's 2004 medal marking the society's move to lower Manhattan honored benefactor Donald Partrick with a portrait, and showed a heroic figure rolling huge medals. More than 240 other exquisite medals issued by numismatic groups, past and present, are listed in the computer database of the ANS collection.

Medals have been struck to recall disasters as well as grand occasions. An 1872 relic medal designed by William Barber of the U.S. Mint commemorated the Chicago Fire. It was made of bronze from the city's ruined courthouse bell. The 1906 "Resurrection of San Francisco" medal conveyed France's sympathy to the people of California for the city's destruction by earthquake and fire. A 1915 *Lusitania* medal by Karl Goetz of Germany depicted the sinking of the vessel by a German U-boat. Goetz issued this medal not out of sympathy for the victims, but to question the role of the Cunard Line, which Germany had accused of carrying military armament in disregard of passenger safety. The reverse of this medal shows Death (represented as a skeleton) selling fares at a Cunard ticket window. At World War I's end in 1918, France replied with a *Lusitania* medal of its own; this one, by Rene Baudichon, with its dramatic rendering of loss of life, shows a ferocious Statue of Liberty bursting from the sea with a sword, under a Latin legend meaning "America, avenger of the law."

American soldiers' coming home from war was another occasion for presenting medals. The citizens of New York City and Charleston, South Carolina, each hired Charles C. Wright to cut dies for medals for their volunteer regiments on their return from Mexico in 1848. Other communities have done the same many times since then. The largest series of community-issued service medals came in the 20th century, struck for soldiers returning from World War I's European battlefields. The format and content of these medals varied widely—the one universal message being gratitude and appreciation for service.

YEAR	COMMEMORATING	ARTIST / MINT	METAL	F	EF	MS-63
1826	Completion of Erie Canal*	Wright/Pelletreau	Silv	$1,250	$3,500	$10,000
1848	Charleston's Mexican-American War volunteers	Wright / U.S. Mint	Silv	2,000	5,000	9,000

* Voted No. 8 in *100 Greatest American Medals and Tokens* (Jaeger/Bowers).

Major-Event Medals *(continued)*

Actual size 80 mm

YEAR	COMMEMORATING	ARTIST / MINT	METAL	F	EF	MS-63
1864	Cathedral of Peter and Paul, Philadelphia	Paquet / U.S. Mint	Silv	—	$500	$1,000
1864	Great Central Fair of U.S. Sanitary Commission	Paquet / U.S. Mint	Bz	—	200	600
1869	Oceans united by railway	Barber / U.S. Mint	Bz	—	250	700

Major-Event Medals *(continued)*

Actual size 69 mm

Actual size 77 mm

YEAR	COMMEMORATING	ARTIST / MINT	METAL	F	EF	MS-63
1871	Chicago Fire (copper from courthouse bell)	Barber / U.S. Mint	Cop	—	$200	$500
1886	Statue of Liberty / Friendship with France	Roty / Paris Mint	Bz	—	—	600
1892	400th anniversary of Columbus's voyage	Whitehouse/Tiffany	Bz	—	300	500

Major-Event Medals *(continued)*

Actual size 77 mm

YEAR	COMMEMORATING	ARTIST / MINT	METAL	F	EF	MS-63
1899	Spanish American War volunteers	Unknown	Bz	—	$50	$100
1902	NY Chamber of Commerce new building	Whitehouse/Tiffany	Bz	—	—	300
1913	Panama Canal opening	John F. Newman Co.	Bz	—	—	150
1915	*Lusitania* (German)**	Goetz	Bz	—	125	250

** Many modern copies of this medal exist. Valuations are for originals.

Major-Event Medals *(continued)*

Actual size 63 mm

YEAR	COMMEMORATING	ARTIST / MINT	METAL	F	EF	MS-63
1918	"*Lusitania* avenged" (French)	Baudichon/Paris	Bz	—	—	$200
1919	Peace of Versailles	Beach/ANS	Silv	—	—	350
1919	World War I veterans	Whitehead & Hoag	Bz	—	$30	50
1920	Opening of Manila Mint	Morgan / U.S. Mint	Bz	$100	400	1,200

MAJOR-EVENT MEDALS *(continued)*

Actual size 89x66 mm

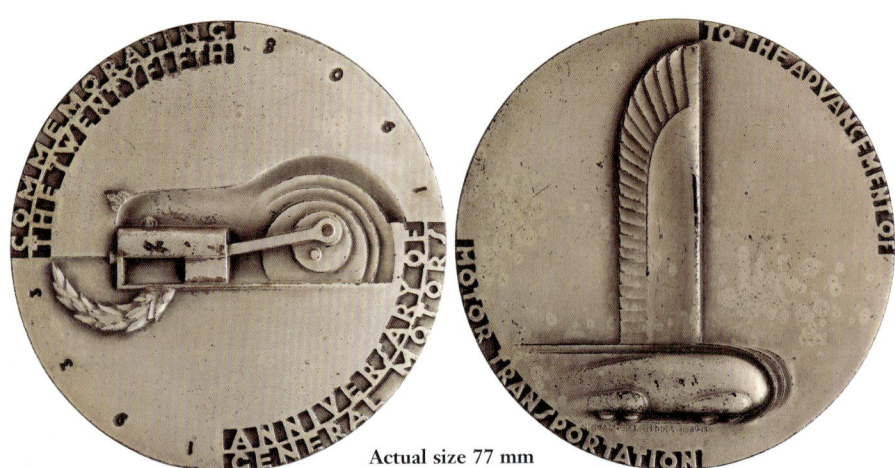

Actual size 77 mm

Actual size 77 mm

YEAR	COMMEMORATING	ARTIST / MINT	METAL	F	EF	MS-63
1930	300th anniversary of Massachusetts	Robbins Mint	Svd Bz	—	$30	$50
1933	25th anniversary of General Motors	Bel Geddes / MACo	Svd Bz	—	600	1,000
1942	100th anniversary of Schaefer Brewing	Chambellan/MACo	Bz	—	—	50

Major-Event Medals *(continued)*

Actual size 90×110 mm

YEAR	COMMEMORATING	ARTIST / MINT	METAL	F	EF	MS-63
1977	125th anniversary of American Numismatic Society	Jovine/MACo	Silv	—	$250	$500

Celebration Souvenirs

The very first Peach Day festival of Grand Junction, Colorado, was held in September 1891, for peach growers to celebrate the importance of their product in the local economy. Bands played, speakers orated, children and adults participated in spirited games and contests, and free baskets of ripe peaches were given to all. For Peach Day 1894, a medal was ordered from S.H. Quint & Sons of Philadelphia, to commemorate what had become an annual event.[47]

Other groups sharing common interests met to hold festivals and conventions as well. Sangerfests (song festivals) were popular gatherings for 19th-century singing groups. Participants looked forward all year to these combination sightseeing trips / musical holidays, and happily purchased token souvenirs in whichever city hosted their event. The medal and token issues of annual conventions of national fraternal and professional organizations recall many long-disbanded groups, such as the Brotherhood of Blacksmiths, Dropforgers and Helpers, or the Knights of the Golden Eagle. Military organizations also produced medals and tokens for attendees of their gatherings to bring home and collect. One such issuer was the Confederate Veterans of the Civil War, and another was the Grand Army of the Republic (G.A.R.) for Union veterans. As might be expected, numismatic organizations and coin clubs were, and still are, prolific issuers of convention and anniversary souvenirs. A search of the American Numismatic Society computerized object database, using "coin club" as the keywords and "tokens" as the category, yields more than 2,000 examples.

Many celebration tokens, such as G.A.R. encampment pieces or Mardi Gras doubloons, fall into series of their own, since each recurring event produced new issues. Others, such as souvenirs of monument openings or Revolutionary War battle centennials, may be collected as thematic series. Most official celebration issues carried symbols pertinent to the event (such as the harp, the international symbol of music, on many sangerfest issues), with descriptive legends and very often a year or day date. These, if they are close in size to a U.S. silver dollar, are pursued by "so-called dollar" enthusiasts. Commercial issues often combined an event-themed reverse with a merchant-advertising obverse, or some popular stock reverse such as the Lord's Prayer, a calendar, a schedule of events, or a good-luck symbol. Many depicted the buildings or grounds on which the gatherings were held, or symbols important to the particular group.

Actual size 63 mm

YEAR	SOUVENIR OF	METAL	COMMENTARY	F	EF	MS-63
1868	A church opening in Brooklyn	Br	Methodist shell card depicts Methodist founder John Wesley	—	$250	$400
1882	Baltimore oriole celebration	Bz	Well-struck medal by a talented unknown diesinker	—	10	20
1884	Cattlemen convention, St. Louis	WM	Mermods & Jaccard Jewelry Co. produced this	—	200	350
1886	National sangerfest, Milwaukee	WM	Beautiful memento of a good time for singers	$7	15	30

CELEBRATION SOUVENIRS *(continued)*

YEAR	SOUVENIR OF	METAL	COMMENTARY	F	EF	MS-63
1886	Centennial of Portland, Maine	Bz	Bearing the familiar fishes of G.H. Lovett	—	$40	$50
1890	Army of West Virginia reunion, Parkersburg	WM	Military reunion issues form their own series	—	25	40
1891	National sangerfest, Newark, N.J.	WM	Most sangerfest issues have a harp in the design	$5	10	20
1894	Peach Day, Grand Junction, Colo.	WM	S.H. Quint & Sons of Philadelphia was the maker	—	20	50
1900	GAR 34th encampment, Findlay, Ohio	Bz	GAR medals make a nice series for Civil War buffs	10	35	50

CELEBRATION SOUVENIRS (continued)

YEAR	SOUVENIR OF	METAL	COMMENTARY	F	EF	MS-63
1901	Tarriff League banquet	Bz	Tremendous artistry for a political-banquet souvenir	—	$200	$300
1907	ANA triennial convention, New York City	Br	C.H. Hanson struck these Thomas Elder giveaways	—	30	75
1908	Visit of U.S. Fleet to San Francisco	Br	The "Great White Fleet" came with 14,000 sailors	—	20	40
1909	Portola Festival, San Francisco	Bz	For the anniversary of San Francisco Bay's discovery	—	10	20
1916	Gasparilla Carnival, Tampa	Br	Schwaab of Milwaukee filled many souvenir orders	—	20	30
1929	National Air Races, Cleveland	Bz	Made by the Bastian Brothers of Rochester, New York	—	7	10

CELEBRATION SOUVENIRS *(continued)*

YEAR	SOUVENIR OF	METAL	COMMENTARY	F	EF	MS-63
1961	Shrimp Festival, Morgan City, La.	Silv	Like "Peach Day," but for a different harvest	—	—	$30
1963	Diamond Jubilee, Aberdeen, Wash.	Silv	Jubilee issues make a series all their own	$1	$2	3

MARDI GRAS DOUBLOONS

Starting in the 1880s, tourist souvenir medals were occasionally struck for Mardi Gras in New Orleans. However, the carnival club known as Krewe of Rex was the first to employ the familiar silver-dollar-sized (39 or 40 mm) aluminum tokens issued annually since 1960. These beautiful, brightly colored tokens show a high degree of artistry and detail, and many were designed by New Orleans artist H. Alvin Sharpe. Rex ordered 83,000 of them the first year, to throw to the crowds instead of the bead necklaces and other trinkets usually tossed from the floats. They caught on immediately with krewe members, who collected them as mementos of their participation in the carnival, as well as with parade attendees. Soon representatives of various krewes were designing tokens with imagery on one side devoted to the annual Mardi Gras theme, and on the other side naming the krewe and conveying its yearly float theme. In Mobile, Alabama, which also holds an annual Mardi Gras celebration and where carnival clubs are known as *mystic societies*, doubloons began being issued in 1965. Cataloger Arthur Hardy, of the collector's organization Crescent City Doubloon Traders, records the new issues each year, and the group holds its first annual swap meet the day after Mardi Gras.

YEAR	KREWE	THEME OR SUBJECT	METAL	COMMENTARY	F	EF	MS-63
1884	None	Celebration Souvenir	Bz	Earliest souvenirs were not sponsored by krewes	—	$60	—
1962	Rex	Year of the Circus	Silv	Rex and H.A. Sharpe originated the doubloon concept	—	—	$30

MARDI GRAS DOUBLOONS (continued)

YEAR	KREWE	THEME OR SUBJECT	METAL	COMMENTARY	F	EF	MS-63
1968	Hex Doctor Man	Voo Doo Queen	Bz	Another of Sharpe's many fascinating issues	—	$2	—
1968	Mystic Nites of Juma	Bullfighter	Bz	The krewes chose the content of their doubloons	—	1	$1
1968	Arabi	Tales of Superstition	Alum	Mardi Gras organizers chose the annual themes	—	1	—
1970	Carnival Club	A Dutch Treat	Alum	Popularity of these issues grew with each parade	—	1	—
1978	Pegasus	Marco Polo	Alum	Doubloons are inexpensive, but their designs are rich	—	1	—

TOURIST-SITE SOUVENIRS

Collectors of tourist souvenirs may seek issues struck more than a century ago, a few decades ago, or just yesterday. Most every tourist attraction from the Alamo to Hoover Dam, amusement park from Coney Island to Disneyland, and natural wonder from Niagara Falls to the Grand Canyon, has issued souvenir medals or tokens at some point in its history. Cathedrals, museums, zoos, and historic sites often have gift shops that are the last things seen as visitors leave the premises, and where souvenir medals and tokens are sold. Even the official visitors' centers at U.S. national parks and monuments offer souvenir medals. (These fine pieces, designed and struck at Medallic Art Company, make up an interesting subcategory.)

Major agricultural show venues, including the Sugar Palace of Omaha, Nebraska, the Corn Palace of Sioux City, Iowa, the Interstate Grain Palace of Aberdeen, South Dakota, the Interstate Hay Palace of Momence, Illinois, and the Cotton Palace of Waco, Texas, all sold souvenir medals and tokens to visitors. A type of novelty "coin," the oversize lucky penny (or nickel, dime, etc.), which could be as large as 76 mm in diameter, has appeared in some tourist shops since around 1913. These heavy, paperweight-size objects were cast, not struck from dies, and usually had a scene of, or at least the name of, the attraction on the obverse, with blown-up designs from particular U.S. coins on the reverse. These are cataloged by Stephen Alpert in his 1979 work, *Large Lucky Souvenir Coins*.

YEAR	ATTRACTION / SUBJECT	METAL	COMMENTARY	F	EF	MS-63
1880s	Liberty Bell / Lord's Prayer	Silv	The Lord's Prayer was a feature of many souvenirs	$5	$10	$15
1885	Old North Church, Boston (relic)	Lead	Not the loveliest issue—but very collectible	15	25	40
1890	Sioux City, Iowa, Corn Palace	Bz	A new one was built from corn each year, 1887–1891	8	15	25
1890s	Coney Island's Colossus	WM	One leg contained a cigar store, another housed a diorama	—	80	150
1894	Waco, Texas, Cotton Palace	Alum	Schwaab of Milwaukee created this keepsake	25	90	125

Tourist-Site Souvenirs *(continued)*

Actual size 70 mm

Actual size 71 mm

YEAR	ATTRACTION / SUBJECT	METAL	COMMENTARY	F	EF	MS-63
1900s	Niagara Falls / Bragging piece	Alum	Every conceivable subject was struck in metal	—	$125	$200
1906	Cliff House, San Francisco	Br	It survived the quake of 1906, only to burn down in 1907	$10	30	75
1923	Washington, DC / U.S. Capitol	Cop	A giant lucky coin of the one-cent denomination	—	—	5
1925	Washington, DC / U.S. Capitol	WM	These may bear contemporary or historical coin designs	—	—	5

TOURIST-SITE SOUVENIRS *(continued)*

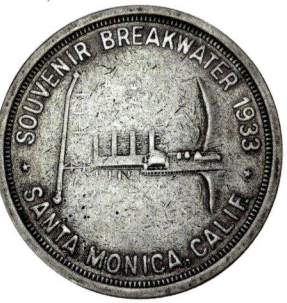

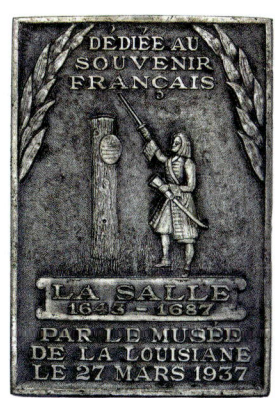

YEAR	ATTRACTION / SUBJECT	METAL	COMMENTARY	F	EF	MS-63
1933	Ocean Park, Santa Monica pier	WM	L.A. Rubber Stamp Co. was a prolific token issuer	$3	$5	$12
1937	La Maison Creole, New Orleans	Silv	Classic wrought-iron–balconied Creole architecture	—	—	100
1939	Sites throughout North Carolina	Alum	Whitehead & Hoag defined the state's attractions	5	10	20
1953	Oldest house in St. Augustine, Fla.	Gilt Bz	Today it houses the St. Augustine Historical Society	—	4	8

Tourist-Site Souvenirs *(continued)*

Actual size 63 mm

YEAR	ATTRACTION / SUBJECT	METAL	COMMENTARY	F	EF	MS-63
1969	Grand Canyon National Park / 50th anniversary	Bz	MACo created medals for many national parks	—	—	$20
1993	American Museum of the Moving Image	Br	Inside the famed Astoria, New York, studios built in 1920	—	—	1

Performance Souvenirs

On a smaller scale than most major-event medals, perhaps—but still marking special occasions in American life—are souvenir medals and tokens issued for various performing arts.

19th-Century Souvenirs

Like today's rock stars, whose t-shirts, clothing patches, and other merchandise are hawked to fans after a concert, 19th-century performers distributed tokens bearing their names, the names of their acts, or views of their performance locations. In the case of "Swedish Nightingale" Jenny Lind, private diesinkers found it opportune to strike tokens bearing her image, to seize profit from her popular 1850 American tour. Leonidas Westervelt first cataloged the populous Lind issues in 1921. Since then, several authors have added European issues, coins, anniversary issues, and other commemoratives to the corpus of Lind documentation.

Dog trainer H.B. West (1853), minstrel-show directors G. Christy and H. Wood (1857), and comedian / traveling showman Fayette "Yankee" Robinson (1863) were also the subjects of souvenir tokens. Those who attended the March 18, 1897, heavyweight-boxing title fight in Carson City, Nevada, could choose between two tokens: one had an obverse portrait of "Gentleman Jim" Corbett, while the other featured his opponent, Robert Fitzsimmons. (See the 1910 Nevada store card of Jack Givens in chapter 1, for another prizefight example.) The white metal keepsake of comedian Henry Dixey's 400th New York performance of "Adonis" in 1885 marks the first major credit in the career of a man who would become a huge theatrical celebrity.

19th-Century Souvenirs (continued)

YEAR	PERFORMER / OCCASION	METAL	COMMENTARY	F	EF	MS-63
1844	Tom Thumb / Barnum tour	WM	Allen & Moore of England struck these at Barnum's order	—	$100	$225
1850	Jenny Lind / Castle Garden debut	WM	Jenny Lind issues form their own subcategory	—	35	90
1853	West's Dog show at Crystal Palace	Br	A fairly common issue of an early animal act	$10	20	65
1864	Yankee Robinson's Big Show	Cop	Shows featured minstrel acts plus live animals and curiosities	15	35	75
1868	Stone and Murray's Circus	Svd Br	Stone and Murray were American; circus toured worldwide	—	350	500
1885	Henry Dixey's Burlesque Show	WM	*Adonis* reviewed as "one of the best American performances"	15	50	75

19TH-CENTURY SOUVENIRS (continued)

YEAR	PERFORMER / OCCASION	METAL	COMMENTARY	F	EF	MS-63
1892	Buffalo Bill's London tour	Cop	Baddleby & Reynolds struck this handsome medal	$125	$250	$400
1897	Corbett/Fitzsimmons title fight	Br	"Gentleman Jim," of course, took the honors	100	250	750

MOVIE TOKENS

A popular 20th-century collectible series consists of motion-picture studio tokens given away at movie previews and openings. According to Q. David Bowers, most were made of brass or copper, and ranged from the size of a quarter to a half dollar. Some bore a film's title, such as Charlie Chaplin's *Gold Rush*, the name of the studio that produced it, and sometimes an image of its star. Others listed several cast members. Some named the theater location and date when the film was scheduled to open (necessarily creating many varieties). Smaller, cheaper aluminum movie tokens with movie stars on them were packaged inside products such as ice cream, so people would keep buying ice cream until they had collected all the stars. Examples of movie promo tokens are known from the 1920s, but the majority came from the 1930s and 1940s.

YEAR	PERSONALITY / FILM	METAL	COMMENTARY	F	EF	MS-63
1915	Charlie Chaplin / *A Jitney Elopement*	GS	A jitney was a bus; it's in chapter 7!	$10	$20	$30
1915	Harry Schumm / *Broken Coin* (serial)	WM	Universal Studios' first serial had 22 episodes	—	10	15
1925	Gloria Swanson / *Madame Sans Gene*	Br	By Whitehead and Hoag. "Sans gene" = no worries	2	3	5
1925	Eric von Stroheim / *Greed*	Br	The great masterpiece of the silent era	5	7	12

MOVIE TOKENS (continued)

YEAR	PERSONALITY / FILM	METAL	COMMENTARY	F	EF	MS-63
1926	William Fairbanks / *Vanishing Millions*	Br	Serial with Fairbanks as "Monk" is now lost	—	$5	$12
1931	*10 Cents a Dance*	Alum	Barbara Stanwyck starred in this feature presentation	$3	4	5
1930s	Jean Harlow / MGM star / Popsicle token	Alum	An MGM star came with every box of Popsicles	—	5	10
1933	Frederic March / *Design for Living*	Alum	The portrait work on these cheap trinkets isn't half bad	2	4	6
1933	*Gold Diggers of 1933*	Br	They are Ginger Rogers, Ruby Keeler, and Joan Blondell	—	5	10
1934	Johnny Weismuller / *Tarzan and His Mate*	Alum	Weismuller was the sixth actor to play Tarzan	2	4	6

MAGICIANS' TOKENS

The fascinating magician-token category also includes medals, advertising pieces, and trick coins—in short, any item having to do with the magic arts. Toward the end of the 19th century, famous tricksters such as Howard Thurston and Harry Kellar manipulated tokens in their acts, and then threw them into the audience or sold them after the show. Some of these pieces were specially weighted for ease of palming, and bore magic symbols, a portrait of the magician, or the logo of the magic-supply company (such as Mysto or Martinka) that produced them. A very early token with a magician as its subject was struck by C.C. Wright to honor Herr Alexander Heimberger in 1847. F. William Keuthe's "Magician's Tokens and Related Items: An Illustrated Check-List," in the *TAMS Journal* of October 1978 is the major reference for this popular category, and the collectors' organization is known as the Magic Token Society.

YEAR	MAGICIAN OR MAGIC COMPANY	METAL	COMMENTARY	F	EF	MS-63
1847	Alexander Heim	Gilt Bz	Charles C. Wright struck this as a gift to Heim	$50	$100	$300
1880s	C. Milton Chase, magic supply	WM	The bull's-eye on the eagle was for spinning on a stick	25	50	100

MAGICIANS' TOKENS (continued)

YEAR	MAGICIAN OR MAGIC COMPANY	METAL	COMMENTARY	F	EF	MS-63
1890s	Martinka Magic (store card)	Svd Br	Major New York magic store with a mail-order trade	$75	$250	$400
1920s	Eli Hackman	GS	Thomas W. Yost & Co. sponsored Hackman, issued tokens	40	60	100
1920s	Robert Houdin (commemorative)	WM	Yost-issued show coin honoring a 19th-century master	15	30	60
1920s	Balmberger (show coin)	GS	German manufacturer imported magic supplies in the U.S.	—	5	7
1920s	Mysto Magic Company (show coin)	Alum	Company formed in 1909; its magic sets are collectible today	—	3	—
1928	Howard Thurston	Br	Thurston enjoyed worldwide fame with his touring stage show	5	7	10

MEDALS OF THE SPACE PROGRAM

America's forays into space have been amply recorded in exonumia. Private producers such as the Franklin Mint, Galaxy Medals, Medallic Art Company, and others produced collector medals in the formats and metals typical of their firms, to take advantage of public fascination with humanity's "giant leap." Some were made of "flown metal," that is, space-age alloys salvaged from scrapped rockets. Others used "flown silver" that was carried on space missions in ingot form, for the express purpose of being later struck into medals. Others were "ground relic" issues made from salvaged parts of launch pads and solid-rocket boosters.[48] Two series of space medals are considered extremely desirable: the Balfour medals and the Robbins medallions.

The National Aeronautics and Space Administration (NASA) was created in 1958, after the launch of the Soviet satellite *Sputnik* demonstrated to the United States that it was falling behind in the "space race." By 1961, NASA had a regular schedule of missions, and commissioned L.G. Balfour Co. of Attleboro, Massachusetts, to recognize the importance of each one by striking silver and pewter medals in very deep relief, for distribution to the personnel involved. The 13 Balfour issues employed designs from sketches and photographs reviewed by NASA's official artist. The public had no access to these until 1973, when the International Numismatic Agency marketed leatherette-boxed sets in silver and bronze.[49] To space memorabilia collectors, however, actual relics of space flights generate the greatest interest, along with artifacts once belonging to the astronauts. The medallion issues of The Robbins Company fit both requirements, because they were struck for the astronauts, who carried them into space. In collectors' eyes, the Robbins medallions are *the* official American space issues, even though NASA itself did not endorse them.

According to Howard C. Weinberger, author of *The Robbins Medallions—Flown Treasure from the Apollo Space Program*, and its 2006 sequel, *Flown Treasure from the Manned Space Programs*, the medals came in gold and silver, and the gold strikes were available only to members of the flight crew of each mission. These are sometimes called *wives' medals* because some astronauts presented them as gifts to their wives upon returning from space. Any astronaut affiliated with the NASA Astronaut Flight Office could purchase the silver strikes. The series began with the first manned Apollo launch, No. 7, in 1968. It has continued unbroken through all of the Apollo, Soyuz, Skylab, and Space Shuttle missions, and recent expeditions to the International Space Station. There are now 140 varieties, with about 350 pieces struck per variety. There have been from 80 to 450 silver strikes taken aboard each mission, as compared to 3 to 7 of the gold.

Robbins produced no sets, so any collections seen offered for sale have been assembled one at a time by the individual astronauts purchasing them, a provenance that dramatically heightens their value! The fact that they are serially numbered, and each can be certified to a particular flight, separates them from most other space-related memorabilia. As the minimum number of silver medallions carried per flight was 80, there are a possible 80 complete flown sets in existence. In 1999, the Wally Schirra collection of 11 medals covering Apollo flights 7 to 17 sold for $27,600.[50] Auction activity is increasing as original owners die and their estates enter the market, and as of 2006, the Robbins medallions are being certified and slabbed, similar to coins, by the Numismatic Guaranty Corporation of America (NGC).

Actual size 70 mm

YEAR	ASTRONAUT / MISSION	MINT	METAL	COMMENTARY	F	EF	MS-63
1962	Glenn/*Mercury,* first earth orbit	Wendell	WM	First human space traveler commemorated	—	—	$5
1969	*Apollo 11,* first lunar landing	MACo	Bz	JFK's dream; by sculptor Karen Worth	—	—	30

Medals of the Space Program (continued)

YEAR	ASTRONAUT / MISSION	MINT	METAL	COMMENTARY	F	EF	MS-63
1969	Conrad, Gordon, Bean / *Apollo 12*	Robbins	Gold	Bean's gold strike, carried on the mission	—	—	$20,000
1973	Apollo lunar missions 1968–1972	Galaxy	Bz	The entire Apollo program for collectors	—	—	25
1973	Bean, Garriott, Lousma / *Skylab II*	Robbins	Gold	Only flight crew received gold strikes	—	—	12,500

Medals of the Space Program *(continued)*

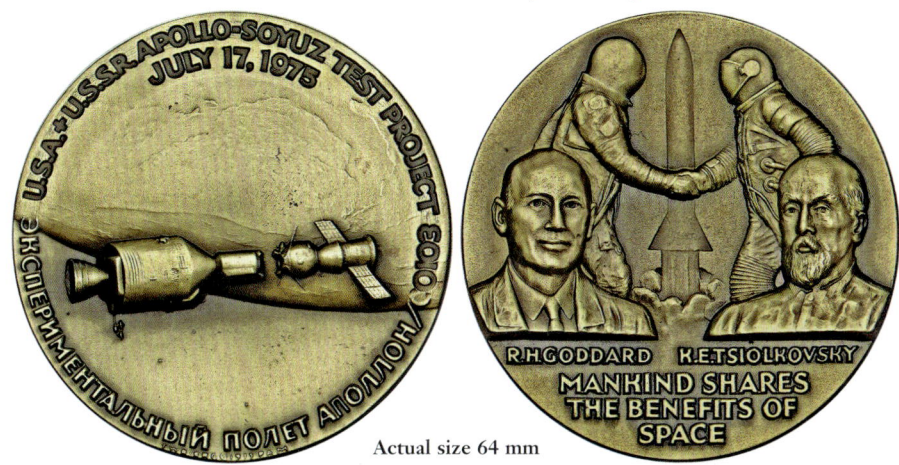

Actual size 64 mm

YEAR	ASTRONAUT / MISSION	MINT	METAL	COMMENTARY	F	EF	MS-63
1975	*Apollo–Soyuz* capsule link	AMI	Bz	Marking a new international cooperation	—	—	$20
2005	Space shuttle *Discovery*	Robbins	Silv	One of just 40 flown silver strikes	—	—	2,000

10
EXPOSITION SOUVENIRS

Historian Warren Susman has suggested that the 19th- and 20th-century urban expositions and world's fairs represented rites of passage for Americans, to ease their transition to new ways of living. The astonishing wonders viewed at these immense showplaces would soon become features of everyday life. In a memoir of his visit to the World's Columbian Exposition in 1893, brilliantly educated world-traveler Henry Adams called it "more surprising than anything else on the continent, Niagara Falls, the Yellowstone geysers, and the whole transcontinental railway system thrown in. . . . Education ran riot at Chicago, for retarded minds who had never faced in concrete form so many matters of which they were ignorant."[51]

To civic leaders, the economic promise of inviting hundreds of thousands of visitors to their cities for extended periods was just as great a motivator. Years of design and planning, and fortunes in construction capital, were invested in these ventures, and anyone who had a trade to ply, an innovation to market, or an art or a craft to exhibit, wanted to be part of the once-in-a-lifetime opportunity. Manufacturers and tradesmen created souvenir medals to be handed out to visitors. Restaurateurs, department-store owners, and other merchants of the host city created their own issues to take advantage of the influx of new customers and encourage their return. Some producers set up medal presses right on the premises, so their patrons could observe the coining process and receive a freshly minted souvenir. At the 1876 Centennial Exhibition in Philadelphia, a U.S. Mint exhibit in the Nevada building featured "Nevada Dollars" from dies by William Barber. These were made of pure silver, crushed from Nevada ores at a quartz mill on the grounds.

Starting with America's first international fair in 1853—New York's Crystal Palace Exposition of the Industry of All Nations—organizing committees arranged for the creation of official commemorative medals (not to be confused with the *award* medals covered in part V). Even expos lasting just a day, like the October 24, 1932, Philadelphia event marking the 250th anniversary of William Penn's arrival in America, issued at least one collectible medal. Harold Hibler and Charles Kappen cataloged many of the official specimens in their 1963 work, *So-Called Dollars*, but they omitted merchant issues from their classification.[52] (A much-expanded online archive of so-called dollars can be found at so-calleddollars.com. Also, in 2008 the Coin & Currency Institute published a new edition of the Hibler-Kappen book.)

Many collectors feel that to get the full flavor of what expositions had to offer, it is important to reach beyond the dollar-size limitation and to include merchant advertising pieces. (In this book, examples of merchant "expo dollars" are included in chapter 1.) Some collectors specialize in just the issues of a single exposition, and incorporate special U.S. and foreign commemorative coins in their quest. The events that generated the greatest number of die-struck items were the U.S. Centennial Exhibition in Philadelphia (1876), the World's Columbian Exposition in Chicago (1893), the California Midwinter Exposition in San Francisco (1894), and the Louisiana Purchase Exposition in St. Louis (1904). Information for collectors is available on the Web sites of the So-Called Dollar Collectors Club and the World's Fair Collector's Society.

Exposition Souvenirs 155

YEAR	EXPOSITION	METAL	COMMENTARY	F	EF	MS-63
1872	Boston Peace Jubilee	WM	Organizer Gilmore was also the "father of the concert band"	—	$20	$35
1876	U.S. Centennial Exhibition, Philadelphia*	Silv	Smaller of two official medal sizes from the U.S. Mint	$20	125	300
1889	Piedmont Exposition, Atlanta	WM	Atlanta burned, but rose from its ashes like the phoenix	5	10	30
1892	World's Columbian Exposition, Chicago	WM	A bird's-eye view of the "White City" built for the exposition	15	45	100
1893	World's Columbian Exposition, Chicago	Alum	The Ferris wheel: one of many wonders seen at the fair	5	30	125

* Voted No. 52 in *100 Greatest American Medals and Tokens* (Jaeger/Bowers).

156　A GUIDE BOOK OF UNITED STATES TOKENS AND MEDALS

YEAR	EXPOSITION	METAL	COMMENTARY	F	EF	MS-63
1893	World's Candy Exposition, New York	WM	Featuring candy makers, machines, and delicious samples	$15	$45	$75
1907	Tercentennial of Jamestown, Va.	Br	Celebrating maritime and colonial history at Hampton Roads	10	15	30
1919	Alaska-Yukon-Pacific Exposition	Br	Showcasing the glories of the Pacific Northwest in Seattle	—	50	75

Exposition Souvenirs

YEAR	EXPOSITION	METAL	COMMENTARY	F	EF	MS-63
1929	U.S. Sesquicentennial, Philadelphia	Nick	Many types of souvenirs honored George Washington	$10	$20	$60
1933	Century of Progress Exposition, Chicago	Bz	Swastika was a good-luck symbol of Native American origin	—	7	10
1962	Seattle World's Fair	Bz	Showing off the landmark Space Needle	—	—	15
1964	New York World's Fair	Br	Unisphere implied global influence for U.S. Steel Corporation	—	2	3

11
PERSONAL MEDALS AND TOKENS

Any medal struck to commemorate the life or deeds of a person who did not achieve the presidency may be considered a personal medal. Statesmen, performers, inventors, scientists, writers, businesspeople, and sports figures have been accorded this honor, some because of their historical importance, and others because of their popularity. Ordinary citizens have been the subjects of personal medals as well, in celebration of births, weddings, anniversaries, and professional accomplishments. Engravers, sculptors, and numismatists who routinely handled medals honoring important and powerful figures got a kick out of creating private issues to honor their very own important figures, such as children, colleagues, or spouses.

Medals expert D. Wayne Johnson once calculated, in numbers of medals and tokens, the most honored Americans after the presidents. They were Benjamin Franklin, the Marquis de Lafayette (as a friend of America), Thomas Edison, Mark Twain, Albert Einstein, and Charles Lindbergh. Personal medals have been issued individually or in series, for official or commercial reasons, and during or after the honoree's lifetime. The typical format has the subject's portrait on the obverse, with explanatory legends, symbolic images, or perhaps a family crest on the reverse. Some are masterpieces of bas-relief portraiture, while others bear almost comically inaccurate portrait attempts. Some of the more respected 20th-century series, such as the Signers of the Declaration of Independence (by sculptor Ralph Menconi) and the New York University Hall of Fame for Great Americans (by various renowned sculptors), were struck at the Medallic Art Company. In the 1960s, the Franklin Mint struck numerous "coin medals" commemorating important Americans, as discussed in chapter 13.

At least one uncomplimentary personal medal was the 1933 "toilet medal" by George de Zayas, struck at the expense of then–U.S. senator and former Louisiana governor Huey Long. Joseph Levine relates the background to this piece:

> Long, the venerable "kingfish," was attending a party at a country club in Sands Point, Long Island. A heavy drinker, Long proceeded to imbibe a bit too much, and could not retain his customary control over his physical movements. While standing in front of the urinal, his unsteadiness caused him to soak the lower pants and shoes of a fellow relief-seeker. The surprised and angered victim turned and promptly punched Long in the eye. The incident received wide publicity, and one national magazine started a campaign for public subscriptions for a medal to reward the unknown assailant.[53]

The medal, pictured on page 160, depicts a clenched fist striking a fish, whose crown has been knocked off its head. A toilet seat encircles the scene. According to Johnson, former research director at Medallic Art Co., a plaque-sized version was mounted above the urinals in the men's executive bathroom.

Personal Medals and Tokens 159

Actual size 77x58 mm

YEAR	PERSON	ARTIST / MINT	METAL	COMMENTARY	F	EF	MS-63
1853	Edward-Willis Parsons	G.H. Lovett	WM	A made-to-order family keepsake	—	$50	$125
1878	Baron von Steuben	F.B. Smith / U.S. Mint	Bz	Struck at the order of J. Colvin Randall	—	100	250
1882	Sharpless family	Unknown	Nick	Souvenir of a family reunion	—	50	75
1885	William and Mary Key	William Key	Bz	Marking the artist's silver anniversary	—	—	25
1903	Amerigo Vespucci	V.D. Brenner / MACo	Bz	Master sculptor honors Italian explorer	—	—	400

Actual size 77 mm

Actual size 75 mm

YEAR	PERSON	ARTIST / MINT	METAL	COMMENTARY	F	EF	MS-63
1933	Huey Long, "the Kingfish"	G. de Zayas / MACo	Bz	Issued in response to a satirical contest	—	$35	$75
1935	Mark Twain	Kilenyi/Robbins	Bz	Struck for the writer's birth centennial	—	—	50
1948	Babe Ruth	Whitehead & Hoag	Gilt Bz	Sold to raise funds for the Ruth Foundation	—	8	15
1969	Thomas Paine	M. Lantz / MACo	Bz	From the Hall of Fame for Great Americans	—	15	40

YEAR	PERSON	ARTIST / MINT	METAL	COMMENTARY	F	EF	MS-63
1989	Russell Rulau	Pobjoy Mint	Silv	Author and cataloger marks a half century	—	—	$3
1999	Art Kagin	Unknown	Cop	A birthday piece for a beloved coin dealer	—	—	3
2007	R.S. Yeoman, Kenneth Bressett	C. Daughtrey / Silver Towne	Pew	Longtime editors of the *Guide Book of United States Coins*	—	—	35

ARRAS TOKENS

Some Hispanic Americans observe an old Spanish Catholic wedding tradition that involves the groom presenting his bride with a gift of 13 tokens called *arras*. (In the Philippines, where the custom was also brought from Spain, these are sometimes known as *arrhea*.) When the tradition began, coins were used—a wealthy groom might afford gold, a man of means silver, and the average groom gold-plated or plain bronze or brass. The number 13 represents Christ and his disciples. During the wedding service the tokens, kept in a fancy box, are carried in by a godmother (the *madrina de las arras*, one of several patrons and attendants with special roles in the wedding), and given to the priest for blessing. Then the groom trickles them into the bride's palms. The exchange of arras symbolizes the groom's commitment to support his family, and the bride's commitment to manage their household. In the past, if actual coins were used, the couple might donate them to the church. Today's bride will keep her tokens as mementoes of her wedding—*recuerdos matrimoniales*. Common themes on arras tokens include a bride and groom, a portrait of Christ, a cross, intertwined hearts, a church or cathedral, clasped hands, and other symbols of love, devotion, and piety.[54] The specimens displayed here come from Mexico, but all may be found in the Southwestern United States as well. An interesting online catalog of arras and other international wedding tokens is maintained by Forrest Stevens at users.pullman.com/fjstevens/tokens/ArrasTokens.

YEAR	OBVERSE / REVERSE	METAL	F	EF	MS-63
1930s	Bride and groom before a church / Clasped hands over heart, no legend	Br	$5	$10.00	$15
1950s	Bride and groom before a church / Clasped hands, RECUERDO MATRIMONIAL	Br	—	10.00	15
1950s	Basilica de Virgen Guadelupe (Mexico City) / Mexican eagle with olive branch	Gilt base metal	1	2.50	5
1970s	Bride and groom / Clasped hands over heart, NUESTRA BODA (Our Wedding)	Gilt base metal	1	2.50	5
1978+	Popo John Paul II / Clasped hands, RECUERDO MATRIMONIAL	Svd base metal	1	2.00	3
1970s+	Emperor Maximilian / Linked wedding rings, RECUERDO DE MI BODA	Gilt base metal	1	2.00	3

Note: A typical plated, base-metal arras token set (new) may sell today for as little as $7–$10.

12

THE HISTORICAL COMMEMORATIVE CRAZE OF 1858–1861

This chapter was contributed by Q. David Bowers.

In the summer of 1858, several elements came together to initiate what became a passion for collecting newly made medals. The successful laying of the Atlantic Cable, completed on August 5, 1858, spurred George H. Lovett of New York (see introduction) to create a commemorative medal. The obverse depicted a stylized view of John Bull, representing England, exchanging electrical sparks with Brother Jonathan, representing America. The inscriptions, HOW ARE YOU JONATHAN to the left is seemingly answered by PURTY WELL OLD FELLER. HEOW'S YERSELF at the right. The reverse included the inscription ATLANTIC TELEGRAPH / SUCCESSFULLY LAID / 5TH OF / AUGUST / 1858. Although details are scarce today, these souvenir medals probably proved to be popular with American citizens, whose wild celebrations included a gala held at New York's showplace, the Crystal Palace, where an official Tiffany & Co. medal (dies also made by Lovett) was presented to cable progenitor Cyrus Field. (The cable connection sputtered out in a few weeks, however.)

The medals became popular with numismatists as well. In 1858, the coin hobby was just beginning to be widespread, fueled by the rapidly disappearing old "large" copper cents, which came to have a nostalgic value, and the advent of the new smaller-size Flying Eagle cents, launched on May 25, 1857. By 1858, more than a dozen coin dealers were active in New York City, Philadelphia, Boston, Baltimore, and elsewhere. Most handled other items as well, such as popular prints, books, and antiques. By 1859, in New York, such dealers as Augustus B. Sage, Ezra Hill, and John Curtis were enjoying a lively trade, while in Philadelphia the newly established William K. Idler was doing well, and in Boston the main factor was Henry Cook. Medalists in New York and Philadelphia included the sons of Robert Lovett (George H., John D., and Robert Jr.), William Bridgens, Smith & Hartmann, and F.C. Key & Sons, while in Boston Joseph H. Merriam enjoyed a brisk business, and in Cincinnati, Benjamin True and others were at work. Each of these, and others as well, tapped into the growing numismatic market and created small medals depicting people and events from the past as well as current events. These diesinkers often issued medals on their own, in addition to making them on commission from patrons, usually coin dealers.

It was soon discovered that by mixing dies in combinations never intended to be mated with each other, "rarities" could be made. Generally, these were struck in very small numbers and often years after the original issues. Today, these illogical pieces are highly prized by collectors. Some dealers mixed dies from different engravers, such as combining Lovett's with those of Bridgens, Key, and Merriam. In addition, some dies fell into private hands and were used to make restrikes and fantasy issues. Many if not most of the dealers of this era issued store cards, often combining an advertisement on one side with an unrelated building or a famous portrait (most often that of George Washington) on the other. Augustus B. Sage, the teenaged rare-coin enthusiast who was instrumental in founding the American Numismatic Society in 1858, was New York City's leading dealer. In 1859 and 1860, he issued three store cards and several series of numismatic medals, and seems to have been the first to institute a program of making numismatic medals.

In 1859, Sage issued four coin-auction catalogs, more than any other firm in America. It seems reasonable to conclude that he began publishing his own copper tokens in the autumn of 1858, having been inspired by current events, with articles in *Harper's New Monthly Magazine* providing the impetus. George Lovett prepared the dies and struck the pieces. The first issues, called the Odds and Ends series, featured the burning of the Crystal Palace in October. This was a sugar house used as a Revolutionary War prison that had been mentioned in a recent *Harper's* article. The Odds and Ends series also celebrated the continuing chess triumphs of Paul Morphy. The reverse inscriptions of these tokens seem to have reflected Sage's emotions and compassion, as with ALL IS VANITY on the reverse of No. 1, the plight of the patriots in a British prison on the second issue, and an observation concerning Staunton's discourtesy on the third token. These three subjects, as interesting as they may have been to Sage himself, met with a mixed or lackluster reception on the part of intended customers.

Meanwhile, in the final days of 1858, Sage conceived his Historical Tokens series with a sharper focus. Featured were early American structures, which eventually took the form of 13 different buildings plus one ship, most of which had to do with the Revolutionary War. Sage's Historical Tokens are believed to have been the first lengthy private series of commemorative tokens produced in the United States for sale to collectors (an American equivalent of various European series including Edward Thomason's products in England and the Series Numismatica in France). By February 1859, Lovett had prepared nearly a dozen varieties, per this advertisement: "Aug. B. Sage's Historical Tokens. This series will consist of about 25 tokens, each one giving a correct representation of some public building, around which there is any thing of an historical interest. Eleven pieces in this series have thus far been published. . . ." The Historical Series petered out with No. 14.

Two of the 14 obverses in the regular series are each combined with two reverses, as Lovett cut the first dies erroneously. The obverse of each illustrates the subject, and the reverse has a brief explanatory text. Most subjects were inspired by descriptions and/or illustrations in Benson J. Lossing's 1852 *Pictorial Field Guide to the Revolution*. Historian Lossing was an acquaintance of Sage's, and an honorary member of the American Numismatic Society. In early 1859, Sage's Historical Tokens with Washington-related *buildings* seem to have had a fine reception, but not nearly on the order of what might have been, had such pieces featured Washington *portraits*. Later numismatists including James Ross Snowden (1861), William Spohn Baker (1885), and George J. Fuld with Russell Rulau (1985), prepared detailed listings of tokens and medals featuring *portraits* of Washington. Had Sage or Lovett thought of inserting even a tiny portrait of Washington as part of the motif of buildings, etc., the scenario would have been different, and Sage's pieces would be much better known today.

Sage's third series was the Numismatic Gallery, which had its beginning in early 1859, and which eventually depicted eight different numismatists, or possibly nine (if the James R. Chilton token was, indeed, issued). From the aspect of numismatic history this series is one of the most important of its era. Today, examples are scarce. In addition to copper, original white-metal impressions were made for certain of the later issues. The number of pieces known today varies widely, with the Henry Bogert medal being the most often seen (perhaps Bogert ordered extra examples to give out?). Probably, interest waned as the series went on, prompting it to be discontinued after the Robert J. Dodge issue. Pieces are sufficiently elusive that only a few collectors have been able to assemble a full set of portraits.

In spring 1859, Sage announced his fourth and apparently final series, known as the Masonic Medalets. However, only No. 1 ever saw the light of day. In 1859 and 1860, other dealers and collectors who had caught the "bug" published dozens of new varieties of tokens and medalets. In general, latecomers selected subjects they thought would be *popular* and thus aid in sales. Portraits of presidents in particular were widely used (see chapter 17).

Issued in an era before coin holders and protective containers became popular, most of these medals were handled casually. Often they were carried in pockets, dropped, mixed loosely with others, and otherwise neglected. They were souvenirs in their time and were meant to be passed around. Today, most medals are seen in coin grades in and around MS-60 or PF-60. Grades of AU to MS-62 cover perhaps 80% of the medals issued by Sage, Hill, Curtis, Lovett, and others in New York City.[55] Medals issued in Philadelphia tend to exist in higher average grades, this being particularly true of dealers' store cards. Average weights vary considerably: given a group of 10 similar tokens, scarcely any two weigh precisely the same, a curious situation indicating that such pieces were often made one at a time, rather than in extended runs. The most-often seen metals of striking are those illustrated herein. Although there were many exceptions, most medals or medalets were of a size from 28 mm to 31 mm and were struck in copper, brass, or white metal. Silver strikings were sometimes produced on special order. Edges were either plain (usually) or reeded.

For the most complete listing of these pieces in a single source, refer to Rulau's most recent *Standard Catalog of U.S. Tokens 1700–1900*, which describes many mulings, metal combinations, and the like. The listing here indicates just a few of the more important and popular numismatic medals of 1858 to 1860, with some produced into early 1861, after which time the Civil War (declared on April 16, 1861) occupied everyone's attention, and the issuance of numismatic medals diminished greatly.

DIESINKERS AND COIN DEALERS

RULAU NO.	PERSON / SUBJECT	METAL	COMMENTARY	F	EF	MS-63
630J-2A	William Bridgens store card	Cop	This New York diesinker's card was a Civil War token	$20	$40	$100
Pa 89	Edward Cogan store card	Bz	Cogan thrived in first in Philadelphia, then New York	20	40	100

DIESINKERS AND COIN DEALERS *(continued)*

RULAU NO.	PERSON / SUBJECT	METAL	COMMENTARY	F	EF	MS-63
Ma-Bo 19	Henry Cook store card	Bz	Cook sold and repaired shoes *and* dealt in coins	—	$200	$500
NY 180	John K. Curtis store card	Cop	"The Antiquary" operated in Greenwich Village	$20	35	100
NY 312	Ezra Hill store card	WM	Another active New York coin dealer / token issuer	20	40	100
Pa 212a	William Idler store card	WM	Idler often used U.S. Mint facilities to strike medals	40	75	200
Baker 551B	F.C. Key & Sons store card	Br	One of many store-card mulings for the Keys	15	30	125
NY 495	G.H. Lovett's Atlantic telegraph	WM	Souvenir of the occasion made to A.B. Sage's order	15	35	100
NY 491B	G.H. Lovett's hobbies*	Br	Lovett knew this one would be irresistible	20	35	75
NY 498	J.D. Lovett store card	Br	Showing a seal press, tool of the issuer's trade	15	35	55
Pa 355	R. Lovett Jr. store card	C-N	Many store cards featured this French liberty head	20	40	80

* Voted No. 47 in *100 Greatest American Medals and Tokens* (Jaeger/Bowers).

DIESINKERS AND COIN DEALERS *(continued)*

RULAU NO.	PERSON / SUBJECT	METAL	COMMENTARY	F	EF	MS-63
Ma-Bo 73	J. Merriam store card	Cop	A self-portrait store card is always interesting	$25	$75	$150
NY 2052	Merriam's *Great Eastern*	WM	Sidewheeler's visit was a sensation in New York	20	50	125
	Merriam's Prince of Wales	Bz	A visiting prince warranted a souvenir token issue	15	35	75

AUGUSTUS B. SAGE TOKEN SERIES

RULAU NO.	SUBJECT	METAL	COMMENTARY	F	EF	MS-63
NY 768	Sage's Washington store card	WM	One of many mulings to this Washington bust	$20	$30	$75
NY 757	Sage's library card	Br	Offering library access for a specified fee	20	30	75
Odds/Ends 1	Crystal Palace Fire	Bz	Marking the ruination of a great exposition hall	20	30	75
Odds/Ends 3	Paul Morphy, chess champion	Bz	Sage shows his admiration by striking a token	25	40	90

Augustus B. Sage Token Series (continued)

RULAU NO.	SUBJECT	METAL	COMMENTARY	F	EF	MS-63
Num. Gall. 1	Charles I. Bushnell*	Bz	Sage honors a fellow researcher and friend	—	$125	$200
Num. Gall. 2	Henry Bogert	Bz	Striking tokens for colleagues began with Sage	$20	30	75
Num. Gall. 9	Robert Dodge	Bz	To build interest in collectors as well as collecting	20	30	75
Mas. Med. 1	Masonic Hall, New York City	Bz	Hosted the first American Institute fair in 1828	23	30	75
Hist. Tok. 1	Old Provoost	Bz	Revolutionary War buildings a favorite Sage subject	15	30	75
Hist. Tok. 5	Old Jersey / Prison ship	Bz	Prisoners of war starved and died in "floating hell"	15	30	75
Hist. Tok. 6	Philadelphia State House	WM	Another building important to revolutionary history	—	25	75
Hist. Tok 11	Headquarters at Valley Forge	Bz	Sage charged 25¢ each; $4 for 14-piece set	15	30	75

* Voted No. 58 in *100 Greatest American Medals and Tokens* (Jaeger/Bowers).

Odd Mulings

OBVERSE / REVERSE BY	OBVERSE / REVERSE	COMMENTARY	F	EF	MS-63
G. Lovett / G. Lovett	Daniel Webster / We All Have our Hobbies	Here's where it gets confusing. . . .	$20	$35	$75
F.C. Key / G. Lovett	Edwin Forrest / We All Have our Hobbies	Why strike these illogical mules?	20	35	75
Bridgens / G. Lovett	Boy and Dog / Brother Jonathan	To attract collectors, of course!	15	35	100

13

COIN MEDALS OF THE FRANKLIN MINT

More than 100 years after Augustus B. Sage piqued America's interest in medals struck just for collectors, a second fad on a far larger scale was born in much the same way: with an idea in the mind of a single entrepreneur. The history of the Franklin Mint commemorative "coin medal" phenomenon encompasses the stories of founder Joseph Segel, his talented board chairman Gilroy Roberts, a star-studded roster of medallic artists, and of course, the coin medals themselves. An array of forces brought an end to the Franklin Mint's spectacular success: a high-stakes 1980 silver-market cornering stunt, a fateful *60 Minutes* television episode, the saturation of the market by competitors, and changes in mint ownership leading to changes in product direction. The medallic issues covered in this chapter were minted in the "glory days" of 1964 to 1980, while the Franklin Mint was a publicly owned company whose product lines were dictated by its collector/members and stockholders.

THE FOUNDER AND HIS PLAN

In a September 2005 interview, 14-year Franklin Mint president Charles Andes told the author, "If you want to write the history of the Franklin Mint, it's him," and jerked his thumb towards Joe Segel sitting in the next chair. The company Andes took on in 1972 was a $100-plus-million-dollar-a-year operation that owned mints in the United States, Canada, Britain, France, and Japan. By 1980 it would have its own bookbindery, furniture plant, and museum, and produce many other lines of collectibles such as porcelain plates, crystal cameos, die-cast cars, and bronze figurines. Thousands of gifted people were involved in its incredible success, but like Andes, most would readily hand credit to Segel, whose uncompromising philosophy underlay the whole empire: create a quality product, support it with quality marketing, and "always give the customer more than he expects."

Segel was a 34-year-old advertising executive when he got the idea for a mail-order medals business from a 1964 *Time* magazine photo showing a line of collectors waiting to buy the last issues of the U.S. silver dollar. Segel knew the recently issued Kennedy half dollars were also a big success with collectors. But the Treasury was about to abandon 90% silver for copper-nickel and silver-clad coinage compositions, and this would leave the market for sterling-silver commemoratives wide open to whoever stepped up to produce them. General Douglas MacArthur had just died, and a silver coin honoring him might make a good starting point. Since it would be commemorative in nature, and a little larger than a dollar, it would be by definition a medal; but since Segel was certain he wanted a Proof surface, it would have to be minted more like a coin. He decided to describe his intended product as a *coin medal*.

Segel included three additional important aspects in his business plan: guaranteed rarity; guaranteed exclusivity; and letting customers decide the subject matter to be commemorated. Each medal would be designed by a different, famous sculptor, and only one numbered specimen would be available to each member of the society that was formed to issue the medals. Membership would be open only for a short period, and after the member rolls closed, the total edition of each issue would be permanently limited to the number of members who had subscribed. Members would nominate and vote for the subjects to be commemorated, and their medals, weighing just under an ounce and priced at $6.60 apiece, would be mailed out once a month. Orders for medals would be given to a manufacturer of promotional coins that Segel knew. A monthly newsletter would keep members abreast of the nominees and the results of voting, and would include a forum for suggestions and reactions to the product.

In June 1964, Segel took out a striking four-page ad in the numismatic journals for his National Commemorative Society (NCS). Six weeks later, he balloted the 5,252 new members for their choice of subjects, and landed five important sculptors for the first issues: Calvin Massey, Gilroy Roberts, Dexter Jones, Frank Gasparro, and Anthony deFrancisci. When the first medals were shipped out, subscribers were amazed at the results. Wrote one member, "Like most of the rest, I joined the society on a hunch and I have been commending my good fortune more and more each month." Segel swiftly implemented members' suggestions for improvement, such as moving from an overall mirror finish to a two-tone finish and switching from coin alignment to medal alignment of the obverse and reverse. The subscriber newsletters and almanacs described how the minting equipment worked, profiled the artists, and exposed the ups and downs of the creative process, allowing members to participate in the production of their coin medals from start to finish. Altogether, it was a savory collecting experience and a smash hit.

Segel began coming up with ideas for other series. He hired U.S. Mint Chief Sculptor-Engraver Gilroy Roberts as chairman of the board, called his company the General Numismatics Corporation, and opened his own mint. It began with a single coining press and a small machine shop, but soon other commemorative societies formed and began placing orders for series. All editions were limited to a certain number of strikes and the dies were always destroyed at the end of the edition. In 1965, Nevada casinos began placing orders for slot-machine tokens (see chapter 6), and the company took off. In 1967 Segel renamed the growing firm the Franklin Mint.[56]

By 1968 it was the Franklin Mint, not the Treasury, that had lines of collectors stretching down the block to acquire its products. Its plant occupied 13 buildings, with 900 employees, and struck medals and coins of the realm for foreign countries in multiple sizes and eight different alloys besides sterling silver. These included "Karatclad" (gold on .925 fine silver), aluminum, platinum, bronze, brass, nickel-silver, and Franklinium I and II. There were four available finishes: full Proof, prooflike, mint quality, and antiqued. Admiring representatives of foreign mints came to examine Segel's setup, and this led to alliances and the acquisition of the John Pinches Organization of England, the Wellings Mint of Canada, and Le Medallier in France (manufacturers of the Janvier pantograph). In 1969 Segel broke ground for a huge new mint facility in Pennsylvania and formed the Franklin Mint Collectors' Society. In 1972 he placed the helm in the able hands of Charles Andes and "retired." Now known as the "king of the startups"[57] for the number of other companies he formed, Segel's greatest legacy is in his coin medals. The support and exposure he gave sculptors in the 1960s and 1970s sustained the world's appreciation of coin art, and his gigantic sales figures indicated the degree of thirst people had for it.

The Artists

Gilroy Roberts's reputation as designer of the Kennedy half-dollar coin, and his connections in the sculpting/engraving world, assured that a steady stream of talented artists would work on Franklin Mint medals, and he designed and engraved many company products himself. Sculptors considered it a privilege to be invited to create a Franklin Mint medal or series, and enjoyed the unique challenge it presented. Some were young but exceptionally talented, like Karen Worth, whose Franklin Mint medals were among the first of more than 600 lifetime medal credits. Others, like Elizabeth Jones, Thomas Lo Medico, and EvAngelos Frudakis, were seasoned professionals, performing their Franklin Mint work in the midst of other major assignments such as monumental sculpture commissions and teaching sculpture to students. (Jones would later become chief sculptor-engraver of the U.S. Mint.) C. Paul Jennewein, Donald DeLue, Felix Schlag, Robert Weinman, Carl Schmitz, Paul Vincze, and dozens more were already world renowned for their coin and medal designs, and took the Franklin Mint commissions for the fun of it. For Anthony De Francisci, designer of the 1921–1935 Peace dollar, the NCS coin medal honoring John F. Kennedy was the last work of his life—completed just three days before his death in October 1964.

By 1973, the company had a staff of 19 sculptors working full time.

The Coin Medals

The mission of the mint was to create a series for every taste and budget. The Medical Heritage Society issued the History of Dentistry, History of Pharmacy, and Pioneers in Medicine. For hunters, there was the Big Game series, and for animal lovers, Wildlife of North America and Birds. Military personnel could collect the History of the Army, Navy, or Marine Corps, and there were series dealing with the history of flight, spacecraft, and NASA's space programs. Sports lovers could choose Pro Football's Immortals, while celebrity followers subscribed to the Hollywood Hall of Fame. African and Native Americans had their series: the American Negro Commemorative Society, the Indian Chiefs, and the Indian Tribes of America. The American Numismatic Association ordered annual souvenir medals for its convention banquets, and the United Nations issued annual medals, in five languages, on subjects of worldwide interest. Some series were aimed at foreign markets, such as the 1970 World Cup soccer-team portrait medals for Great Britain.

Each commemorative society was structured along the same lines, allowing its members to choose subjects, define edition limits, and specify metals in which its series would be struck. Segel's mother and aunt conceived a society to honor historically important women, the Société Commemorative des Femmes Célèbres (SCFC). Said Segel, "These two ladies developed and ran SCFC completely on their own. I had no involvement with it, except to occasionally answer questions. It was fun to watch them do their thing." Other groups, such as the Catholic Heritage Society and the Jewish Heritage Society, struck series on the events and figures important to their faiths. Art treasures were a frequent in-house series theme, including the works of Michelangelo, Rembrandt, Da Vinci, Rubens, Van Gogh, and more. By 1981, the final year for Chester Krause's annual *Guidebook of Franklin Mint Issues*, the sculpting and engraving staff had created 169 different coin medal series, coins of the realm for 21 countries, 55 art ingot series, and 267 issues of gaming tokens.

The Conclusion

In 1976, public interest in mail-order medals peaked. According to Andes, "the Bicentennial was such a huge year for historical commemoratives, for our medals and across the board, and it was difficult to follow that with more of the same thing. We branched out into other lines of collectibles." Franklin Mint competitors, including the Danbury Mint, the Kennedy Mint, and the Lincoln Mint, were using the lucrative mail-order format with equal success. Says Segel, "I have no knowledge of whether those competitors really limited their editions as religiously as we did. I suspect they did not. Moreover, most of them . . . had no real coin-making facilities of their own."

Then, in 1978 *60 Minutes* television segment, CBS reporter Morley Safer implied that people were buying the medals as an investment, only to learn they had little actual resale value. Safer interviewed collectors who were disappointed when they discovered dealers wouldn't pay better than retail value for their collections, and dealers who stated they would not pay more than bullion value for any modern coin medals. The segment ended with a view of a stream of coin medals being poured into a smelter, with Safer advising: "If you are buying for investment reasons . . . there are a lot of questions you should ask before you buy."[58] Says Segel, "*60 Minutes* made the grievous error of comparing what coin dealers were willing to sell a piece for, with what they were willing to pay for it, then concluding from that bid/offer comparison that Franklin Mint pieces were always going to be worth less than one would pay for them. The same unfavorable comparison could be made for any collectible, at any given point of time. And *60 Minutes* completely ignored the historical, educational, and aesthetic values of Franklin Mint issues."

The event to have the greatest impact on surviving populations of Franklin Mint medals was the "silver bubble" of 1979 and 1980, when the Hunt brothers of Texas bought up 200 million ounces, or half the world's supply, driving the price of silver from $4 to nearly $50 per ounce in a few month's time. Says well-known exonumist Clifford Mishler, "Very large quantities were consigned to melting during the *party*. At that time, nothing that was bought for silver value was held back, not Franklin Mint material, not common U.S. coins, not even *stickered* dollars! That means that, today, there are undoubtedly quite a few Franklin Mint issues that are legitimately scarce." There is no published hobby research on just how scarce silver Franklin medals have become. They may be found for sale on the Internet at just over bullion value, and complete sets of popular series such as Roberts's Presidents and Norman Rockwell's Spirit of Scouting medals have increased in value handsomely. Segel accounts for the apparent lack of strong aftermarket value on the other issues this way: "In the early years, there was a concerted effort by coin dealers to belittle Franklin Mint issues, I think primarily because it cut into their business. And, I think that many of them did not believe that the issues were truly limited in edition."

In 1981, Warner Communications, Inc., acquired the Franklin Mint, discontinued producing silver coin medals, and in 1984 sold the mint to corporate giant Roll International. In 1994 the Franklin Mint began offering bronze and silver holiday-themed medals for $75 to $475 each and a series of "starter set" collections priced from $90 to $2,200.[59] The firm ran into trouble in 1997, when it used the image of pro golfer Tiger Woods on a medal without a licensing agreement, and again in 1998 for its commemorative plate featuring an unlicensed image of Princess Diana.[60] In 2003 Roll closed the mint, terminating 200 employees and selling its corporate center and museum building to a developer, concluding what has been called "the greatest numismatic success story of all time."[61]

Franklin Mint Coin Medals

SERIES / SOCIETY	SUBJECT	SCULPTOR	METAL	COMMENTARY	MS-63*
Bicentennial History of the United States	Year 1797	Philip Nathan	Bz	One of a series of 200 medals	$3
	Year 1869	Ernest Lauser	Bz	Issued in silver and bronze	3
	Year 1930	Vincent Miller	Bz	The series took 100 months to complete	3
Spirit of Scouting	Thrifty	Richard Baldwin	Silv	Norman Rockwell's design	20

* Since Franklin Mint medals were issued in plastic holders and did not circulate, they are invariably found in pristine, high grades. A bit of tarnish is typically the only defect.

Coin Medals of the Franklin Mint 175

Franklin Mint Coin Medals (continued)

SERIES / SOCIETY	SUBJECT	SCULPTOR	METAL	COMMENTARY	MS-63*
Spirit of Scouting (continued)	Loyal	Richard Baldwin	Silv	The set contained 12 medals	$20
	Clean	Richard Baldwin	Silv	These have high appeal to scouting collectors	20
Catholic Commemorative Society	Prince of Peace	EvAngelos Frudakis	Silv	The sculptor won a design competition	20
Negro Commemorative Society	Mahalia Jackson	Gilroy Roberts	Silv	Portraits of historic figures	20
	Richard Wright	Elizabeth Jones	Silv	Made by world-renowned sculptors	20

* Since Franklin Mint medals were issued in plastic holders and did not circulate, they are invariably found in pristine, high grades. A bit of tarnish is typically the only defect.

Franklin Mint Coin Medals (continued)

SERIES / SOCIETY	SUBJECT	SCULPTOR	METAL	COMMENTARY	MS-63*
National Commemmorative Society	Paul Revere	Thomas Lo Medico	Silv	NCS members selected the subjects	$20
	Lafayette	Karen Worth	Silv	The NCS set had 150 medals in all	20
Medical Heritage Society	Schweitzer	Elizabeth Jones	Silv	60-medal series on physicians and medicine	20
Femmes Celebres	Eve	EvAngelos Frudakis	Silv	From a 50-medal series honoring women	20

* Since Franklin Mint medals were issued in plastic holders and did not circulate, they are invariably found in pristine, high grades. A bit of tarnish is typically the only defect.

FRANKLIN MINT SPECIAL ISSUES

SUBJECT, YEAR	SCULPTOR	METAL	COMMENTARY	MS-63
Christmas, 1975	Ernest Lauser	Bz	Holiday issues by a different sculptor each year	$5
Bicentennial Day, 1976	Unsigned	Silv	Presented inside a special hardcover book	20

Part III
POLITICAL AND PRESIDENTIAL EXONUMIA

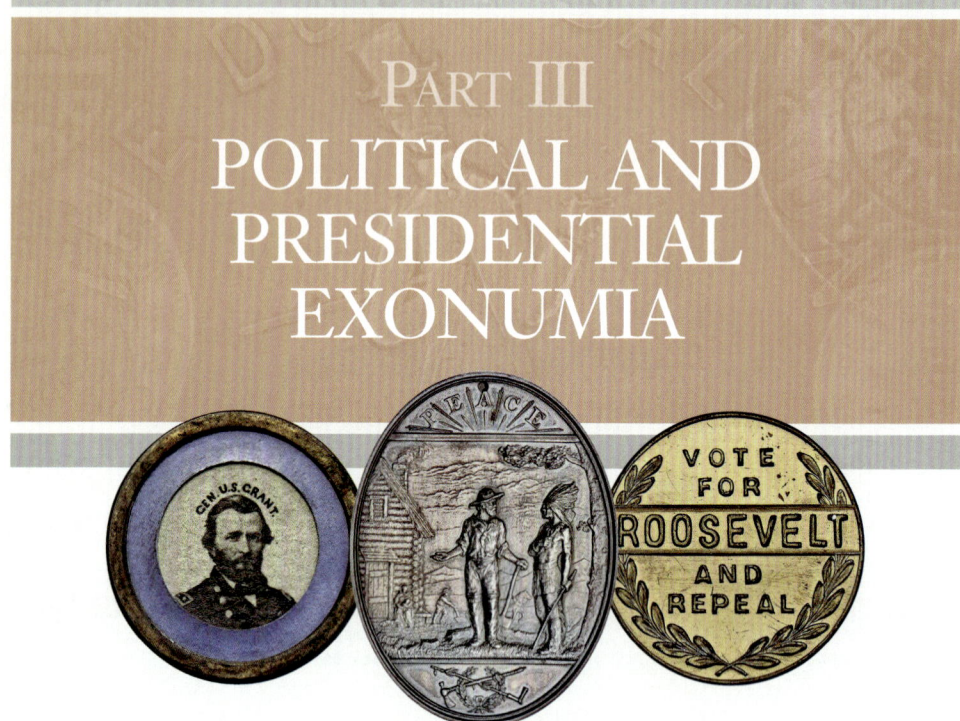

Free public elections are a defining characteristic of the American political system, and specialists in the medal and token culture of presidential elections delight in the fact that they own tangible pieces of American democracy. To find these mostly 19th-century items, collectors patronize medal dealers' auctions and huge expositions devoted to political Americana. The wise presidential collector knows which presidents generate the greatest competition from other collectors. Antiques reporter Dick Friz says this is easy: "Just look at Mount Rushmore"[62] (George Washington, Thomas Jefferson, Abraham Lincoln, and Theodore Roosevelt). Numismatist Edmund Sullivan adds Andrew Jackson, Franklin D. Roosevelt, and John F. Kennedy to the short list.[63] However, demand is not always tied to popularity. In the election of 1840 that pitted Martin Van Buren against William Henry Harrison, more than 135 different tokens endorsed Harrison, but fewer than 20 supported Van Buren. Political dealer Charles McSorley notes, "The strong demand for Van Buren items is due to their scarcity, not to Van Buren's popularity as a president."

Die-struck items pertaining to James Knox Polk, elected in 1844, and Lewis Cass, who ran against Zachary Taylor in 1848, are scarce and considered key issues. Since candidates in early American elections did not issue tokens, contemporary die-struck items of any kind relating to John Adams, James Madison, James Monroe, and Thomas Jefferson, though they do exist, are expensive and hard to come by. Competition from collectors in other specialties can also drive up cost: Hard Times token collectors want political items generated between the years of 1832 and 1844, and Civil War token collectors have a thirst for presidential issues from the 1860 and 1864 elections, some of which circulated as wartime money.

Two distinct categories are followed: *presidential election campaign* items, and *presidential commemorative* items generated after a candidate achieved the presidency. Presidential commemorative items separate further into two categories: *contemporary* items issued during a president's term of office, which include Indian peace medals and inaugural medals; and *historical commemoratives* issued after his term. Understandably, contemporary presidential pieces fetch higher prices than commemoratives, and 19th-century commemoratives are worth more than later ones. The Indian peace medals are included in Part III because they fit the definition of contemporary presidential items, and are sought by presidential collectors as such. Readers should be aware, however, that the presidential Indian peace medals are part of a much larger peace medal series.

A third type of American political exonumia is *political-cause* medals and tokens. These served a function similar to the modern day t-shirt or bumper sticker, as a means of putting a political opinion into people's hands and pockets.

The most complete reference for 19th-century political exonumia is Edmund Sullivan's 1981 *American Political Badges and Medalets*, incorporating the research of H. Doyle DeWitt. The American Political Items Collectors (APIC) organization publishes two periodicals: *The Keynoter* and *The Political Bandwagon*. The *Political Collector* quarterly magazine is another good source of information.

14

PRESIDENTIAL CAMPAIGN MEDALS AND TOKENS

To our generation, accustomed almost to the point of immunity to the sophisticated products of American "campaign science," it is hard to understand the potent impact little die-struck campaign medals had on the 19th-century voter. Pro- and anti-candidate tokens, political-cause medals, and other pieces of propaganda first made their way into the nation's presidential campaigns almost 200 years ago.

Supportive Pieces

Candidates did not begin to understand the potential of placing their image or slogan on manufactured goods until the 1824 election pitting Andrew Jackson against John Quincy Adams. Though no campaign medals were struck for Adams, who had the weight of his distinguished family name in his favor, three varieties of brass medals bearing a bust of Jackson portrayed him as "The Hero of New Orleans" and linked him to "Our Nation's Pride" and "Our Nation's Good." His supporters wore these suspended from a pin at their lapels. Adams carried the day in 1824, but for diesinkers a precedent had been established, and for the next election, in 1828, they struck bigger, showier Jackson medals in white metal, and at least one created a matching piece for Adams.

Campaign medals became more popular with each presidential contest. The election of 1840, featuring the spirited "log cabin and hard cider" platform of William Henry Harrison, generated a cascade of medals, buttons, badges, and jewelry, and incumbent Van Buren, who chose not to answer this frenzy with campaign products of his own, was defeated. It became clear that candidates who failed to project some catchy, displayable image or persona for themselves did so at their peril, and nicknames such as "Tippecanoe," "the Little Giant," and "Honest Abe," emblazoned on metal, became the norm.

Since the election of 1852, diesinkers had produced matching medals for all the candidates, so they would have a product to sell to proponents of every party. Often the design differences between these companion pieces were limited to the portrait bust and choice of slogan; other characteristics such as size, border type, and decorative elements were identical. Medal production for the election of 1844 was lopsided in favor of Henry Clay, and for the election of 1848, in favor of Zachary Taylor, but eventually the numbers of medals generated for each candidate became fairly equal.

DEWITT NO.*	METAL	COMMENTARY	F	EF	MS-63
AJACK 1824-5	Br	Struck by Scovill of Waterbury, Connecticut	$75	$150	$300

* The candidate's initials and election year are expressed in H. Doyle Dewitt's numbering system of 1959 (amplified by Edmund Sullivan in 1981).

Supportive Pieces *(continued)*

DEWITT NO.*	METAL	COMMENTARY	F	EF	MS-63
AJACK 1828-1	WM	Campaigning on the candidate's military record	$750	$2,500	$4,000
JQA 1828-2	WM	The distinguished incumbent couldn't beat "Old Hickory"	750	2,500	4,000
AJACK 1832-1	Cop	First in the Low Hard Times series is this Jackson campaign piece	2,000	7,500	25,000
HC 1832-2	WM	Recalling Clay's first run in a four-candidate race; two known	200	—	—
MVB 1836-3	WM	With Jackson's backing, Van Buren defeated four opponents	100	250	400
HC 1836-1	WM	Clay was the foremost among Van Buren's 1836 rivals	100	200	350

* The candidate's initials and election year are expressed in H. Doyle Dewitt's numbering system of 1959 (amplified by Edmund Sullivan in 1981).

SUPPORTIVE PIECES *(continued)*

DEWITT NO.*	METAL	COMMENTARY	F	EF	MS-63
MVB 1840-5	WM	The incumbent fell victim to a persistent, energetic Harrison campaign	$300	$700	$1,500
WHH 1840-8	WM	One of more than 130 different die-struck Harrison issues	40	100	275
JP 1844-1	WM	Success did crown Polk and Dallas's efforts	200	350	650
HC 1844-2	Cop	Poor Henry Clay's third presidential bid didn't succeed either	—	350	700
ZT 1848-8	WM	Military prowess once again carried a candidate to victory	—	150	350

* The candidate's initials and election year are expressed in H. Doyle Dewitt's numbering system of 1959 (amplified by Edmund Sullivan in 1981).

SUPPORTIVE PIECES *(continued)*

DEWITT NO.*	METAL	COMMENTARY	F	EF	MS-63
LC 1848-1	Cop	Any tokens of Lewis Cass are scarce and desirable	$225	$500	$1,250
MVB 1848-2	Svd Br Shell	Van Buren tried it again with the Free Soil party, and lost	200	450	1,000
FP 1852-5	WM	Dies for this Franklin Pierce piece were by Smith & Hartmann	30	65	125
WS 1852-1	Silv	Winfield Scott's Mexican battle successes listed to his credit	75	150	350
JB 1856-2	WM	Engraver Key presented the candidate's name in a rebus	—	1,500	2,200

* The candidate's initials and election year are expressed in H. Doyle Dewitt's numbering system of 1959 (amplified by Edmund Sullivan in 1981).

Supportive Pieces (continued)

DEWITT NO.*	METAL	COMMENTARY	F	EF	MS-63
JF 1856-2	Cop	Smith & Hartmann cut the dies; Ball, Black & Co. distributed the medals	$85	$220	$450
MF 1856-1	Cop	Millard Fillmore won the day on a strong platform of unity	100	200	425
AL 1860-2	Svd WM	This is the rail splitter; 129 other designs helped Lincoln best three rivals	—	450	1,000
SD 1860-1	Cop	Henning & Eymann's Douglas portrait is one of the finest of the era	—	135	350
JBELL-1860-1	Silv	B. True made matching pieces for Lincoln, Douglas, and Breckinridge	—	—	1,500

* The candidate's initials and election year are expressed in H. Doyle Dewitt's numbering system of 1959 (amplified by Edmund Sullivan in 1981).

SUPPORTIVE PIECES (continued)

DEWITT NO.*	METAL	COMMENTARY	F	EF	MS-63
JCB-1860-1	Silv	True's pugnacious portraiture makes his tokens all the more likable	—	—	$1,500
AL 1864-5	WM	Equating the candidate with Washington: a tried and true campaign theme	$100	$200	450
GMcC 1864-24	Silv	The *Monitor* was the Navy's pride: good imagery for one hoping for victory	—	—	900
JF 1864-1	Silv	G.H. Lovett fit as many accomplishments as possible on this advertisement	—	—	1,000
USG 1868-19	HR	Black vulcanite was a cheap expedient for Grant and his rival, Seymour	—	75	175
HS 1868-6	HR	Seymour's piece was very similar in design to Grant's—but smaller	—	75	175

* The candidate's initials and election year are expressed in H. Doyle Dewitt's numbering system of 1959 (amplified by Edmund Sullivan in 1981).

SUPPORTIVE PIECES *(continued)*

DEWITT NO.*	METAL	COMMENTARY	F	EF	MS-63
USG 1872-1	Leather	Leather piece heralds Grant's and Wilson's associations with the material	—	$100	$150
HG 1872-2	Silv	Greeley wielded more power as a journalist than a presidential candidate	—	—	1,250
RBH 1876-1	Cop	Some of these pieces were gilded or silvered, as were companions for Tilden	$25	50	100
SJT 1876-2	Svd Cop	Tilden won the popular and electoral votes, but not the presidency!	50	75	125
JG 1880-10	Br	A nicely struck piece for the second president to be assassinated	10	20	45
WSH 1880-4	Cop	Hancock campaign items of any kind are scarce, but not tokens!	—	20	45
GC 1884-9	WM	This candidate for the White House had a one-word platform: REFORM	—	30	60
JGB 1884-2	Cop	A handsome, elaborate medal didn't help Blaine and Logan win	—	60	125

* The candidate's initials and election year are expressed in H. Doyle Dewitt's numbering system of 1959 (amplified by Edmund Sullivan in 1981).

SUPPORTIVE PIECES *(continued)*

DEWITT NO.*	METAL	COMMENTARY	F	EF	MS-63
BH 1888-9	WM	The Washington comparison makes this piece even more collectible	$10	$20	$75
GC 1888-10	WM	The First Lady appeared on the incumbent's medal, but her man lost this time	10	20	40
BH 1892-2	WM	The qualities listed on this medal didn't help him retain the office	15	25	60
GC 1892-8	Alum	An appealing portrait and a slogan to inspire renewed trust	10	25	40
FDR-1932 unlisted	Cop	Tavern "good-fors" disappeared in Prohibition; FDR would bring them back	—	10	10
FDR-1932 unlisted	Cop	Classic FDR prosperity token implied hope amidst economic depression	1	2	3

* The candidate's initials and election year are expressed in H. Doyle Dewitt's numbering system of 1959 (amplified by Edmund Sullivan in 1981).

Supportive Pieces (continued)

DEWITT NO.*	METAL	COMMENTARY	F	EF	MS-63
RMN-1968 unlisted	Cop	A 20th-century return to tradition: strike a token for your candidate!	—	—	$10
RMN-1972 unlisted	Br	Gilroy Roberts gave these reelection campaign pieces a sleek, modern look	—	—	5

* The candidate's initials and election year are expressed in H. Doyle Dewitt's numbering system of 1959 (amplified by Edmund Sullivan in 1981).

Satirical Pieces

Some campaign tokens, instead of supporting a candidate, took aim at the political platform or persona of his opponent. The earliest satirical medals to circulate in the United States were the so-called Paine medalets, which were, in fact, anti-Paine. In the early 1790s, British Tories published these copper tokens depicting the death of Thomas Paine by hanging or beheading, with the legend THE WRONGS OF MAN, in mockery of Paine's controversial book *The Rights of Man*. Paine's text blamed Europe's problems on the political system of monarchy supported by aristocracy, and advocated a system in which all classes of men had a voice in government and a right to vote to choose their leaders. European crowned heads condemned his ideas as treasonous, but the working classes, some of whom were diesinkers, embraced them and produced medalets in his support. In the post-revolutionary United States, the freedoms suggested by Paine were already in place, but there was disagreement as to how they should be administered. Federalists such as John Adams and Alexander Hamilton believed in a strong centralized government that made decisions on the people's behalf, and in 1796 they imported quantities of satirical Paine tokens to carry as pocket pieces. Anti-Federalists like Thomas Jefferson and George Clinton felt a strong centralized system was nothing but monarchy in disguise. They countered the satirical Paine medalets with their own pro-Paine medalets, also imported from England.

Nearly 40 years later, as discussed in chapter 2, the satirical content of Hard Times tokens addressed disagreements over American monetary and banking practices. This era saw the introduction of humor as a political weapon, in a far gentler approach than employed by the scorching anti-Paine medalets. In 1876, Isaac Wood of New York commissioned satirical medals at the expense of reform candidate Samuel Tilden. Though Tilden won the popular vote, he lost the presidency in the Electoral College. One of

Woods's pieces crowed, IN THE 60TH YEAR OF ITS AGE / DEMOCRATIC PARTY DIED OF TILDENOPATHY / LET IT R.I.P. Satirical tokens were employed to brilliant effect in the election of 1896, which pitted Republican William McKinley against Democrat William Jennings Bryan. The most contentious campaign issue was whether America should adopt the gold or the silver standard, and almost 150 different tokens satirizing Bryan's opposition to the gold standard were produced. These pieces, called *Bryan Dollars* or *Bryan Money*, derided the candidate's proposal for a monetary standard based on a ratio of 16 parts silver to one part gold. According to Edmund Sullivan:

> Despite their name, these pieces are actually anti-Bryan. . . . Bryan money exists in base or type metal, cast iron, aluminum, lead, and silver, and ranges in diameter from one to four inches. Many pieces are technologically crude. Most of them portray on the obverse the same profile of Liberty that appeared on the regular coinage [silver dollar] of the day; the reverses show a spread eagle. The combination of a cheap metal and an exaggerated diameter was intended to demonstrate what would happen to our coinage if Bryan were elected president: it would be debased and inflated.[64]

In 1908, voters who had trouble deciding which candidate to back could always toss a "decision maker" token. One side featured a bust of William Howard Taft with the legend I'LL TOSS YOU and the other side sported a bust of William Jennings Bryan with the legend I'LL MATCH YOU. This concept was reused in 1980, with the issuance of "The President Picker." One side featured a bust of Jimmy Carter, the other side featured Ronald Reagan. A legend on each side read IF COIN LANDS ON EDGE / VOTE ANDERSON. In the 1968 campaign, jocular tokens reading KEEP AMERICA HUMPH-FREE / DUMP THE HUMP appeared, alongside SUPPORT THE VIET CONG / McCARTHY FOR PRESIDENT and LBJ COIN / NO GOLD, NO SILVER, JUST PURE BRASS.[65]

Other political perspectives have been hashed out on medals and tokens from time to time. The Aaron White satirical medal of 1857 and Alex Shagin Intelligent Design medal of 2006 are but two collectible examples.

YEAR	SUBJECT	METAL	COMMENTARY	F	EF	MS-63
1796	"Wrongs of Man"	Cop	Some hoped for a swift end to Thomas Paine and his "Rights of Man"	$100	$200	$350
1796	Gallows scene	Br	Monarchists considered Paine's supporters as traitors to the Crown	—	500	750
1857	Use Coins Not Paper	Br	Strange anti-paper satire from hard-money advocate Aaron White	—	150	450

SATIRICAL PIECES (continued)

YEAR	SUBJECT	METAL	COMMENTARY	F	EF	MS-63
1878	"Shammy Tilden"	Lead	One of a trio of anti-Tilden smear pieces that Isaac Wood issued	—	$75	$100
1896	16-to-1 "dime"	Iron	A hunk of "Bryan Money" was not a thing of beauty—intentionally	$35	75	150
1896	Cartwheel dollar*	Silv	"Cartwheel dollar" belittled Bryan's silver as a substitute for gold	125	275	450
1912	President picker	WM	When all candidates disappoint, flip this token to decide your vote	—	25	50
2005	A complex question	Silv	Alex Shagin's take on a controversy: evolution or intelligent design?	—	—	20

* Voted No. 22 in *100 Greatest American Medals and Tokens* (Jaeger/Bowers).

Ferrotypes

The presidential election of 1860 saw the appearance of a new form of political lapel piece, one highly prized by collectors today and priced accordingly: the campaign ferrotype. This consisted of a gilt brass or tin frame surrounding a little tintype portrait of the candidate. Each was holed at the top for suspension from a ribbon, and they were produced in sets representing all the candidates. Often they bore merchant advertising on the reverse. The chance to own an original photographic portrait of a presidential candidate, especially Abraham Lincoln, is a strong part of the campaign ferrotype's appeal. Some portraits were made at live sittings, and these fetch the highest prices (especially beardless photos of Lincoln). Others were simply daguerreotypes of famous lithographs, such as those produced by Currier and Ives. Around 300 pieces survive from the 1860 campaign, and all are extremely fragile. Ferrotypes were produced for every presidential election through the end of the century.

DEWITT NO.	METAL	COMMENTARY	F	EF	MS-63
AL-1860-90	Br shell	Beardless Lincoln portraits are highly prized; here Hamlin joins him	$200	$750	$2,000
GMC 1864-49	Br shell	McClellan and Pendleton lost despite this well-made supportive piece	300	1,500	3,500
AL-1864-94	Br shell	The 1864 maker's companion piece for Lincoln and Hamlin	350	2,000	4,000
USG 1868-69	Br shell	Grant and Colfax portraits printed on cardboard, framed in blue paper	—	400	750
HG 1872-25	Gilt Br	Greeley and Brown ferrotypes framed with a gilt brass shell	—	500	2,000

Private diesinkers used whatever materials came to hand as planchets for campaign pieces, and overstrikes (see the introduction) are relatively plentiful in this category. In a 1979 article in *The Political Collector*, Charles McSorley noted:

> Sometimes it's possible to make a find right in your own collection. . . . I was looking at a medalet of Horatio Seymour struck by Peter Jacobus of Philadelphia. The workmanship on this piece is truly a masterpiece of

the die cutter's art. The detail and realistic representation of Seymour's almost-facing bust is a delight to behold. . . . On turning the piece over, still looking at it with a magnifying glass, I detected some traces of lettering in the blank field. I began to decipher the letters "upport" and "ittle." It had been "Support the Little Giant"—this Seymour medalet had been struck over an earlier 1860 brass piece of Stephen Douglas by Robert Lovett Jr., also of Philadelphia. So here we have a Democrat in 1868 having his image struck over that of another Democrat from 1860. Two losers on one medal! . . . In my collection are also two Douglas copper medalets by Robert Lovett Jr. that are overstruck on coins. One is on a five-centime French coin of Napoleon III, the other on an 1832 Nova Scotia half penny of George IV.

In July 1896, Newark manufacturer Whitehead and Hoag acquired the 1893 patent of Bostonian Amanda Lougee, adapting it to a product that quickly swept die-struck campaign pieces into the past.[66] The company's campaign button, which featured a printed paper disc under celluloid affixed to a metal pin-back, was much cheaper to produce than a medal or a token, and allowed greater design versatility and the unprecedented use of color. A few 20th-century manufacturers still struck metal campaign tokens for distribution as pocket pieces. These, however, were generally inexpensive items lacking in artistic quality. The Franklin D. Roosevelt campaigns of 1932 and 1936 issued better-made brass and nickel "prosperity tokens," which implied that FDR's programs would succeed in pulling the country out of the Great Depression. Still, the great era of the campaign token was over.

15

POLITICAL-CAUSE MEDALS AND TOKENS

Two celebrated causes of the 19th century to be widely promoted on tokens were the abolition of slavery, and temperance.

ABOLITION PIECES

The well-known abolitionist "Am I Not a Man and a Brother?" theme, with its kneeling slave bound in chains, had circulated in England since 1795. New tokens with the same device were imported to the United States in the 1830s, and were followed in 1837 by their American companion pieces reading, "Am I Not a Woman and a Sister?" (The famous 1851 "Ain't I a Woman" speech by Soujourner Truth, which brought international renown to the ex-slave–turned–abolitionist public speaker, may have been inspired by this very token. Truth lived in New York City, where the majority of the tokens circulated, from 1838 to 1843. It is likely that she saw and handled some, and took their legend to heart.) Another antislavery medal was struck in 1850 to honor abolitionist Isaac Hopper, a Philadelphia Quaker who put action behind his sentiments. He founded a society for the employment of the poor and a school for black children. A famous 1860 medal issued after the Harper's Ferry incident showed the execution of abolitionist John Brown.

YEAR	SUBJECT	METAL	COMMENTARY	F	EF	MS-63
1833	American Colonization Society	Cop	Freed slaves heading for Liberia used this copper coinage	$70	$135	$275
1834	Encouraging U.S. emancipation	Silv	Britain led by example, freeing its colonial slaves in 1833	75	150	350

Abolition Pieces *(continued)*

YEAR	SUBJECT	METAL	COMMENTARY	F	EF	MS-63
1838	Am I Not a Man and a Brother?*	Cop	Struck in Belleville, N.J.; a widespread Northern sentiment	—	$80,000	—
1838	Am I Not a Woman and a Sister?**	Cop	The woman/sister mintage far outnumbered the man/brother	$150	250	$800
1850	Isaac Hopper, abolitionist	Svd WM	Portrait of "Father of the Underground Railroad" by S. Ellis	—	750	1,250
1859	John Brown, abolitionist	Silv	French medal to the assassinated extremist of Harper's Ferry	—	4,000	8,500

* Voted No. 10 (with the token below) in *100 Greatest American Medals and Tokens* (Jaeger/Bowers). Very few specimens are known. All are in the VF-EF grade range.

** Voted No. 10 (with the token above) in *100 Greatest American Medals and Tokens*.

Temperance Pieces

Temperance societies pledged to end the use of alcohol. They issued tokens for their members to wear pinned to their lapels, or to take home as souvenirs of important society functions and anniversaries. The medals and tokens of the Washington Temperance Societies usually bore renditions of the first president. In 1919, while federal legislators were debating passage of the Volstead Act, coin dealer Thomas L. Elder exhibited 250 examples of temperance medals and tokens before the New York Numismatic Club. The earliest of these were struck in the 1830s by James Bale (alone, and in his partnership with Frederick B. Smith), and featured a scene of a man retrieving fresh water from a well with the "old oaken bucket." Elder held more than 50 varieties of this type, signed by various diesinkers including Benjamin True and Joseph F. Thomas, and issued by several temperance societies including the National Christian Temperance Union, the Total Abstinence Society, and The Cold Water Army. Several varieties struck for the Catholic Temperance Society bore a portrait of its leader, Father Matthew, and one token of 1855 showed an upside-down wineglass. Others showed fountains spewing water, and some version of the pledge WE AGREE TO ABSTAIN FROM THE USE OF ALL INTOXICATING LIQUORS AS A BEVERAGE.

YEAR	SUBJECT	METAL	COMMENTARY	F	EF	MS-63
1840s	The old oaken bucket	Br	Tokens by Bale glorified spring water for its purity	$5	$8	$15
1840s	Washington Temperance Society	WM	Most pledges were similar to the one on the reverse	—	25	50
1850s	Anti-tobacco	Br	Another pledge struck in metal for the strong willed	10	20	40
1893	Father Mathew Association	WM	Issued for 1893 meeting in Pittsburgh, honoring the founder	20	50	100
1915	Rum-soaked citizens of New York	Silv	Thomas L. Elder made it clear he advocated Prohibition	—	—	350*

* This value is for silver. More typically this piece is found in aluminum.

16

CONTEMPORARY PRESIDENTIAL COMMEMORATIVES

After the votes are cast and counted, and one presidential contender is elected to the nation's highest office, it is time for an official medal to honor the new chief executive. Inaugural medals have a long tradition among American exonumia, as did the Indian peace medals struck for presentation by early presidents.

Inaugural Medals

The formal practice of having an inaugural medals committee decide upon an artist, agree upon a design, gain the approval of the president-elect, and produce a splendid medal in his honor was not launched until William McKinley's term of office commencing in 1901. Collectors desiring a complete contemporary series must fill in with early issues from the hands of private diesinkers, and some inauguration-committee souvenir medals issued beginning in the 1880s. In the case of George Washington, only a few varieties of decorative die-struck buttons and cufflinks bearing his initials survive from his first term of office. Some bear the phrase LONG LIVE THE PRESIDENT or PATER PATRIAE. From his second term, there are a few medalets bearing his portrait with the phrase SUCCESS TO THE UNITED STATES. (The first large medallic portrait of Washington ever struck in the United States is thought to be the Manly medal of 1790.) John Adams merited just a few styles of buttons and cufflinks, but Thomas Jefferson was the subject of a beautiful 1801 silver inaugural medal by immigrant German engraver John Reich. This was offered for sale out of a Philadelphia shop, and was probably created not just to honor the new president, but also to showcase Reich's substantial diesinking talent.

Presidents Madison and Monroe have no *contemporary* inaugural medals to represent their positions in the series, however, another German immigrant, Moritz Furst, engraved medals for these two in the 1820s. In 1825, Furst did a fine medal for John Quincy Adams. In the following decades, says Joseph Levine,

> The inaugurations of Martin Van Buren, John Tyler, James K. Polk, and Zachary Taylor are represented by a curious series of four similar medals, all struck by the U.S. Mint. All used for the obverse the medium-size Indian peace medal die for the respective president. The reverses bore a wreath enclosing the date of each respective inauguration. These four medals, all struck by order of the chief coiner, Adam Eckfeldt, are extremely rare and their use has never been known. Perhaps they were

ordered by Eckfeldt to be given as personal medals to the president and other VIPs. The absence of such a medal from William Henry Harrison, whose short-lived presidency fell between those of Van Buren and Tyler, lends credence to this theory. Subsequent inaugurations through that of Rutherford B. Hayes in 1877 are represented by a variety of private medallic commemoratives struck in different sizes and metals.

In 1889, 1893, and 1897, inaugural committees struck portrait medals for their members to wear at the inauguration festivities. McKinley's inauguration in 1901 launched the "official" gold inaugural medal, presented to the president and vice president, with 3,000 silver strikes distributed to government dignitaries and inaugural committee members. America's greatest sculptors vied for the honor of designing inaugural medals, and America's most respected commercial mints competed for production privileges. Presidents serving more than one term had more than one inaugural medal. The presidential medals listed in the U.S. Mint online product catalog were designed for sale to collectors, and are not the official inaugural medals. The best way to distinguish the many commercial presidential inaugurals from the official ones is to review the images posted on the Web site inauguralmedals.com, which lists both "contenders" and "pretenders."[67]

YEAR	PRESIDENT	MAKER	METAL	COMMENTARY	F	EF	MS-63
1793	Washington	Unknown	Bz	Not an inaugural medal per se, but celebrating Washington's presidency	$300	$900	$3,500
1801	Jefferson*	John Reich	Silv	Beautiful die work, issued privately, showcased Reich's talent	7,500	20,000	40,000
1833	Jackson	U.S. Mint	Gold	Portrait was from a James B. Longacre drawing	—	3,000	4,500

* Voted No. 26 in *100 Greatest American Medals and Tokens* (Jaeger/Bowers).

INAUGURAL MEDALS *(continued)*

Actual size 62 mm

Actual size 76 mm

Actual size 68 mm

YEAR	PRESIDENT	MAKER	METAL	COMMENTARY	F	EF	MS-63
1837	Van Buren	U.S. Mint	Bz	Engraved by German Moritz Furst, on contract with the Mint	—	$500	$1,000
1905	T. Roosevelt**	Tiffany & Co.	Bz	Roosevelt considered Saint-Gaudens's work masterful	—	20,000	40,000
1913	Wilson	Whitehead & Hoag	Bz	Private mints competed for presidential-medal commissions	—	200	400

** Voted No. 27 in *100 Greatest American Medals and Tokens* (Jaeger/Bowers).

Inaugural Medals *(continued)*

YEAR	PRESIDENT	MAKER	METAL	COMMENTARY	F	EF	MS-63
1933	F.D. Roosevelt	U.S. Mint	Bz	Manship's sculpting services were in high demand in the 1930s	—	$350	$700
1969	Nixon	MACo	Bz	By Ralph Menconi, talented presidential-portrait artist	—	10	20

Indian Peace Medals

In colonial days, European monarchs struck gilt copper or solid-silver medals as diplomatic gifts for chiefs of Native American tribes. British, French, and Spanish peace medals depicted the reigning monarch on the obverse and the national coat of arms, a slogan of peace, or a scene of Native American life on the reverse. The first U.S. Indian peace medal, engraved in 1789, continued this tradition. It depicts not George Washington but the American eagle on the obverse, and on the reverse, a scene of a Native American and an armor-clad soldier sharing a peace pipe. Subsequent medals show the president in place of the soldier. These Washington medals were not struck, but hand engraved by silversmith Joseph Richardson and possibly others, so each example is different from the rest.

The earliest round, die-struck peace medals presented to Indians by this nation were the "Seasons" medals, a set of three honoring George Washington in his second term and struck in England in 1798. Beginning with Thomas Jefferson, round silver peace medals in three sizes were struck from dies made by U.S. Mint engravers. Until 1846, when the dies were replaced due to wear, reverses featured a handshake/peace-pipe design by John Reich.⁶⁸ Because the round-format series lacked the first two presidents, Mint staff created medals for Washington and Adams many years after their presidencies. The use of peace-medal diplomacy waned after the term of Andrew Johnson, and the last official gifts of medals to Native Americans were made in the term of Grover Cleveland in 1893.

For original silver Indian peace medals, condition is not always important to value. Since some chiefs wore these gifts all their lives on chains around the neck, this is one numismatic instance where wear can actually enhance price—if provenance is authenticated. Medals bearing portraits of "scarce" presidents can be very dear, such as a dented silver example of James K. Polk's 1845 medal, which fetched $24,000 at a Stack's auction in 2005. One large-format John Reich Jefferson medal, which had been featured as the cover plate in Francis Prucha's standard reference on the subject, brought $115,000 at a Bowers and Merena auction in 2001. Original engraved Washington medals may fetch sums in the $50,000 to $75,000 range.⁶⁹ More affordable to the average collector are bronze restrikes of the entire struck series, made and sold in two sizes (beginning around 1860) by the U.S. Mint. "List" peace medals available from the Mint today sell for $38 for the three-inch format and $3.50 for the 1-5/16-inch format. Images of the entire restrike series are visible in the Mint's online catalog, at usmint.gov.

Actual size 127x171 mm

Common reverse used with three obverses (see images and entry, next page).

YEAR	PRESIDENT	ARTIST	METAL	COMMENTARY	F	EF	MS-63
1792	Washington*	Unsigned	Silv	Washington himself awarded some of this type to chiefs	$125,000	$250,000	—

* Voted No. 5 in *100 Greatest American Medals and Tokens* (Jaeger/Bowers).

Contemporary Presidential Commemoratives

INDIAN PEACE MEDALS *(continued)*

The three obverses of the Washington "set."

Actual size 76 mm

YEAR	PRESIDENT	ARTIST	METAL	COMMENTARY	F	EF	MS-63
1796	Washington**	Trumbull	Cop	Common reverse for three obverses; first "set" of U.S. medals	$3,000	$9,000	$15,000
1801	Jefferson***	Reich	Silv	Launching the reverse design used for half a century	50,000	75,000	—
1825	J.Q. Adams†	Furst	Silv	Adams didn't like this portrait, but collectors love it today	10,000	15,000	30,000

** Voted No. 6 in *100 Greatest American Medals and Tokens* (Jaeger/Bowers). Silver medals range from $7,000 to $60,000.
*** Voted No. 3 in *100 Greatest American Medals and Tokens*.
† Voted No. 67 in *100 Greatest American Medals and Tokens*.

Indian Peace Medals *(continued)*

Actual size 76 mm

Actual size 76 mm

YEAR	PRESIDENT	ARTIST	METAL	COMMENTARY	F	EF	MS-63
1862	Lincoln‡	Ellis/Willson	Silv	Note the brave operating the plow—wearing a peace medal!	$12,500	$22,000	$37,500
1865	Johnson	Paquet	Silv	Engraver Paquet had a fondness for classical imagery	12,500	17,500	30,000

‡ Voted No. 57 in *100 Greatest American Medals and Tokens* (Jaeger/Bowers).

Indian Peace Medals *(continued)*

Actual size 60×76 mm

Actual size 76 mm

YEAR	PRESIDENT	ARTIST	METAL	COMMENTARY	F	EF	MS-63
1881	Arthur	Barber	Silv	A new oval format; its design centered on the settler, not the Indian	$25,000	$40,000	$80,000
1890	Harrison	Barber	Silv	A return to the round format, with the awardee's name incused	35,000	65,000	—

17

POST-PRESIDENCY COMMEMORATIVES

Campaign medals and tokens illustrate a candidate's presidential aspirations and the dramatic road to the White House. An inaugural medal commemorates his successful rise to the highest office in the land. After these pieces come the medals and tokens that honor the president's life and accomplishments, mark his death, and commemorate his place in the line of chief executives stretching back to the late 1700s.

Life, Death, and Accomplishment Pieces

When Philadelphian Joseph Sansom published a medal honoring George Washington in 1805, engraved by John Reich, struck at the U.S. Mint, and priced at $50 in gold and $5 in silver, the publicity surrounding it and the success of its sales kicked off a 200-year tradition that has produced a vast, rich field for collectors. There are thousands of varieties of presidential commemoratives, intended to convey esteem to the honoree and fix his deeds in memory. They marked not just their subject's birth, presidency, and death, but also the major events of his career, such as landmark speeches, pivotal military battles, familiar patriotic sayings, or beloved life fables, like Washington telling the truth about the cherry tree or Lincoln splitting rails. The first known presidential memorial medal, by Jacob Perkins, was dedicated to Washington with the legend HE IS IN GLORY, THE WORLD IN TEARS, and placed on sale in early January 1800, only slightly more than two weeks after Washington's death on December 14, 1799. An 1866 portrait medal by Franky Magniadas, struck in Switzerland, commemorated Lincoln's Emancipation Proclamation. (Forty thousand French citizens raised the money to pay for this issue, which depicted a winged Liberty extending a wreath of freedom to a pair of slaves. A gold copy was struck for presentation to Mary Todd Lincoln.) Other standard medallic devices were the chief executive on horseback, his family arms, his first lady, or scenes of his military headquarters, residence, or tomb.

Our first president has earned the most die-struck issues, and is by far the most widely collected. Flipping through the pages of this book the reader will find many Washington portrait pieces, in practically every category. Following Washington in varieties of medals and tokens are Lincoln and Kennedy. There were booms in presidential-medal production for the commemorative craze of 1858 to 1861 (see chapter 12); for the nation's anniversaries in 1876 and 1976; and for the World's Columbian Exposition in 1892 and 1893. Other sources for presidential portraits are the award medals of the hundreds of public and private institutions that have been named for U.S. presidents over the years. These include high schools, colleges, social clubs, fraternal organizations, towns, counties, newspapers, corporations, fire companies, and so on. Of course, merchant tokens (see chapter 1) and patriotic Civil War tokens (chapter 3) might feature presidential portraits, but so did calendar tokens, Lord's Prayer tokens, street-car tokens, and souvenirs of tourist attractions. Portraits of Washington, Jefferson, Lincoln, Franklin Roosevelt, Eisenhower, and Kennedy can all be found on U.S. coins, which means they may also be found on play money produced by game manufacturers (see chapter 6) or paperweight-sized "lucky coins" (see chapter 9).

WASHINGTON MEDALS

YEAR	REF. NO.	ARTIST / MAKER	METAL	COMMENTARY	F	EF	MS-63
1790	Baker 61C*	Brooks/Manly	Gold	Sold in bronze, silver, and white metal; gold example is unique	$750	$1,500	$5,000
1799	Baker 166**	J. Perkins	Gold	Mourning badge issued holed; gold strikes are quite rare	15,000	20,000	50,000
1805	Baker 57***	Reich/Sansom	Silv	Part of a commemorative series planned by Sansom	—	25,000	60,000
1832	Baker 160A	Philadelphia Artificers	WM	Sold as souvenirs of Washington's birth-centennial parade	—	75	150

* Voted No. 17 in *100 Greatest American Medals and Tokens* (Jaeger/Bowers). Valuation is for base metal. The gold strike pictured resides at the Massachusetts Historical Society.
** Voted No. 11 in *100 Greatest American Medals and Tokens*.
*** Voted No. 71 in *100 Greatest American Medals and Tokens*.

Washington Medals (continued)

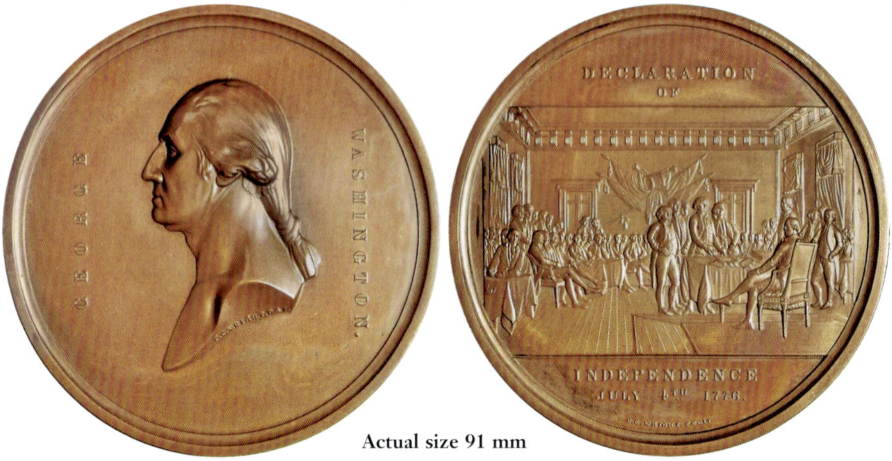

Actual size 91 mm

Actual size 65 mm

YEAR	REF. NO.	ARTIST / MAKER	METAL	COMMENTARY	F	EF	MS-63
1851	Baker 53†	Wright	Cop	Preeminent diesinker Wright's take on the nation's origins	—	$12,000	$20,000
1860	Baker 326‡	Paquet	Cop	Celebrating establishment of Mint's Washingtonia collection	—	200	450
1876	Baker 119B	Smith & Horst	WM	Frederick Smith sold these at Philadelphia's Centennial Exposition	—	250	400

† Voted No. 66 in *100 Greatest American Medals and Tokens* (Jaeger/Bowers).
‡ Voted No. 75 in *100 Greatest American Medals and Tokens*.

Washington Medals *(continued)*

YEAR	REF. NO.	ARTIST / MAKER	METAL	COMMENTARY	F	EF	MS-63
1902	Baker O-297	August Frank	Bz	Masonic orders loved to honor Washington, a famous Mason	—	$50	$125
1904	Baker 1828	U.S. Mint	Silv	One of a Monument Association series Congress authorized	—	15	50

Lincoln and Kennedy Medals

Actual size 240×180 mm

YEAR	SUBJECT	ARTIST / MAKER	METAL	COMMENTARY	F	EF	MS-63
1865	Lincoln mourning	J.A. Bolen	Br	The assassination precipitated many struck mementos	—	$100	$250
1907	Lincoln plaque	V.D. Brenner	Bz	A plaque by the designer of the 1909 Lincoln cent	—	700	1,250

LINCOLN AND KENNEDY MEDALS (continued)

Actual size 76 mm

YEAR	SUBJECT	ARTIST / MAKER	METAL	COMMENTARY	F	EF	MS-63
1909	Log cabin memorial	J.M. Clarke	Svd Bz	Souvenir sold during Lincoln's birth centennial	—	—	$100
1937	Lincoln Tunnel	J. Kilenyi	Bz	A president's name was recalled in many ways	—	—	60
1967	Kennedy mourning	A. De Francisci	Silv	Another piece prompted by an assassination	—	—	20
1967	Kennedy Peace Forest	P. Vincze	Silv	Struck for the dedication of the famous site in Israel	—	—	20

PRESIDENTIAL SERIES

Around 1926, boxes of Little Duchess Laundry Blue soap powder included "gift tokens" featuring portraits of different presidents. These were redeemable at markets for discounts, like modern coupons clipped from newspapers. In the 1930s, Charms Candy Company expanded on the idea by packaging an entire series of aluminum presidential "coins" inside its candy wrappers, to encourage children to keep buying Charms until they had collected all 30 presidents. More than 250,000 children participated in a similar promotion for Cracker Jack popcorn confection. In the 1960s, Shell Gasoline's Mr. President Coin Game featured a cardboard holder with slots for 36 aluminum presidential coin medals, one of which could be obtained with each full tank of gas.

Using presidential series to sell products was a 20th-century concept, but selling presidents as a group to collectors was nothing new. In 1840 diesinker W.H. Bridgens created a handsome medal bearing a central image of George Washington ringed by portraits of his seven successors. In 1859 George Lovett, who produced more Washington medals than any other diesinker, may have been the first to realize that collectors might also buy medals of the other presidents. He embarked on his well-known presidents/residences series, which covered the first 16 chief executives. In the 1860s, the U.S. Mint made itself into the nation's biggest medals dealer, in part by offering restrikes of its presidential series. In 1960 Max Humbert's Presidential Art Medals company commissioned sculptor Ralph Menconi to design a presidential series to be struck by Medallic Art Company. Incumbent John Kennedy, who was very pleased with his own medal, purchased a supply as gifts for friends, sparking a great demand for the entire series. In 1971 the White House Historical Association (WHHA) authorized the Franklin Mint to produce a 40-medal series of First Ladies, designed by sculptor Harold Faulkner, and used the royalties to acquire furnishings and works of art for the White House. This fundraiser was so successful that the WHHA followed it in 1972 with a 36-medal presidential series designed by former U.S. Mint chief sculptor-engraver Gilroy Roberts. Roberts took two years on the undertaking, and considered it the high point of his medallic career. Afterward just about every private mint in the business of selling medals to collectors issued a presidential series of its own.

YEAR	PRESIDENT	ARTIST / MAKER	METAL	COMMENTARY	F	EF	MS-63
1840	Washington–Van Buren	Bridgens	Bz	Bridgens's idea to group the presidents started a trend	—	$300	$800
1859	JQA/Residence	G.H. Lovett	Bz	Sold from Lovett's shop on Fulton Street, New York	—	15	40

Presidential Series *(continued)*

YEAR	PRESIDENT	ARTIST / MAKER	METAL	COMMENTARY	F	EF	MS-63
1859	Washington/Residence	G.H. Lovett	WM	From a series of the first 16 presidents	—	$25	$50
1860	Van Buren / Residence	G.H. Lovett	WM	W.C. Prime's 1861 price: 50¢ each in copper	—	18	50
1893	23 presidents	Ryden	Bz	It would be tough to fit them all on a medal today!	$15	30	60
1904	Washington / Jefferson / Roosevelt	Whitehead & Hoag	Bz	Candy maker's giveaway; St. Louis Exposition	3	5	11
1930s	Jefferson	Charms Candy	WM	Children collected them then; adults do now	—	1	2
1940s	Tyler	Cracker Jack	Alum	Kids kept buying Cracker Jack to acquire them all	—	1	—
1940s	Taylor	Cracker Jack	Alum	Completing this series may take a while, but it's fun	—	1	—

Post-Presidency Commemoratives

YEAR	PRESIDENT	ARTIST / MAKER	METAL	COMMENTARY	F	EF	MS-63
1960	Pierce	Menconi	Bz	Of the highly regarded Presidential Art Medals series	—	—	$5
1960	Wilson	Menconi	Silv	Menconi sculpted through Nixon; others to Clinton	—	—	20
1960s	T. Roosevelt	Shell Oil	Br	Came with your tank of gas, kept you coming back	—	$1	—
1960s	F.D. Roosevelt	Shell Oil	Br	Hollow pieces are often seen dented or bent	—	1	—
1972	Lady Bird Johnson	Faulkner/FM	Silv	Fundraising series of White House Historical Association	—	—	20
1973	Truman	Roberts/FM	Silv	Commissioned by White House Historical Association	—	—	20

NGC offers comprehensive services for collectors of medals and tokens, including variety attribution.

Medals and Tokens
Grading From NGC

Many series are currently eligible for grading:

- Early American
- Hard Times
- Merchant and Trade Tokens
- Civil War Tokens
- So-Called Dollars
- Bryan Money
- U.S. Mint Medals
- Robbins Space Medals

And many more!

Visit **www.NGCcoin.com** for a complete list of eligible types and submission details.

P.O. Box 4776 | Sarasota, FL 34230 | 800-NGC-COIN (642-2646) | www.NGCcoin.com

An Independent Member of the Certified Collectibles Group

PART IV
ART MEDALS

The medal has a long—indeed an ancient—history as an art form. According to Mark Jones in his acclaimed 1979 work for the British Museum, *The Art of the Medal*, an Italian coiner of the court of the Lords of Carrara produced the first commemorative medal having no monetary function. This was struck to celebrate Francesco II Novello's capture of Padua on June 15, 1390. In the same era, Venetian engravers of the Sesto family produced medals honoring their own medieval rulers. Italian painter Antonio Pisano, known today as Pisanello, is widely credited with ushering in the medal as an art form in the 1430s. His beautiful large-format medals, made by the casting method for the ruling Gonzaga family of Mantua, launched the courtly tradition of issuing medals for the pleasure of the wealthy and powerful. Through the Renaissance, Baroque, Rococo, and Neo-Classical periods, European medallic art flourished as minting technologies improved. By the 19th century, distinguished engravers of the United States had begun to add their contributions to this tradition. In the late-19th century, sculptors got into the act.

18

ART AND EXHIBITION MEDALS

Texas sculptor EvAngelos Frudakis trained under Paul Manship, Walker Hancock, and Jo Davidson at New York's Beaux-Arts Institute of Design in the 1930s. Now in his late 80s, he is still working. Over his long career he received many medal commissions, and created several series of coin medals for the Franklin Mint. Frudakis regrets, however, turning down the Society of Medalists' invitation to create a medal for their celebrated series. "At the time, my work schedule was too heavy to allow it, but now that it's over, I wish I could have been part of it—they let you do pretty much what you wanted."

To Frudakis, having unfettered artistic license is the key to truly effective medallic work. It is also the key to the art-medal category, which includes the works of sculptors who have had the freedom to take their own conceptualizations through every phase of execution, from making the initial drawing, to sculpting the model, to overseeing the production of the object in metal. Numismatists have long appreciated the medal as a fine-art medium that accounts for some of America's richest sculptural treasures. Luckily for collectors, the secret is not well known in the wider art world, and today's staggering price tags on paintings, sculptures, and other works of famous artists have not yet been attached to art medals.

According to California medalist Eugene Daub (see introduction), there is a reason why competent medallic sculptors are few: "First you have to learn drawing, life drawing, and anatomy, then modeling sculpture in the round. Then you must master bas-relief rendering of figures and scenes. It could take 15 years for a student to reach the point of being an effective relief artist capable of creating medals." Sculptors of wide reputation make medals infrequently, between commissions for monuments or other large, time-consuming projects. Interest in the form has been sustained, for the most part, by collector/sculptor groups organizing shows, hosting competitions, and sponsoring series of medals to which the public may subscribe.

In 1909, wealthy New York collector Robert Hewitt Jr. and his friend, *New York Times* literary critic and National Arts Club founder Charles de Kay, inaugurated the first American art-medal series, called the Circle of Friends of the Medallion. Their aim was to awaken Americans to the renaissance of medallic art that had been in full swing in Europe for more than a decade. That same year, the American Numismatic Society invited sculptors from around the world to compete in their International Exhibition of Contemporary Medals, to be held in New York in 1910. An unprecedented 200 artists participated.

THE AMERICAN NUMISMATIC SOCIETY EXHIBITION OF 1910

In the late 19th century, French medalists began featuring classical figures wearing flowing, diaphanous clothing, surrounded by leaves and flowers arranged in sinuous lines. They called their dreamlike, lyrical style *Art Nouveau*. Other French and European medalists worked in the Beaux-Arts tradition, which emphasized classical forms, symmetry, rich ornamentation, and grandeur. Both traditions were strongly influenced by painting. Artists like Louis-Oscar Roty and Alexandre Charpentier, who were among the first in the world

Art and Exhibition Medals 215

to employ sculptural modeling in making medals, applied painting's principles of perspective to wonderful effect, through modulation of relief from very high to very low. The ANS international exhibition, held in the Society's grand New York City building at Audubon Terrace in 1910, showcased these and other techniques. A Belgian who had mastered them, Godefroid Devreese, won the $10,000 grand prize and the right to design the show's commemorative plaquette. Agnes Baldwin's gorgeous exhibition catalog was published by the ANS in 1911.

Many of the 53 Americans who exhibited their recent work had been schooled in France, like their mentor Augustus Saint-Gaudens, who had just died in 1907. (As a young man in 1867, having completed his course of study at New York's National Academy of Design, Saint-Gaudens traveled to Paris to train at the École des Beaux-Arts. His later accomplishments in both monumental and medallic sculpture and his stature as Theodore Roosevelt's preferred coin designer made it almost compulsory for aspiring American artists to do the same.) Chester Beach, John G. Borglum, Victor David Brenner, Edward Sawyer, John Flanagan, Frederic MacMonnies, Janet Scudder, and many others studied in Paris, and what they learned there contributed greatly to the Beaux Arts movement in America, which persisted into the World War I years. Barbara Baxter's catalog of a 1987 New York exhibition of more than 300 early-20th-century medals, *The Beaux Arts Medal in America*, and Susan Luftschein's 1995 catalog of the John Marqusee collection at Cornell University, are required reading for anyone interested in the period.

Actual size 60x100 mm

Actual size 100x180 mm

YEAR	TOPIC	ARTIST	METAL	COMMENTARY	EF	MS-63
1897	American Gas Institute	Chester Beach	Silv	Showing Art Nouveau and Beaux Arts influences	—	$250
1900	Alice Jones	Janet Scudder	Bz	Uniface portraits were Paris-trained Scudder's forte	—	300
1901	Wm. Keen, M.D.	R.T. McKenzie	Bz	Beaux Arts portraiture at its best	—	750

ANS Exhibition of 1910 *(continued)*

Actual size 64 mm

Actual size 71 mm

Actual size 90x65 mm

YEAR	TOPIC	ARTIST	METAL	COMMENTARY	EF	MS-63
1903	Chicago Society of Artists	J. Bracken-Wendt	Bz	Chicago artists embraced Beaux-Arts influences	—	$250
1904	Chief Tja-Yo-Ni	Edw. W. Sawyer	Silv	Sawyer's 40-medal chief series was completed in 1922	—	500
1905	James McNeill Whistler	V.D. Brenner	Bz	A master sculptor's personal tribute to a friend	—	300

ANS Exhibition of 1910 *(continued)*

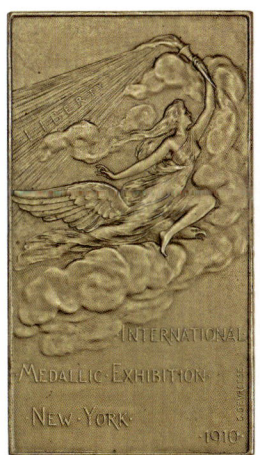 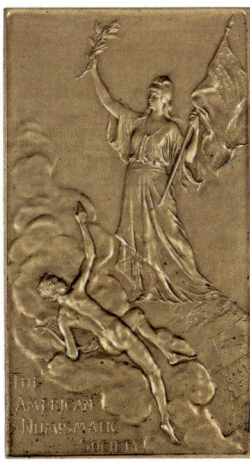

Actual size 50x88 mm

YEAR	TOPIC	ARTIST	METAL	COMMENTARY	EF	MS-63
1900s	Niagara	F. MacMonnies	Svd Bz	Indian subjects were popular in the new century	—	$200
1910	Official Exhibit Plaque	G. DeVreese	Bz	Winner's plaque proved unpopular; only 3 struck	$300	600

The Circle of Friends of the Medallion

The Circle of Friends issues were made first by Davison's Sons, then by Deitsch Brothers, whose mint was taken over by Henry and Felix Weil during the course of the series and renamed Medallic Art Co. These 12 issues were mailed twice a year to subscribers (who paid $10 in annual dues), in book-like holders that opened to a description of the medal and its artist on one page, with the medal itself set into a hole cut out on the facing page. It is estimated that there were about 500 complete sets struck in bronze, and from 50 to 100 in silver. Because they were stored in books, the medals today are generally in pristine condition.

All of them showcased the exciting developments in medallic art. The reverse of Issue No. 1, by John Flanagan, commemorated New York's three-week-long Hudson-Fulton Celebration. It bears a softly draped reclining female figure of the type so popular with Nouveau artists. The cityscape spreading behind her has the three-dimensional perspective of a good painting. In all the COF issues, variations in depth of relief and heaviness of outline were used to convey a range of feeling, from the warm sensuality of Victor David Brenner's Issue No. 4, "Motherhood," to the ethereal mystery of Sigurd Neandross's Issue No. 8, "The Ocean." The bold figures depicted on Paul Manship's Issue No. 11, published in December 1914, burst from their background and exude power. Perhaps the concerns of a world at war precluded excessive romanticism for Manship. As always in wartime, the arts suffered, and the 12th issue of the COF would be its last.

Actual size 69 mm

Actual size 69 mm

ISSUE	TOPIC	ARTIST	EF	MS-63*
1	Hudson-Fulton celebration	John Flanagan	$100	$200
2	There's No Place Like Home / Homecoming	Isidore Konti	105	210
3	St. Brendan / Irish navigator	John Mowbray-Clark	75	175
4	Motherhood	Victor David Brenner	100	200

* For specimens bound as issued in their original book, add $20.

CIRCLE OF FRIENDS *(continued)*

Actual size 69 mm

Actual size 70 mm

ISSUE	TOPIC	ARTIST	EF	MS-63*
5	Plaquette to Lafayette	Jules E. Roiné	$90	$175
6	Charles Dickens and his work	John S. Conway	65	135
7	Bahai leader Abdul Bahá	Louis Potter	75	175
8	Okeanos / Tribute to the oceans	Sigurd Neandross	75	175
9	John C. Frémont, explorer of the West	René T. de Quelin	90	175
10	Centennial of peace between U.S. and U.K.	John Mowbray-Clark	90	175
11	Tercentenary of New York City	Paul Manship	175	350
12	St. Joan of Arc / Honor to France	Allan G. Newman	50	100

* For specimens bound as issued in their original book, add $20.

The Society of Medalists

The next major stylistic influence on world art originated once again in France, since it was first widely seen at the 1925 Exposition International des Arts Décoratifs et Industriels Modernes. The Art Deco movement expressed an elegant, streamlined style featuring large, crisply defined forms and sweeping lines, in step with the progressive, "thoroughly modern" Roaring Twenties mentality. In the United States, commercial artists, architects, and designers wholeheartedly embraced Art Deco, but with the exception of a lucky few medalists who received commemorative or award-medal assignments and could experiment with the new style, the art of making medals was practically dead. Explains Daub, "There were just a few people left doing it, like James Earle and Laura Gardin Fraser, Herbert Adams, and Adolph Weinman, and they were well known and their work was respected, but with the impact of photography, modern design, and so many new styles and formats in which artists could work, interest in traditional medallic art with its old-fashioned principles and use of classical symbolism began to wane. It was viewed as fuddy-duddy."

Under the aegis of the American Federation of Arts, a group of sculptors calling themselves the Society of Medalists organized to create a forum for medal makers to experiment with new styles *or* perpetuate traditional ones, each according to his or her preference. The group decided to offer, by public subscription, two medals per year, using Medallic Art Co. as its mint. Beginning with Laura Gardin Fraser in 1930, sculptors would create medals by invitation only—and they relished that invitation because it came from their respected peers, and the choice of subject, design, shape, and finish was entirely up to them. The result of all that unleashed talent and imagination was a magnificent 65-year-long dream series of 129 medals, representing 129 different artistic approaches and as many creative visions. The Art Deco influence is visible in Lee Lawrie's issue No. 5 of 1932, and Richard Recchia's issue No. 29 of 1944, among others.

Artists addressed themes ranging from deprivation (Hermon MacNeil's 1931 Dust Bowl reference, "Hopi Prayer for Rain") to abundance (Albert Laessle's 1934 "American Turkey"). They showed their pride in humanity's achievements (Carl Schmitz's 1943 "Four Freedoms") and their deep political concerns (Elbert Weinberg's 1971 "Pandora"). Some acknowledged industrial progress, as in Mahroni Young's 1944 "Riggers and Riveters," while others celebrated nature, pictured in Don Everhart's 1982 "Dance of the Dolphins."

With the retirement of Joseph Veach Noble, the Society's administrative guiding light of the final 30 years, the series came to an end in 1995. The dies survive in the possession of the Medallic Art Co., which has no immediate plans for making restrikes.[70] A standard reference on SOM issues does not exist, but the Web site of the Medal Collectors of America is a good place to view images of those not depicted here.

Individual SOM medals struck in silver and bronze were edge-marked with the issue number and year. Most of the artists subscribed to the series, so a good place to find these medals is in the estates of sculptors. According to dealer Joseph Levine, the SOM artists currently in greatest demand are Paul Manship, Donald DeLue, and Robert Tait MacKenzie. The artists whose medals fetch the highest prices overall are the pre-SOM sculptors, Augustus Saint-Gaudens, Victor D. Brenner, and Daniel Chester French. Says Levine, "It's a natural progression from sculpture to medallic art, so if you are a collector interested in a particular sculptor, then you are interested in that sculptor's medals as well. It only follows that America's most famous sculptors are the most demanded medalists."

Art and Exhibition Medals 221

Actual size of larger Society of Medalists pieces is 71 mm

ISSUE NO. / DATE	ARTIST	SUBJECT OR THEME	EF	MS-63*
1 / 1930	Laura G. Fraser	Hunter and prey	$75	$155
2 / 1930	Paul Manship	Magic of the grape	200	375
3 / 1931	Hermon MacNeil	Hopi prayer for rain	75	150
4 / 1931	Fred MacMonnies	Charles Lindbergh	85	175
5 / 1932	Lee Lawrie	Sowing/Reaping	60	125

* Values given are for original bronze issues. Many, but not all, medals in the series were also struck in silver—some in the original year of issue, others as later restrikes. Availability of silver strikes is spotty, and dealer pricing is "catch as catch can."

The Society of Medalists *(continued)*

Actual size of larger Society of Medalists pieces is 71 mm

ISSUE NO. / DATE	ARTIST	SUBJECT OR THEME	EF	MS-63*
6 / 1932	John Flanagan	Torch race	$60	$125
7 / 1933	Carl Jennewein	Gloria	45	90
8 / 1933	Gaetano Cecere	No Easy Way to the Stars	60	125
9 / 1934	Herbert Adams	Fishing	45	85
10 / 1934	Albert Laessle	Abundance	40	80
11 / 1935	Lorado Taft	Great Lakes	50	100
12 / 1935	Anthony DeFrancisci	Creation	55	110
13 / 1936	R. Tait McKenzie	Track and field events	105	215
14 / 1936	Albert Stewart	Peace	40	75
15 / 1937	Robert Aitken	Lovers	50	100
16 / 1937	Chester Beach	Peace/War	75	150
17 / 1938	A. Stirling Calder	Dance of life	30	60
18 / 1938	Gertrude Lathrop	Conserve wildlife	45	90
19 / 1939	Edward McCartan	Peace/War	40	80
20 / 1939	John Gregory	Ceres blessing	30	55
21 / 1940	Edmond Amateis	Aesop's Fables	35	70

* Values given are for original bronze issues. Many, but not all, medals in the series were also struck in silver—some in the original year of issue, others as later restrikes. Availability of silver strikes is spotty, and dealer pricing is "catch as catch can."

The Society of Medalists *(continued)*

ISSUE NO. / DATE	ARTIST	SUBJECT OR THEME	EF	MS-63*
22 / 1940	Walker Hancock	Overcoming adversity	$65	$125
23 / 1941	Joseph Renier	Pro Patria / Prometheus	25	50
24 / 1941	Edwin Springweiler	Arctic/Antarctic	40	80
25 / 1942	Janet Decoux	Sluggard/Worker	40	80
26 / 1942	Brenda Putnam	Plane/Bird	50	100
27 / 1943	Anna Huntington	Elephant / Water hole	140	275
28 / 1943	Carl Schmitz	The Four Freedoms	20	45**
29 / 1944	Richard Recchia	Bust outlasts throne	20	45**
30 / 1944	Mahroni Young	Riggers/Riveters	65	125
31 / 1945	René Chambellan	Marines / Iwo Jima	50	95
32 / 1945	Berthold Nebel	Ravages of war	35	70
33 / 1946	Joseph Kiselewski	World peace	20	40
34 / 1946	Sidney Waugh	Privacy	25	45
35 / 1947	Bruce Moore	Vigilance vs. destruction	25	55
36 / 1947	Henry Kreis	Wise / Foolish virgins	25	50
37 / 1948	Michael Lantz	John the Baptist / Salome	30	60
38 / 1948	Thos. Lo Medico	Happiness / Good will	30	60
39 / 1949	Adolph Weinman	Genesis/Destiny	45	85
40 / 1949	Leo Friedlander	Harmony/Tranquility	25	45
41 / 1950	Donal Hord	Sowing/Reaping	35	70
42 / 1950	Cecil Howard	Peace/War	50	95
43 / 1951	Albert Wein	God the creator	25	55
44 / 1951	Wheeler Williams	Madonna/Lamb	20	35

* Values given are for original bronze issues. Many, but not all, medals in the series were also struck in silver—some in the original year of issue, others as later restrikes. Availability of silver strikes is spotty, and dealer pricing is "catch as catch can."

** Original bronze issues were struck at a smaller diameter due to the wartime metal shortage. These strikes were silvered to make up for their smaller size. The value shown is for original silvered-bronze issues. Later restrikes at 71 mm in solid bronze are valued at $250 to $300 in MS-63.

THE SOCIETY OF MEDALISTS *(continued)*

Actual size of larger Society of Medalists pieces is 71 mm

ISSUE NO. / DATE	ARTIST	SUBJECT OR THEME	EF	MS-63*
45 / 1952	J. Earle Fraser	Pony Express	$125	$225
46 / 1952	Karl Gruppe	Boy Scouts	35	70
47 / 1953	G. M. Proctor	Fish/Bait	45	85
48 / 1953	Peter Dalton	Brotherhood/Peace	15	30
49 / 1954	Abram Belskie	Art/Sculpting	45	85
50 / 1954	Ivan Mestrovic	Socrates and Plato	50	95
51 / 1955	Malvina Hoffman	No man is an island	40	80
52 / 1955	Georg Lober	Hans Christian Andersen	20	40
53 / 1956	John Angel	Genesis/Annunciation	30	60
54 / 1956	Paul Fjelde	Walt Whitman	30	55
55 / 1957	Pietro Montana	St. Francis of Assisi	20	35
56 / 1957	Donald De Lue	Creator	175	350
57 / 1958	Charles Rudy	Years/Days	20	35
58 / 1958	Jean de Marco	Music and drama	30	55
59 / 1959	Allan Rouser	Apache Indians	110	215
60 / 1959	Katherine Weems	Puma/Wildfowl	30	55
61 / 1960	Leo Lentelli	Romulus and Remus	30	60
62 / 1960	Adlai S. Hardin	The Nativity	25	50
63 / 1961	Adolph Block	Pilgrims/Liberty	20	40
64 / 1961	Nat Chote	David and Goliath	30	55
65 / 1962	Oronzio Maldarelli	Bathers and dancers	30	55
66 / 1962	Carl Mose	Our land / Our heritage	20	35
67 / 1963	Karen Worth	Spirit of the Space Age	25	50
68 / 1963	Joseph Coletti	Great frigate bird	20	35
69 / 1964	Robert Weinman	Socrates/Knowledge	45	85
70 / 1964	Frank Eliscu	Swimming/Sea	30	55
71 / 1965	Margaret Grigor	Alaska/Hawaii	25	45
72 / 1965	Elizabeth Weistrop	Homage to squirrels	20	40
73 / 1966	Robert Lohman	Nature/Creativity	30	60
74 / 1966	Ralph Manconi	Thomas Jefferson / Liberty	25	50
75 / 1967	Herring Coe	Beyond sky / Beneath sea	30	60
76 / 1967	Donald Miller	Life forms / Preservation	35	65
77 / 1968	Nina Winkel	Boys and girls	20	40
78 / 1968	Terry Lies	Perseverance/Dedication	30	55

* Values given are for original bronze issues. Many, but not all, medals in the series were also struck in silver—some in the original year of issue, others as later restrikes. Availability of silver strikes is spotty, and dealer pricing is "catch as catch can."

The Society of Medalists *(continued)*

Actual size of larger Society of Medalists pieces is 71 mm

ISSUE NO. / DATE	ARTIST	SUBJECT OR THEME	EF	MS-63*
79 / 1969	Bruno Mankowski	Bunyan/Appleseed	$20	$35
80 / 1969	Boris Buzan	Astronauts / Space travel	20	40
81 / 1970	Julian Harris	Uncle Remus	20	35
82 / 1970	Tom Allen Jr.	The elements / Life	20	35
83 / 1971	Hal Reed	Unleashing the atom	20	40
84 / 1971	Elbert Weinberg	Pandora: One and two	20	45
85 / 1972	Sten Jacobsson	The saved and the fallen	10	20
86 / 1972	John E. Svenson	Chilkat Indians	30	55
87 / 1973	Mico Kaufman	War/Peace	20	40
88 / 1973	Edward Grove	Alphabets and language	25	45
89 / 1974	Laszlo Ispanky	Youth and age	15	25
90 / 1974	Stanley Bleifeld	Chinese wisdom	20	40
91 / 1975	Frederick Shrady	Courage/Hope	30	55
92 / 1975	Bruno Lucchesi	Couples/Parents	30	55
93 / 1976	Harvey Weiss	Creatures great and small	35	65
94 / 1976	Anthony Notaro	Pilgrims/Mayflower	25	50
95 / 1977	Harry Marinsky	Sleeping cyclist / Castle	20	40
96 / 1977	Stephen Robin	Tutankhamun	45	85
97 / 1978	Robert Cook	Music and dance	30	55
98 / 1978	Moissaye Marans	Dawn and Dusk	30	55
99 / 1979	Donald Borja	Helios / Solar energy	40	75
100 / 1979	Linda Harper	Laughter/Tears	25	50
101 / 1980	Marcel Jovine	Dreamers/Dreams	40	75
102 / 1980	Edward Hoffman	Ill Alice and Winnie	20	40
103 / 1981	Laci de Gerenday	Cougar/Deer	40	80
104 / 1981	Elizabeth Gordon Chandler	Arts enrich life	35	70
105 / 1982	John Cook	Shallowness/Conceit	35	65
106 / 1982	Don Everhart	Dance of Dolphins	40	75
107 / 1983	Joseph Di Lorenzo	Arthurian legend	45	85
108 / 1983	Carter Jones	Balanchine/Dance	45	85
109 / 1984	Dexter Jones	Clown/Harlequin	25	50
110 / 1984	Margaret Ellison	Zodiac	40	80
111 / 1985	Donald De Lue	Imprisonment/Effort	250	400
112 / 1985	R.M. Miller	Escape/Capture	30	55

* Values given are for original bronze issues. Many, but not all, medals in the series were also struck in silver—some in the original year of issue, others as later restrikes. Availability of silver strikes is spotty, and dealer pricing is "catch as catch can."

The Society of Medalists (continued)

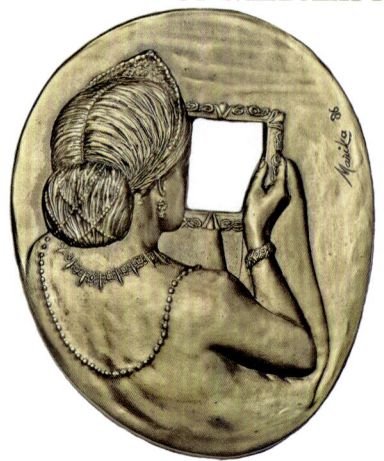

Actual size of larger Society of Medalists pieces is 71 mm

ISSUE NO. / DATE	ARTIST	SUBJECT OR THEME	EF	MS-63*
113 / 1986	Marika Somogyi	Vanity/Evil	$40	$75
114 / 1986	Alex Shagin	Children/Earth	35	65
115 / 1987	Robert Weinman	Cat and mouse	95	185
116 / 1987	Robert Cronbach	Sunrise/Moonrise	35	65
117 / 1988	Leonda Finke	Prodigal son	40	75
118 / 1988	P. Lewis-Verani	Snow/Sand	40	75
119 / 1989	Nicola Moss	Darwin/Galapagos	120	240
120 / 1989	Keiichi Uryu	Man/Woman	110	215
121 / 1990	Eugene Daub	Fire/Ice	40	75
122 / 1990	Marcel Jovine	God and man / All creatures	140	275
123 / 1991	M. Meszaros	Staircase perspectives	75	150
124 / 1992	Joseph Sheppard	Icarus	150	300
125 / 1993	Don Everhart	Tyrannosaurus Rex	60	115
126 / 1993	Karen Worth	Arrogance/Punishment	150	300
127 / 1994	A. Haiderzad	Old Kabul bazaar	150	300
128 / 1994	Don Everhart	Dinosaurs (set of 6)	220	440
129 / 1995	Geri Gould	Gospel scenes	200	400

* Values given are for original bronze issues. Many, but not all, medals in the series were also struck in silver—some in the original year of issue, others as later restrikes. Availability of silver strikes is spotty, and dealer pricing is "catch as catch can."

Evolving Medallic Art Today

Even with the Society of Medalists alive and active, a number of sculptors and enthusiasts felt that more could be done to revive the medallic art form. Bev Mazze, Gary Eriksen, Carter Jones, and Alan Stahl felt that "the lights were almost out." In 1982 they formed the American Medallic Sculpture Association (AMSA) to encourage the creation and study of medallic sculpture in North America. AMSA now has about 200 sculptor members, and hosts shows such as the American Numismatic Association Money Museum (Colorado Springs) international medallic art show of 2001, and the "Beyond Two Dimensions" exhibit at Forest Lawn Museum (Los Angeles) in January 2005. It sponsors American competitions and posts international competition notices on its Web site (amsamedals.org), to keep sculptors aware of opportunities. It also maintains close ties with its European sister organization, Federation Internationale de la Medaille (FIDEM). The response to some of AMSA's competitions has been a radical movement that is changing the direction of medallic design. Medals such as Sylvia Pearle's "Mad Cow Disease" (1998) and Antonio Viana's "The Other Century" (2000) display cutting-edge features such as hinged segments that allow the medal to be opened like a book or box. Pieces such as Carole Hodgson's "Bogman" (1987) and Nigel Hall's "Soglio" (2002) feature design elements suspended within a circular frame: that is, the blank fields of the medal are replaced by air. Many artists depart from the circular format altogether, or create design elements that project far out from the planar surfaces of the medal. Readers with Internet access are encouraged to view the explosion of innovative designs in contemporary medallic art by conducting an image search on the term "art medal." The printed catalog of the September 2007 FIDEM Exhibition in Colorado Springs, packed with photos from this international show, is another fine resource.

Since 1913, the American Numismatic Society has awarded the J. Sanford Saltus medal to sculptors for distinguished achievement in the art of the medal. Beaux-Arts master Adolph Weinman designed the prize, which, through 1983, was bestowed on 31 American artists. After 1983, the ANS expanded eligibility to include international sculptors, and the medal is now awarded for lifetime achievement in medallic art. Another organization supporting the form is Brookgreen Gardens Center for American Sculpture in Myrtle Beach, South Carolina. Since 1972, Brookgreen has sponsored a fine-art medal series for subscription by its patrons, with subject matter emphasizing sculpture, the natural world, and the history of South Carolina.

The major organization uniting medal enthusiasts, on the consumer end, is the Medal Collectors of America.

Actual size 80 mm

YEAR	ARTIST / TOPIC	METAL	COMMENTARY	EF	MS-63
1919	Adolph Weinman / Saltus medal*	Silver	To encourage and foster interest in medallic art	$350	$550

* Voted No. 97 in *100 Greatest American Medals and Tokens* (Jaeger/Bowers). Awarded examples are generally noncollectible. If any enter the market, value will depend on the fame of the recipient.

MEDALLIC ART TODAY *(continued)*

Actual size 76 mm

Actual size 74 mm

Actual size 75 mm

YEAR	ARTIST / TOPIC	METAL	COMMENTARY	EF	MS-63
1985	John Cook / Sculpting centaur	Bz	Sculpting and sculpture are favored Brookgreen themes	—	$150
1986	Alex Shagin / FIDEM conference	Bz	International artists' association keeps the art form alive	—	100
1999	Marion Roller / Plantation life	Bz	Brookgreen artists also emphasized South Carolina history	—	150

Part V
PRIZE MEDALS

A significant attraction of prize medals is their story value. Tied up in each one is the tale of some extraordinary individual, famous or forgotten, who somehow rose above the crowd and achieved something. Another appealing feature is their quality. From the start, America's prize committees realized that important achievements deserved distinguished rewards, and they commissioned some of the most beautiful die-struck objects ever produced. Like major historical commemoratives, many prize medals were struck in precious metals and bestowed in carefully made presentation cases for display on tables, or mounted in frames for display on walls.

It is no surprise that prize medals constitute an enormous body of objects. Medals have been awarded in multiple issues, not only at national events such as manufacturers' expositions and competitions hosted by institutes encouraging excellence in art, literature, invention, and scientific progress, but also at smaller events like farm and mechanics fairs, equestrian competitions, music recitals, regattas, dog shows, shooting matches, and sports tournaments. Added to these are the medals not attached to a particular competition, but awarded in appreciation or recognition of high achievement, like those of the U.S. Congress, colleges, geographic societies, lifesaving and humane societies, and literary, professional, and civic associations. As with historical commemoratives, vintage pieces command prices higher than modern ones, and of course the more famous the prize (or its recipient), the harder it will be to acquire a specimen.

19

ACADEMIC MEDALS

Much can be learned about the history of American education by studying academic prizes and the individuals who established and received them. King's College, later renamed Columbia University, was the first to award a medal to students, in 1760. The College of Philadelphia instituted the Sargent medal in 1766, and in 1770, the baron de Botetourt, British colonial governor of Virginia and rector of the College of William and Mary, left a bequest establishing the next college medals, to be awarded for distinguished achievement in philosophy and classics. He ordered eight gold medals to be struck in England, and all were distributed prior to the Revolutionary War.[71] (The college resumed the award in 1941, and now bestows Botetourt medals, in bronze, annually upon the graduating senior achieving the greatest overall distinction in scholarship.) The next university to establish a medals tradition, with a bequest from Massachusetts governor James Bowdoin in 1790, was Harvard. The Bowdoin Prize for classics is still awarded today, among many other departmental medals endowed by Harvard alumni over the past two centuries.

By the middle of the 19th century, the striking of medals for America's universities was big business. The U.S. Mint engravers can be credited with some dies, and private artists made others, then forwarded them to the Mint medals department, where adequate staff, equipment, and stockpiles of precious metals were on hand to fill orders each year at graduation time. There is no standard reference for college medals, but many medical school awards are cataloged in Malcolm Storer's 1931 *Medicina in Nummis*. The Valentine Mott Medal of New York University School of Medicine, an example instituted in 1856, was named after the surgical pioneer who financed the award. (Mott had been the focus of great controversy in the 1820s as an advocate of dissecting cadavers for study, but after the practice was accepted as a bona fide advance, he was revered as the father of modern surgery.) Mott specified that gold, silver, and bronze medals be awarded annually to the three NYU medical students presenting the best-preserved anatomical specimens.

Busts of philanthropist George Peabody appeared on the medals of "normal schools" that trained teachers across the South, starting around 1877. Peabody provided the funds for these awards, according to his philosophy printed on the medals: EDUCATION IS A DEBT DUE FROM PRESENT TO FUTURE GENERATIONS. Medals were awarded for undergraduate achievement and attendance at public schools, private preparatory schools, Sunday schools, and Jewish academies as well. Of these, the most famous are the various Boston public-school medals, issued from as early as 1799 to as late as 1941. Early examples were entirely hand-engraved, but examples from the 1840s were struck. From 1851 onward, the U.S. Mint handled the work, striking separate medals for boys and girls until 1867.

Academic Medals

YEAR	SCHOOL / MEDAL	MAKER	METAL	COMMENTARY	F	EF	MS-63
1770	William & Mary / Botetourt	T. Pingo	Cop	For achievement in classics and philosophy	—	$18,000	$20,000
1790	Harvard/Bowdoin	Unknown	Silv	Classics prize is still awarded today	—	150	300
1831	Columbia College	James Bale	Silv	Handsome medal a prize worth studying for	—	75	150
1840s	Boston Public / Girls	U.S. Mint	Silv	Annual strikings brought income to Mint's medals dept.	$25	100	200
1850s	Boston Public / Boys	Mitchell / U.S. Mint	Silv	Struck annually from 1851 through 1947	150	300	500

Actual size 63 mm

YEAR	SCHOOL / MEDAL	MAKER	METAL	COMMENTARY	F	EF	MS-63
1855	NYC Free Academy	C.C. Wright	Bz	Today called the College of the City of New York	—	$50	$100
1856	NYU / Valentine Mott	G.H. Lovett	WM	Mott prizes are still awarded, but made of paper now	—	150	250
1867	Pittsburgh Female College	W.H. Key	Bz	Most American colleges did not admit women	—	100	150
1877	Peabody Award	H. Mitchell	Bz	Showing one of America's great educational leaders	—	60	125

Academic Medals

Actual size 80x66 mm

YEAR	SCHOOL / MEDAL	MAKER	METAL	COMMENTARY	F	EF	MS-63
1884	Providence / Anthony Prize	Unknown	Silv	For grammar school kids, an encouragement to read	—	$75	$150
1918	Liberty Loan / Essay	R.B.F.	Bz	Essay contest was part of wartime fundraising effort	—	4	5
1922	Oklahoma City Public Schools	Herbert Adams	Bz	Matchless artwork for a high-school medal!	—	—	50
1990	Bausch & Lomb Science Award		Bz	Awarded since 1933; comes with a University of Rochester scholarship attached	—	—	25

20

MAJOR INSTITUTIONAL AWARDS

America's first learned society for the encouragement of study beyond the college level was the brainchild of Benjamin Franklin in 1743. He patterned his American Philosophical Society (APS) in Philadelphia on the Royal Society of London. Franklin wrote: "The first drudgery of settling new colonies is now pretty well over, and there are many in every province in circumstances that set them at ease, and afford leisure to cultivate the finer arts, and improve the common stock of knowledge." His society would support "all philosophical Experiments that let Light into the Nature of Things, tend to increase the Power of Man over Matter, and multiply the Conveniencies or Pleasures of Life."[72] The APS began awarding medals in 1790. In 1906, for Franklin's birth bicentennial, Congress authorized the Benjamin Franklin medal, designed by Louis and Augustus Saint-Gaudens. Producer Tiffany & Co. struck two in 18k gold and 155 in bronze. President Theodore Roosevelt presented the first gold issue to the Republic of France, and authorized the APS to bestow the rest on noteworthy contributors to American progress. The APS continues to award these and other medals for advances in the sciences, humanities, arts, professions, and public service.

In Cambridge, Massachusetts, another important medal-awarding institution got underway in 1780. John Hancock, John Adams, James Bowdoin, and others founded the American Academy of Arts and Sciences (AAAS), which still awards the Rumford Prize (engraved by Moritz Furst) for outstanding research on heat or light. The first Rumford medal went to Robert Hare in 1839 for his invention of the oxyhydrogen blowpipe. The most recent, in 1996, went to John C. Mather for contributions to understanding the cosmic microwave background.

Through the 19th century, national institutions proliferated to award medals encouraging excellence in the sciences, arts, music, trades, architecture, publishing, and virtually every other discipline. The appearance of the awards changed radically with the shift toward sculpture in the die-making process (as discussed in chapter 18). Among sculptural historians, the period 1876–1917 is known as "the American Renaissance," partly because of innovations in casting and metallurgical technology, but mainly due to the wide public interest in, and support for, the art form. Prize organizations from the 1880s onward vied strenuously for the services of the best-known sculptors. The minuscule sampling given here includes works of Brenner, French, Flanagan, and McKenzie, and all the other major U.S. sculptors contributed specimens to this category.

These illustrious prizes often wind up in museums. Yet buyable examples *can* be located with patience and effort—and these historic pieces are worth the challenge they present to collectors.

Major Institutional Awards 235

Actual size 64 mm

Actual size 70 mm

YEAR	INSTITUTION / AWARD	MAKER	METAL	COMMENTARY	F	EF	MS-63
1839	AAAS/Rumford	Furst/Gorham	Gold	An early incentive to scientific achievement	—	$7,500	$17,000
1887	Architectural League	Unknown	Cop	Attempting a new medallic style in the late 1880s	—	—	150
1897	American Geographical Society	Brenner/Tiffany	Bz	Established in 1896; Robert Peary was first recipient	—	—	400

Actual size 75 mm

Actual size 70 mm

Actual size 70 mm

YEAR	INSTITUTION / AWARD	MAKER	METAL	COMMENTARY	F	EF	MS-63
1904	National Arts Club	Brenner/Gorham	Bz	Uniface plaquettes were popular in this era	—	$250	$1,000
1909	Art Institute of Chicago	V.D. Brenner	Alum	Artist intentionally chose aluminum for novel effect	—	—	450
1915	American Academy of Arts and Letters	J. Fraser / MACo	Bz	The gold medal of this academy is actually bronze	—	200	400

Major Institutional Awards 237

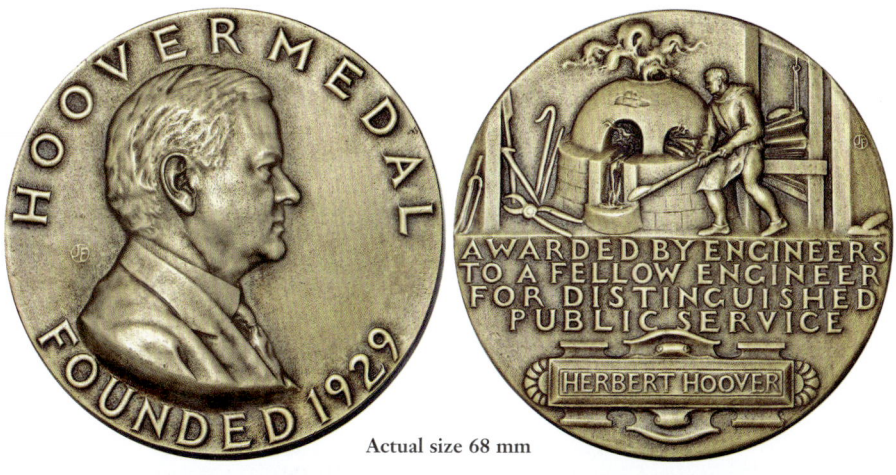

Actual size 70 mm

Actual size 68 mm

YEAR	INSTITUTION / AWARD	MAKER	METAL	COMMENTARY	F	EF	MS-63
1919	Ornithologist's Union	French/MACo	Bz	More 1919 output from the Lincoln Memorial sculptor	—	—	$200
1922	American Chemical Society	Adam Pietz	Bz	Priestley medal returns to a 19th-century styling	—	—	100
1929	Engineering/Hoover	Flanagan / U.S. Mint	Bz	Flanagan was popular choice to design award medals	—	—	300

Actual size 65 mm

YEAR	INSTITUTION / AWARD	MAKER	METAL	COMMENTARY	F	EF	MS-63
1930s	National League Nursing Education	R.T. McKenzie	Bz	Florence Nightingale graces this nursing award	—	—	$50
1938	Library Association / Caldecott	Chambellan/MACo	Bz	Still the pinnacle for children's book illustrators	—	—	75
1950s	International Fine-Arts Council	Kilenyi/Balfour	Gold	Prominent New York–based council is gone today	(bullion value +20–40%)		

21
FAIR AND EXPOSITION MEDALS

Winning a fair-medal commission was a die engraver's dream, because it meant a sizable annual infusion of income: most prize-fair organizing societies awarded precious and base-metal medals year after year, in multiple competition categories.

Fair medals are not only well executed, they are plentiful, easy to find, and relatively affordable.

Agricultural and Mechanics' Society Medals

Unlike the largely recreational farm fairs of today, where people sample country cooking, watch tractor pulls, and admire the blue-ribbon entries of local 4-H clubs, the 19th-century agricultural fair was an event crucial not only to the local economy, but to the United States' success as a republic. Through the first half of the century, the business of America was farming. In the absence of modern communications, the only means farmers had to learn about scientific advances resulting from experiments with seed, soil, irrigation, fertilizers, pomology, and animal husbandry, was by getting together on a regular basis and putting their innovations on display.

Benjamin Rush and Robert Morris founded the earliest organization to encourage agriculture by awarding medals, the Philadelphia Society for Promoting Agriculture, in 1786. Its first gold medal was awarded for an essay on the most efficient way to lay out a farmyard. This society still awards a gold medal annually. The first society to sponsor a prize fair was the Berkshire County Agricultural Society of Massachusetts, whose first cattle show was held in 1810. (The U.S. Mint produced medals for this group between 1872 and 1883.) Finely wrought gold medals by Taylor of Birmingham, England, were awarded by the first state-sponsored agricultural society, based in Syracuse, New York, which held its inaugural fair in 1841.

Meanwhile, mechanics' and tradesmens' societies were forming along the same lines as the farmers' groups, to encourage innovation, exhibit new products to consumers, and serve as rudimentary trade unions. Paul Revere was president of the first of these, the Massachusetts Charitable Mechanics Association, founded in 1795. Its gold and silver prize medals were designed and engraved by Christian Gobrecht and awarded, starting in 1837, at exhibitions in Quincy Hall (and after 1857 at Mechanics Hall in Boston). The New England Society for the Promotion of Manufactures and Mechanic Arts, chartered in 1826, also hosted prize fairs with award medals by Gobrecht. Supported by members' annual dues, such societies maintained year-round offices, libraries, and museums of invention, published inventors' research, and corresponded with other societies. Many inventions were developed for farming, such as specialized tools and mechanized methods of planting, harvesting, and packaging crops. In some regions, agricultural and mechanics' societies combined, hosting a single large exposition that covered everything. The term *mechanic* at the time included fine craftsmen as well, so these expositions featured a wonderful juxtaposition of animal exhibits and heavy machinery, with luxury goods such as ornate silver tea services, delicately cut crystal, or exquisite miniature portraits painted on ivory.

Pictured on the medals are symbols of farming and the trades, such as Ceres (the Roman goddess of agriculture), beehives, cornucopias, hammers, anvils, and machines. Many featured a seated goddess extending a wreath symbolizing the gift of knowledge. Robert Lindesmith published a trial list for this category in the *TAMS Journal* of February 1969, "Medals of U.S. Agricultural Associations, Institutes, and Societies."

Actual size 65 mm

YEAR	ORGANIZATION	MAKER	METAL	COMMENTARY	EF	MS-63
1826	New England Society for Promotion of Manufacturers and Mechanic Arts	Gobrecht / U.S. Mint	Silv	Honoring inventors and inventions	$2,500	$4,500
1837	Massachussetts Charitable Mechanic Association	Gobrecht / U.S. Mint	Silv	Paul Revere was the first president of this group	350	500
1840s	New York State Agricultural Society	Taylor/Birmingham	Bz	High artistic quality seen on fair medals	50	100

AGRICULTURAL AND MECHANICS' SOCIETY MEDALS *(continued)*

Actual size 65 mm

YEAR	ORGANIZATION	MAKER	METAL	COMMENTARY	EF	MS-63
1850	Royal Hawaiian Agricultural Society	Mitchell / U.S. Mint	Bz	Medals awarded only through 1857	$2,000	$4,000
1851	Maine Charitable Mechanic Association	Smith & Hartmann	Bz	Rewarded industrial advances and fine arts	200	300
1852	Connecticut State Agricultural Society	Smith & Hartmann	Bz	Private diesinkers loved prize-fair accounts	75	125

AGRICULTURAL AND MECHANICS' SOCIETY MEDALS *(continued)*

Actual size 61 mm

Actual size 63 mm

YEAR	ORGANIZATION	MAKER	METAL	COMMENTARY	EF	MS-63
1855	Alabama State Agricultural Society	Tiffany & Co.	Bz	Many fair medals were commissioned to jewelers	$350	$600
1855	Columbia County, Pa., Agricultural Society	Unknown	Bz	Today it's called the Bloomsburg State Fair	100	150
1860	Sacramento Agricultural & Horticultural Exhibition	Smith & Hartmann	WM	Ball, Black & Co. minted these medals	100	300

AGRICULTURAL AND MECHANICS' SOCIETY MEDALS *(continued)*

YEAR	ORGANIZATION	MAKER	METAL	COMMENTARY	EF	MS-63
1861	Agricultural Society of Philadelphia	U.S. Mint	Bz	Very rare; no awarded examples known	$100	$200
1869	New York State Poultry Society	R. Laubenheimer	Silv	*Omni animal ex ovo:* all creatures from eggs	100	300
1870	Agricultural, Mechanical & Blood Stock Association	Unknown	Silv	Awarding advances in cattle husbandry	600	800
1874	Western Mass. Poultry Association	Tiffany & Co.	Cop	Tiffany never credited die makers by name	50	100

Agricultural and Mechanics' Society Medals (continued)

Actual size 64 mm

YEAR	ORGANIZATION	MAKER	METAL	COMMENTARY	EF	MS-63
1870s	Georgia State Agricultural Society	Bailey & Co.	Bz	Jeweler Bailey contracted Philadelphia diesinkers	$100	$250
1879	Pennsylvania State Agricultural Society	A. Morin / U.S. Mint	Bz	Struck between 1855 and 1878	75	200

National Prize Fairs and Expositions

Perhaps the most widely available fair medals are those of the American Institute, which performed on the national level the same functions as the mechanics' and agricultural fairs. Starting in 1829, this New York City–based organization hosted annual competitions in four categories: agriculture, commerce, manufacturing, and the arts. From the 1840s onward, these expositions lasted a month to six weeks, featured thousands of exhibitors, and had hundreds of thousands of visitors. On the final day came the elaborate awards ceremony where winners received their gold, silver, and bronze medals, originally designed and engraved by Moritz Furst. The annual medal account passed to C.C. Wright & James Bale in 1831, and then to the Lovett family, who performed the work from 1840 to 1894. The last major prize fair was held in 1897. In an August 1989 study in *TAMS Journal*, "The American Institute: Catalyst for American Greatness," Andrew

Harkness cataloged 20 different medal varieties. The present author supplemented Harkness's research in *Numismatist*, February 2006, "Treasures of the American Institute," and *TAMS Journal*, December 2006, "Exploring the Archives of the American Institute."

Many American Institute medals were sacrificed to the "1980 melt" described in chapter 13, but a rough idea of the original quantity struck can be extrapolated from George Lovett's tally of 1857. That year, he struck 496 medals: 20 large gold, 12 small gold, 100 small silver, 114 large silver, and 250 bronze. Some fairs were much larger and some were much smaller than the 1857 fair, so taking 500 medals per year as an average, and multiplying it by the 67 fairs held in the 19th century, we get a series numbering around 33,500 examples. In the 1930s, the American Institute shifted its emphasis to science. From 1933 to 1951, instead of hosting prize fairs, it awarded one gold medal annually with a $150,000 premium. It didn't completely abandon prize fairs, however. From 1929 to 1982, the Institute hosted annual youth science fairs in conjunction with the New York Academy of Sciences, and student winners received inexpensive token-like medals in brass, white metal, and copper, struck at Medallic Art Co. from Robert Lovett Sr.'s small gold-medal die design.

In Philadelphia, the American Institute's sister organization, the world-famous Franklin Institute, began awarding prize medals to scientific innovators in 1845, and still does so. Its Franklin Gold Medal, instituted in 1914, has gone to such figures as Edison, Marconi, Kettering, and Einstein. The two institutes corresponded with each other and assisted in establishing other regional mechanics' and agricultural societies, one of which was the Colored American Institute for the Promotion of the Mechanic Arts and Sciences. In 1851 and 1852 in Philadelphia, this group hosted exhibitions of inventions, artworks, and handicrafts of black citizens. Its silver prize medals were hand-engraved on smoothed-off U.S. silver dollars of the 1840s.

YEAR	ORGANIZATION	MAKER	METAL	COMMENTARY	EF	MS-63
1831	American Institute	M. Furst	Silv	Agriculture, invention, and arts encouraged	$250	$500
1841	American Institute	R. Lovett Sr.	Gold	Gold awards were far smaller than silver, for cost reasons	1,000	2,000

National Prize Fairs and Expositions *(continued)*

YEAR	ORGANIZATION	MAKER	METAL	COMMENTARY	EF	MS-63
1845	Franklin Institute*	Gobrecht / U.S. Mint	Silv	First exhibition held 1824, first medals struck 1826	$250	$600
1852	Colored American Institute	Unknown	Silv	Hand-engraved on smoothed Liberty Seated dollars	500	—
1883	National Exposition of Railway Appliances, Chicago	Barber / U.S. Mint	Bz	Advances in engineering for the railroads	250	450

* Voted No. 65 in *100 Greatest American Medals and Tokens* (Jaeger/Bowers).

NATIONAL PRIZE FAIRS AND EXPOSITIONS (continued)

Actual size 74 mm

Actual size 73 mm

YEAR	ORGANIZATION	MAKER	METAL	COMMENTARY	EF	MS-63
1883	Southern Exposition, Louisville	Unknown	Bz	Five-summer industrial expo largest since 1876	$125	$175
1885	Three Americas Exposition, New Orleans	Peter Krider	Cop	Krider's Philadelphia plant struck many fine awards	125	300
1895	Cotton States Exposition, Atlanta	P.H. Martiny	Gilt Bz	Sculptor best known for architectural adornments	125	200

NATIONAL PRIZE FAIRS AND EXPOSITIONS (continued)

Actual size 63 mm

Actual size 60x72 mm

YEAR	ORGANIZATION	MAKER	METAL	COMMENTARY	EF	MS-63
1898	Trans-Mississippi Exposition	S.D. Childs	Svd Bz	Showcasing achievements west of the river	$100	$250
1904	Louisiana Purchase Exposition	A. Weinman / U.S. Mint	Bz	Gold, silver, bronze, and grand prizes were bronze	100	250
1909	Hudson-Fulton Essay	Tiffany & Co.	Silv	An essay contest went with the exposition	20	30
1936	International Philatelic Exposition	M. Young / MACo	Bz	Pony Express–themed piece given to all exhibitors	—	30

22

LIFESAVING AND HEROISM MEDALS

Idawalley Lewis inherited from her parents the job of lighthouse keeper at Lime Rock near Newport, Rhode Island. Over the years, she rescued a number of people from the waters around her lighthouse. Still, it was a fairly quiet, routine existence until 1869, when she singlehandedly hauled in a pair of soldiers from an overturned sailboat during a storm. A newspaper picked up the story, then another learned of her prior rescues, and soon Ida found herself on the cover of *Harper's Weekly* under the caption "The Bravest Woman in America." Grateful citizens presented her with a mahogany rowboat and a parade through the streets of Newport; important figures like Ulysses S. Grant and Mrs. William Astor rowed out to Lime Rock just to meet her; and the Life Saving Benevolent Association (LSBA) voted her $100 in cash and their gold medal. Ida's story is typical of many associated with the fascinating category of lifesaving medals. The vivid pictorial content of these objects is often as dramatic as the rescues they commemorate, and their inscriptions provide not only names and dates, but usually also descriptions of specific incidents, giving them great historical value.

At the close of the 18th century, the lighthouse service was the only force keeping watch on American shores. The tall ships plying the coastlines in ever-increasing numbers were enormously expensive to build and crew. When one went down to a total loss of vessel and cargo, maritime insurance companies footed the bill—but there were no benefits whatsoever for families of drowned crewmembers or passengers. In 1796, a Boston-based group of physicians, shipping merchants, and marine insurers formed the Massachusetts Humane Society (MHS) to organize volunteers to keep watch and perform rescues on New England shores. They donated funds to build "huts of refuge" along the coast, where castaways could at least find blankets and shelter if they could manage to drag themselves ashore. In 1807, the MHS built their first lifeboat station, and by 1841 there were 18 stocked with boats and 81 in all. The MHS began awarding medals, struck by the U.S. Mint, in 1880, and continued doing so through 1899.

The busy mid-Atlantic coast had no coastal watch until 1849, when the LSBA formed in New York City. This charitable organization maintained relief stations from Montauk, Long Island, to Cape May, New Jersey. Association member George Lovett designed and struck the gold, silver, and bronze medals for courageous rescuers, and the first gold specimen was presented to John Maxon for his efforts at the January 1850 wreck of the British ship *Aryshire*. A recap of the awards ceremony reported, "This testimonial is given partly to commemorate the first shot sent from a mortar in order to get communication through the surf to a stranded vessel, when boats could not be propelled through the waves, and to reward the skill of Mr. Maxon in directing the operation, which was the cause of landing safely two hundred and one persons from a wreck, during a gale in the middle of the winter."[73] By mid-century, the federal government was helping fund both the MHS and the LSBA, and in 1871 it absorbed their beach stations into the U.S. Lifesaving Service. The

LSBA still functions as an award agency. In 2003, it bestowed one silver and eleven bronze medals (of the original design, and struck at Medallic Art Co.) upon New York area police, fire, and volunteer lifesaving personnel for their involvement with various water rescues.[74]

Starting in 1850, the U.S. State Department authorized the awarding of national lifesaving medals: first class, for saving an American life on the high seas or in a foreign port; and second class, for saving an American sailor along our own coasts. These were designed and struck by U.S. Mint engravers, and are detailed in R.W. Julian's *Medals of the U.S. Mint, the First Century, 1792–1892*. In 1874, and again in 1880, Congress authorized Treasury Department medals for rescues on inland waters and the high seas, as well as various individual medals on occasion. The Philadelphia Owners & Captains Association, patterned on the MHS and LSBA, also awarded medals struck at the Mint, from 1874 to 1889.

Soon all kinds of organizations, such as the Carnegie Hero Fund, magazine and newspaper publishers, civic associations, the Boy Scouts of America, firemen's groups, police agencies, and animal humane societies, were awarding medals for heroism and bravery. A committee of surviving passengers from the most famous shipwreck, the *Titanic* disaster of 1912, ordered 300 medals from goldsmiths Dieges & Clust for presentation to the crew of the first rescue ship on the scene, *Carpathia*. "Unsinkable" Molly Brown herself presented gold medals to Captain Arthur Rostron and the senior officers, silver to the junior officers, and bronze to crew members. The Titanic Historical Society of Indian Orchard, Massachusetts, today sells reproductions of these medals on its Web site.[75]

YEAR	SUBJECT	MAKER	METAL	COMMENTARY	EF	MS-63
1847	Somers rescue	Wright / U.S. Mint	Silv	U.S. warship foundered in a squall; for rescue of her crew	$1,500	$4,000
1849	Lifesaving Benevolent Association	G.H. Lovett	Gold	Line carronade and lifeboats in action on the obverse	5,000	8,000

Lifesaving and Heroism Medals 251

Actual size 71 mm

Actual size 63 mm

YEAR	SUBJECT	MAKER	METAL	COMMENTARY	EF	MS-63
1851	Grinell Expedition	Tiffany & Co.	Bz	For hazardous Arctic rescue of vessel locked in ice	$1,500	$2,500
1859	State Department (Leutze)	U.S. Mint	Gold	Award to foreign nationals for rescuing Americans	—	50,000
1859	State Department (Koehler)	U.S. Mint	Silv	Award to U.S. citizens making coastal rescues	12,000	17,500

252 A GUIDE BOOK OF UNITED STATES TOKENS AND MEDALS

Actual size 82 mm

Actual size 77 mm

Actual size 64 mm

YEAR	SUBJECT	MAKER	METAL	COMMENTARY	EF	MS-63
1866	Creighton, Low & Stouffer	T.B. Welsh / U.S. Mint	Cop	Extremely high relief for the rescuers of the *San Francisco*	$200	$400
1871	George F. Robinson*	Paquet / U.S. Mint	Bz	For the man who prevented Seward's 1865 assassination	300	1,200
1872	Metis Rescue	Barber / U.S. Mint	Bz	Gold medals went to awardees, bronze sold to the public	300	700

* The medal shown is a modern yellow-bronze restrike. Valuations here are for original chocolate-bronze strikes.

Lifesaving and Heroism Medals 253

Actual size 77 mm

YEAR	SUBJECT	MAKER	METAL	COMMENTARY	EF	MS-63
1896	Humane Car Drivers	Unknown	Bz	Rewarding good treatment of working horses	—	$200
1904	Carnegie Hero Medal**	Osborne/Greco	Bz	For selfless acts of ordinary citizens	—	200
1912	Titanic rescuers	Dieges & Clust	Ster	Modern reproductions abound—beware!	$4,000	6,000

** Voted No. 88 in *100 Greatest American Medals and Tokens* (Jaeger/Bowers). Values are for unissued medals, as shown. Medals inscribed to an awardee would be valued at $300 in EF to $500 in MS-63.

WANTED
SERIOUS CUSTOMERS FOR SERIOUS EXONUMIA!

PRESIDENTIAL COIN AND ANTIQUE COMPANY, INC., was formed in 1970 by H. Joseph Levine. Mr. Levine is a Past President of the Token and Medal Society and is a former Vice President & Legal Counsel to the Civil War Token Society. He is a member of many specialized clubs in the broad field of exonumia. He is the author of the Collectors Guide to Presidential Inaugural Medals and Memorabilia and of numerous articles on the subject of tokens and medals published in *The Numismatist*, The Journal of the American Numismatic Association. In addition he has served as a consultant on various subjects to The National Portrait Gallery; The American Numismatic Association; The American Numismatic Society and The Smithsonian Institution - National Numismatic Collection.

PRESIDENTIAL has been known for selling the finest quality tokens and medals in a wide variety of collecting fields.

Through the years, we have handled major rarities in virtually every token and medal area of significance. Below are just a few of the areas in which we deal extensively.

- Hard Times & 19th Century Merchant Tokens
- Civil War Tokens
- Transportation Tokens
- So-Called Dollars
- All Kinds of Political Americana
- Betts Medals
- Indian Peace Medals
- U.S. Mint Medals
- World's Fair & Exposition Items
- Art Medals
- Official Presidential Inaugural Medals

AT AUCTION

We offer material from all of the above areas – plus some. We conduct a major sale each year at Whitman's Baltimore Coin & Currency Convention and have periodic offerings on eBay under the name of MEDALSMAN. If you prefer to sell at auction, there is no better vehicle than our professionally cataloged illustrated sales. Our commission rate is a most reasonable 10%. For many years our catalogs have been considered collectors items themselves. Part I of our Sale of the Charles McSorley Collection of 19th century political tokens earned the Numismatic Literary Guild Award for the Best Exonumia Catalog of 1997 and Mr. Levine was awarded the Carl W.A. Carlson Award for Outstanding Research and Writing in the Medal Field by the Medal Collectors of America. **Please contact us** to request a complimentary copy of our next sale.

PRIVATE TREATY TRANSACTIONS

We both buy and sell on a direct basis. The great majority of coin dealers could care less about tokens and medals and their prices reflect that disinterest. PRESIDENTIAL has specialized in the token and medal field for 35+ years and is positioned to deal fairly and knowledgeably with such material.

PRESIDENTIAL COIN & ANTIQUE CO., INC.
P.O. BOX 277 CLIFTON, VA 20124
571-321-2121 • JLevine968@aol.com

Part VI
FRATERNAL AND MEMBERSHIP-THEMED MEDALS AND TOKENS

As noted in the preface, the orders and decorations of clubs, fraternal societies, and civic organizations have been excluded from this guide. These items frequently employ pinbacks, jewels, hinged sections, and other features that take them away from the definition of medals and tokens as "coin-like objects."

Medals and tokens offer a convenient, distinctive, and attractive way to identify membership in a fraternal group or other organization. They serve purposes similar to uniforms, hats, sashes, and other outward signs of membership, as well as secret handshakes, codewords, and jargon. A fraternal or membership medal says, "I belong to this group, and it belongs to me."

23

FRATERNAL, INCENTIVE, AND MEMBERSHIP MEDALS AND TOKENS

Not every medal was struck to honor some world-changing achievement or act of national importance. The readily collectible category of incentive medals features die-struck items created to acknowledge everyday triumphs. These are awarded to people who stand out from their group, such as firefighters, police, military personnel, or even productive salespeople. They have the dual purpose of commending effort and providing an incentive to "keep up the good work." From the Alcoholics Anonymous member who receives an aluminum token for each new day of sobriety, to the Marine recruit who accumulates "challenge coins" for performing duties with excellence, recipients find their collections meaningful not only as mementoes of success, but as badges of fellowship: their medals indicate they have become part of something bigger than themselves. Membership medals of groups such as social organizations, fraternal societies, private clubs, and fire companies exist specifically for the latter purpose.

FIREFIGHTERS' MEDALS

With the exception of the City of Boston, which funded a professional fire department starting in 1678, communities in pre-federal America required every able-bodied male citizen to be a firefighter. Men from all walks of life would drop everything at the first alarm, and were expected to bring their own buckets to the line leading from the fire to the nearest well.[76] The need for a trained, equipped firefighting force was obvious to Benjamin Franklin, who in 1736 organized the first volunteer firemen's club, the Union Fire Company of Philadelphia. A U.S. Mint medal struck in 1899 acknowledges the fact that George Washington was a founding member of the Friendship Fire Company of Alexandria, Virginia, in 1773. Dues-paying members of these clubs were assured protection for their homes and property, while those who did not join took their chances. In many cases, a membership medal was the proof of support. The oval Northern Liberty Fire Co. medal, likely struck in the 1850s, is an example of marvelous quality (see below).

Starting in the 1840s, communities began sponsoring firefighters' conventions, parades, anniversary celebrations, and tournaments of firefighting skill that generated both prize medals and souvenir pieces, the majority of which were struck in the last two decades of the 19th century. In 1869, publisher James Gordon Bennett instituted an award for bravery, as outlined in the following letter from his son to the New York City fire department:

> My father, being desirous of adding an additional competition to the members of the Metropolitan Fire Department, in the discipline, courage, and honesty with which their duties are now performed, and

Fraternal, Incentive, and Membership Medals and Tokens 257

which was particularly called to his notice at the fire at his country residence during last September, has directed me to enclose the sum of fifteen hundred dollars, and requests that you will pay five hundred dollars to Messrs. Tiffany & Co., for the dies of a medal they are preparing, and use the income of the balance in procuring, annually, a gold medal to be struck from the same, and to be conferred by you and your successors in this trust, upon such members of the Department as you may, in your judgment, consider best entitled to the reward.

The Bennett medal is still the highest award of the New York Fire Department, and since its institution other newspaper and magazine publishers, wealthy individuals, and groups have established many medals for firefighters. In the 21st century, fire companies award challenge coins similar to the military varieties discussed below, to commend individual effort.

YEAR	SUBJECT	MAKER	METAL	COMMENTARY	F	EF	MS-63
1833	Northern Liberty Fire Company	Unknown	Cop	Exquisite die work on this membership piece	$50	$100	$200
1860	New York torchlight parade	Smith/Hartmann	Gilt Br	Obverse paired with other reverses; also in white metal	50	80	—
1860	Fireman's medal	R. Lovett	Cop	12,000 were struck at the order of Alfred Robinson	15	25	50
1869	Bennett medal	Tiffany & Co.	Bz	God of the sea appears, strangely, on the obverse	—	200	400

YEAR	SUBJECT	MAKER	METAL	COMMENTARY	F	EF	MS-63
1873	Rainbow Fire Company	Unknown	WM	A token souvenir of the company centennial	—	$50	$100
1882	Philadelphia F.D. 200th anniversary	William. H. Key	Bz	Engine pictorial lends interest to this hefty piece		50	100
1884	Utica Excursion	A. Demarest	WM	State firemen's conventions created token issues		50	100
1890	Charlotte, N.C., contest	Unknown	WM	Firemen's competitions required award medals		50	100
1891	Hoboken statue	Unknown	WM	Souvenir of the dedication of a statue to firemen		50	100
1897	New York Herald Police & Firemen	R. Stoll	Bz	Newspapers awarded medals for heroic service		75	150

MILITARY AND OTHER CHALLENGE COINS

Anyone looking on the Internet for a definition of the *challenge coin* will encounter a widely duplicated posting entitled, "The History of the Challenge Coin." As the story goes, during World War I a wealthy Army Air Service lieutenant ordered bronze medals to be struck as membership pieces for his squadron's pilots. One of them was shot down over Germany, lost his dog tags, and escaped to France, and was able to prove to suspicious French soldiers that he was an American by showing them the name and emblem of his unit on the medal. Afterward, the lieutenant insisted his pilots carry their medals at all times. Airmen were encouraged to "challenge" their fellows at any time, to ensure they were carrying their medals. If a challenged man could not produce a medal, he had to buy his challenger a drink. If he could produce it, then the challenger would buy the drink. Since this lieutenant's name and the name of his unit are missing from the story, it is unverifiable. There is no evidence for challenge-coin use in World War II or the Korean conflict, so it is safe to assume that this tale has little connection to today's challenge coins.

According to Roxanne Merritt, curator of the John F. Kennedy Special Warfare Museum at Fort Bragg, North Carolina, the American practice of "coining" was born when a member of the 11th Special Forces Group Airborne in Vietnam took old coins, counterstamped them with his unit's emblem, and presented them to the other unit members as souvenirs of duty. In 1969, Colonel Vernon E. Greene, Commander of the 10th Special Forces Group, liked the idea and designed a coin for his unit, putting their symbol, a Trojan horse, on the obverse. Merritt said that the 10th was the only unit to "coin" members until the mid-1980s, when "an explosion took place and everybody started minting coins."[77] Today's military provides a budget for the supply of unit coins for all five branches of service, and to other agencies such as the U.S. Marshals and the CIA, as well as American units of the United Nations peacekeeping forces. Most bear the unit name and crest on the obverse and the commander's chosen design on the reverse.

Early challenge-coin issues were struck in a single base metal. Many current issues are bimetallic, or feature high relief, perforated designs, non-round shapes, or colorful enameling, all intended to convey the unique "personality" of a unit. Says Army veteran Michael McAllister of Washington, DC, "I estimate the current number of challenge coin issues at 10,000 and growing. Many commanders will change the style of their unit's coin when assuming command. The base I go to in Germany every year authorizes four different units to have coins made. Commanders have a two-year cycle, so over a 30-year period, that could mean 15 coins per unit, and 60 coins from just one base." McAllister says that in the Army, the lowest rank that can "coin" is a lieutenant colonel or a sergeant major at the battalion level, and "they use coins as tokens of 'thank you very much.'"

> Say you have a visiting general coming to a base for an inspection. If the general is impressed at what he sees, he might hand some coins out to the key players who made the inspection go well. The base commander may hand out some of his own coins for the same reason. . . . Usually, the higher the command level, the harder it is to get their coin, and earning one signifies you have performed a higher-level type of deed. The president and vice president even have coins (bearing

their seals of office), which they have staff hand out. It is more prestigious if the recipient's name is inscribed on the coin—it indicates that more thought was given to its presentation. . . . Some units are very stingy in handing these coins out, raising the prestige level if you have a coin from that unit, while other units may hand their coins out for very simple accomplishments.[78]

Military personnel must carry their unit coins and may challenge each other, even across services, and the rules for what trumps what are complicated by differing points of view on the relative worth of each unit's coin. Generally, the "value" is tied to the rank of the awarding officer, and a White House coin trumps all. Some military personnel display their collections in elaborate cases in their offices. Bill Clinton kept a case on exhibit in the Oval Office during his presidential term. Oldtimers rue the fact that challenge coins are not as special as they once were. Since Operation Desert Storm, the coins have been sold to the public at military-post gift shops and traded online. The web site of one challenge coin manufacturer boasts, "Today, challenge coins aren't just for the military. They are for everyone! Challenge coins are great for police and fire departments, schools, retirements, weddings, colleges, fraternities, clubs, and many more. Medallions can be designed for your unique organization. You can collect or trade them."[79]

ISSUER	COMMENTARY	METAL	MS-63
United Nations Civilian Police	For award to Bosnia-Herzegovina peacekeepers*	Bz	$20
FBI New Orleans Field Office	Many challenge coins sport colorful, imaginative designs	Enam Bz	10

* Examples showing the awardee's name may fetch double the price of unawarded examples. Bimetal or enameled coins bring a few dollars more than plainer, single-metal specimens.

ISSUER	COMMENTARY	METAL	MS-63
INL Force, Afghanistan	Awarded for excellence in fighting the illegal drug trade	Enam Bz	$10
USAF Thunderbirds Demonstration Squadron	Showing the team's classic bomb burst maneuver	Enam Bz	10

MEMBERSHIP MEDALS

Membership medals and medals marking anniversaries of membership were popular with private clubs, fraternal organizations, benevolent and protective groups, and of course, numismatic clubs, throughout the 19th century. Even earlier pieces are known, such as the 1745 Tuesday Club medal struck for an Annapolis, Maryland, gentlemen's club. The quality of its execution suggests it was made in Europe, and of the five known examples, four are in museums. A 1763 piece, also ridiculously rare and struck in England, was the Charles Town Social Club medal (Charleston, South Carolina). Harvard University's Hasty Pudding Club (1795), Porcellian Club (1800), and Pierian Sodality (1808) medals, as well as Philadelphia's Truth Lovers Society pieces (1813), were hand engraved by silversmiths, but later versions were struck from dies. These and many other membership pieces were holed or looped so members could wear them pinned to their lapels.

One heavy issuer of membership tokens was the Fraternal Order of Freemasons. Starting in the mid-19th century and continuing to the present, some Masonic lodges have presented *mark pennies* to new members, who carried them as pocket pieces which could be produced as proof of membership when visiting other chapters. E.A. King cataloged nearly 10,000 varieties in his 1930 work, *Masonic Chapter Pennies*. Many were struck in copper, but examples are found in white metal, vulcanized rubber, aluminum, and even iron. Some bear portraits of George Washington, the country's most prominent Freemason, who was initiated into the order at Fredericksburg, Virginia, in 1752.[80] Many bear the name of the lodge and some symbol of the Masonic fraternity—such as a draftsman's compass, level, and square, or an uppercase letter G—and leave a blank space on the reverse for inscribing the member's dates of joining and taking the "craft degrees" (rankings which members could attain). Dated and inscribed tokens are more historically interesting than uninscribed ones, since they can be attributed to a particular era and owner.

Outside the membership medal category, Masonic medals were struck as souvenirs of building dedications, anniversaries, and special gatherings, and sold to raise funds for Masonic charities. Many rituals of Masonry involved the conferring of medals, orders, and decorations bearing arcane symbols comprehensible only to the initiated.[81] In the 1870s, well-known collector / medal-issuer Isaac F. Wood commissioned an array of Masonic-themed medals to be sold to collectors, making exonumia with Masonic content a very wide field for collectors.

America's numerous other fraternal orders struck chapter pennies and commemorative medals from time to time as well. Some of these groups printed only their initials on the tokens, such as I.O.O.F. for the International Order of Odd Fellows, or B.P.O.E. for the Benevolent Protective Order of Elks. Attributing these pieces might require a fraternal society reference list.[82] The initials K.K.K., which do appear on a number of authentic tokens, are readily recognizable as an abbreviation for the Ku Klux Klan.

Toward the end of the 19th century, the fashion for die-struck medals waned as many societies shifted to the presentation of jewelry-like orders, decorations, and pins, such as those outlined in *American Society Medals, An Identification Guide*, by Lee Bishop and J. Robert Elliott.

YEAR	GROUP	METAL	COMMENTARY	F	EF	MS-63
1746	Tuesday Club*	Bz	All known 1748 strikes in silver; this unique bronze from the Ford collection	—	—	$45,000
1763	Charlestown Social Club	Bz	Just two are known in private hands; this from the Ford collection	—	—	55,000
1795	Hasty Pudding Club	Silv	Medals of the Harvard group were awarded 1838–1924	—	$150	220

* Voted No. 80 in *100 Greatest American Medals and Tokens* (Jaeger/Bowers).

Fraternal, Incentive, and Membership Medals and Tokens 263

YEAR	GROUP	METAL	COMMENTARY	F	EF	MS-63
1818	Washington Market Chowder Club	Silv	Open-air market in Manhattan hosted members-only dining	—	$10,000	$12,000
1840	Hoboken Turtle Club	WM	Alexander Hamilton and Aaron Burr were members	—	275	300
1861	Pioneer Baseball Club**	Cop	Beloved early baseball relic—a sports collector's prize	—	400	700
1869	Odd Fellows	Sil	Souvenir of Odd Fellows' 50th anniversary	—	75	150
1880	Deadwood Commandery No. 1	Tin	Souvenir of South Dakota's first Knights Templar Masons	$50	75	150
1884	Grand Lodge Iowa A.F.&A.M.	Bz	Masonic lodge's grand masters portrayed on the obverse	—	15	30
1888	Pimlico Driving Club	Bz	Hosted trotter races among members and against other clubs	—	40	80

** Voted No. 84 in *100 Greatest American Medals and Tokens* (Jaeger/Bowers).

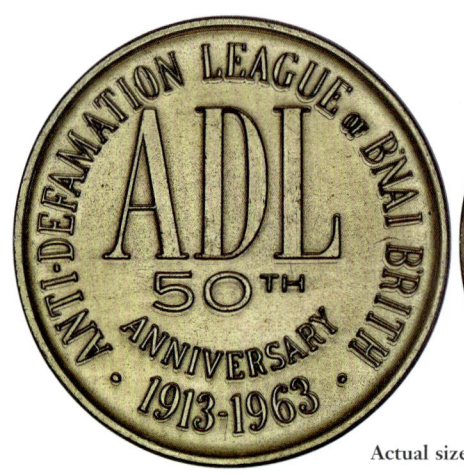
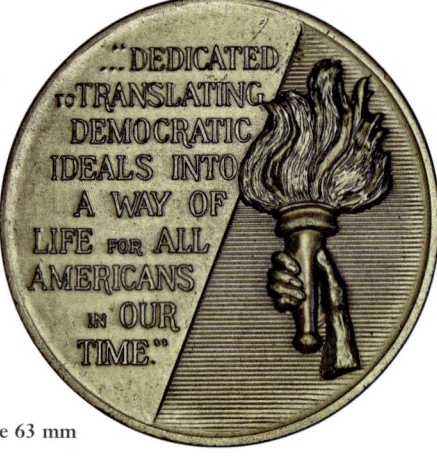

Actual size 63 mm

YEAR	GROUP	METAL	COMMENTARY	F	EF	MS-63
1892	Wolfeboro Arch Masons	Cop	The Arch Masons' calendar begins with the year 530 B.C.	$10	15	20
1963	Anti-Defamation League	Bz	50th-anniversary commemorative medal	15	25	—
1964	Token and Medal Society	Silv	National exonumia-loving group established in 1960	—	—	20

Actual size 63 mm

YEAR	GROUP	METAL	COMMENTARY	F	EF	MS-63
1965	Farthest North Coin Club	Bz	Coin-club membership pieces make a populous category	—	$10	$15
1972	Daughters of the American Revolution	Bz	DAR keepsake for the U.S. Bicentennial, by MACo	—	—	150
1974	American Numismatic Association	Bz	A handsome commemorative of National Coin Week	—	—	10

Actual size 63 mm

YEAR	GROUP	METAL	COMMENTARY	F	EF	MS-63
1978	American Numismatic Society	Silv	ANS member medals occasionally updated; this by F. Eliscu	—	—	$200
1987	Florida United Numismatists	Br	Issued for the 32nd annual FUN convention in Orlando	—	$2	3
1992	Macalester Lodge Masons	Bz	An anniversary collectible for a Minnesota Masonic chapter	—	4	8

Part VII
TOOLED AND ALTERED COINS

Everyone knows that coins are for spending, and numismatists know that coins are for collecting. From time to time since the 1850s, certain individuals have seen coins as blank canvases. They've picked up a sharp instrument, a punch, a hammer, or even a roller press, and gone to work. The resulting category of tooled and altered coins mixes the inherent numismatic interest of the host coin with the added dimension of whatever has been done to it.

Coins have been engraved by artisans into pocket-sized tokens of affection, shaped by prison inmates into tiny teapots, and carved by hoboes into works of folk art. They have had their reliefs pushed higher, their blank fields cut away, their designs enameled in color, and their symbolic elements altered from patriotic to bawdy themes. They have been counterstamped, encased, capped, and stickered by merchants looking for an advertising expedient, and they have been flattened, elongated, and pressed into entirely new designs, to be sold as souvenirs. Coins have been sectioned and fused together to have two heads, two tails, a cent's obverse with a dime's reverse, or a U.S. obverse with a Canadian reverse, among others. Half dollars and dollars have been hollowed out to create tiny hinged boxes, in which to conceal a lock of hair, a photograph, or a message.

Surprisingly, all of these activities are legal, in spite of U.S. Title 18, Section 331, which states, "Whoever fraudulently alters, defaces, mutilates, impairs, diminishes, falsifies, scales, or lightens any of the coins coined at the mints of the United States, or any foreign coins which are by law made current or are in actual use or circulation as money within the United States, shall be fined under this title or imprisoned not more than five years, or both."[83] This law, enacted in 1909, was strictly enforced at first, bringing an abrupt end to some of the above-described practices. The Treasury Department, however, has come to view the decree as hinging on its second word: *fraudulently*. Examples of fraudulent tampering are the ancient practice of shaving metal off the edges of gold coins, or the 1883 practice of making "racketeer nickels." (When the Mint issued a nickel design which did not bear the words FIVE CENTS on the reverse, but instead employed just a Roman numeral V, some miscreants plated gold on their nickels and passed them as $5 pieces.) Section 331 takes aim at these types of deceptions, but not at the creation of coin novelties. A few years ago, the U.S. Mint itself offered watches and other items made by hollowing out coins.

24
MERCHANT ADVERTISING ON COINS

Instead of ordering die-struck tokens like those described in chapter 1, some businesses used the cheaper method of hammering their hallmarks directly onto coins, and giving them out as change for regular transactions. Craftsmen such as smiths, jewelers, watchmakers, and makers of fancy goods used their own punches. Professionals such as surgeons, druggists, dentists, daguerrotypists, and financial brokers had punches specially made. Some proprietors of taverns, stores, and other businesses used individual letter punches to knock their names or initials, or names of products they hoped to sell, into coins. Early in the 20th century, as factory-made goods overtook handmade goods, countermarks on coins dwindled away, and encasements, caps, and ultimately, stickers took their place in coin advertising. Encased and stickered coins are still being made in the 21st century.

COUNTERMARKED COINS

Hallmarks found on U.S. coins, British halfpennies, French centimes, and Spanish *reales* give an added dimension to the material culture of a particular craftsman, by demonstrating the variety of tender he handled in his everyday commerce, and examples can be found from as early as the 1780s. Countermarked coins make interesting "go-withs" for collectors of the products of gunsmiths, silversmiths, swordsmiths, watchmakers, toolmakers, and the like. To collectors of countermarked coins, however, the craftsman's guns, silverware, etc., are considered the go-withs!

One factor important to the cost of countermarked coins is how the marks were made. Single punches of full-name or monogram hallmarks, and punches producing raised lettering on an incuse punched field, impart more value than individual incuse letter punches spelling out the name or initials of the issuer. The latter are harder to attribute to an issuer and location, and they are easier to forge. A second important price factor is by whom the countermarks were made. Marked coins attributable to a known and documented craftsman, professional, merchant, or proprietor are worth more than mavericks (those not so identified), and those made by a famous artisan have additional value added. For example, common coins punched with the EB hallmark of goldsmith Ephraim Brasher, author of the famous Brasher doubloons, fetch five-digit figures.[84]

The condition of the underlying coin is not terribly important to value, since makers often selected circulated coins from their pockets or coin boxes for marking. However, the face value, date, rarity, and provenance of the host coin do matter. Specimens of prolific countermarker James L. Polhemus, a druggist of Sacramento, California, are available in many denominations. Polhemus's stamp on a Liberty Seated silver dime of the 1850s might sell for $150 to $200 in Very Fine condition, but his mark on a $20 gold piece of the 1850s, salvaged from the wreck of the USS *Central America*, fetched $48,300.[85] The most current and comprehensive reference for U.S. countermarked coins is Gregory Brunk's 2003 compilation, *Merchant and Privately Countermarked Coins: Advertising on the World's Smallest Billboards*.

COUNTERMARKED COINS *(continued)*

ISSUER	DATE	HOST COIN	COMMENTARY	F	EF	MS-63
Sachem Oyster Saloon, N.Y.C.	1775	1 real, Charles III	A meeting place for Tammany politicians	$300	$600	—
Gibbs Tiffany & Co., Mass.	1800	Large cent	Sturbridge pistol maker in business 1820–1850	600	800	—
Planters Bank, New Orleans*	1812–15	1/4-slice, 8 reales	Value of 2 reales assured by bank stamp	2,500	5,000	—
J. Martine, North Carolina	1831	Half Dollar	Fayetteville pewterer, 1826–1836	7,000	9,000	—
Dr. G.G. Wilkins, Pittsfield, N.H.	1838	Large cent	Dentist marked 100,000-plus coins, 1857–1876	25	45	—
J. Sidney Miller, Artist, N.H.	1840	Kopeck	Daguerrotypist of Nashua in the 1850s	350	500	—
Shattuck's Water Cure, Maine	1850s	Canada Bank token	Waterford doc cured ladies' ills with cold water	250	400	—
G.G.G. & G.G.G.G., Exeter, N.H.	1851	Large Cent	Goodwin's Grand Greasejuice; Glittering Globules	40	80	—
Moses Hale, ambrotypist	1853	Trime	Hale's studio was in Ellsworth, Maine	—	600	—
Dr. Kidder's Family Pills	1854	Liberty Seated quarter	Dispensing patent medicines in Boston and Lowell	—	500	—
J.L. Polhemus, Sacramento**	1856	Liberty Seated dime	Rulau lists 84 different host coins; many more exist	200	40,000	—
J.B. Schiller, liquor importer	1860	Indian Head cent	Cent marked as dime for the siege of New Orleans	2,300	3,500	$5,500
O.P. Shattuck, Worcester, Mass.	1871	Canada 50 cent	Cigar maker of 1870s, not the Maine physician	—	500	700
D. Maxwell & Son, harness maker	1875	Liberty Seated quarter	West Winsted, Conn., firm thrived through 1890s	500	650	—

* Voted No. 40 in *100 Greatest American Medals and Tokens* (Jaeger/Bowers).
** Voted No. 77 in *100 Greatest American Medals and Tokens*. The counterstamp appears on an incredible variety of host coins. The high figure is for a counterstamped $20 gold coin recovered from the wreck of the SS *Central America*.

Encased Coins

The first U.S. encased coins, or coins socketed into a surrounding metal holder, probably were Indian Head cents of 1901, followed by Lincoln cents in 1909. These early encasements bore merchant advertising, and served the same purposes as merchant tokens. Pre-1901 coins have been encased too, but the practice itself is a 20th-century one. Cents were the most commonly encased denomination, although encased dimes, nickels, quarters, silver dollars, tokens, and even gold coins have been encountered. Some had "good for" values higher than the denomination of the encased coin, such as a cent being good for 5¢ in trade, or 20% off a purchase. Others had no value in trade, but were meant to be kept as souvenirs or good-luck pieces (many featured good luck symbols such as horseshoes, clover leafs, and ancient swastikas).

The metal shortages of World War II interrupted the use of encasements, which resumed in the 1950s with door-to-door distribution by new producers.[86] Their popularity as an advertising novelty gradually waned, but today a few individuals, clubs, and fraternal groups still order them as souvenirs.

Attaching the encasement was accomplished in a coin press, and did some damage to the host coin. Blank ring planchets of aluminum, brass, nickel, copper, or other base metal had central holes sized to accommodate a particular coin, and operation of the press simultaneously struck the advertising designs onto the encasement and forced its adherence to the coin. This could create a slight flattening of design on the coin, especially around its edges. In their 1992 compendium *Tokens and Medals*, Alpert and Elman give some numismatic pointers for encased varieties:

> Over the years, coin collectors have knocked or punched out many coins from their holders because of high-grade condition or rare dates. Sometimes a different coin was put back into the encasement. A switched coin can be spotted by looking for one or more of these tell-tale features: 1) the coin is rotated and not upright relative to the legends on either side of the holder; 2) the coin is much more worn than the holder; 3) the coin is not lying flat, but is slightly tilted; 4) there is evidence of damage on the edge of the coin or on the holder around the coin; 5) when held up to the light, some light comes through between the coin and the holder; 6) the coin pops out easily with slight pressure; 7) a coin of more recent date is in an apparently old-style encasement.

ISSUER	DATE	HOST COIN	COMMENTARY	F	EF	MS-63
Loftis Bros. & Co. Jewelers, Chicago	1901	Indian Head cent	Earliest cents to be encased bring a premium	$15	$40	$125
Underwood Pumps, Philadelphia	1901	Indian Head cent	Encasements came in a number of stock shapes	15	40	125

ENCASED COINS *(continued)*

ISSUER	DATE	HOST COIN	COMMENTARY	F	EF	MS-63
Poli's Theatres (nationwide)	1905	Indian Head cent	A pocket piece kept the business' name in mind	$15	$40	$100
Majestic Saloon, Las Cruces, N.M.	1905	Indian Head cent	Drinking-cup shape on a saloon good-for	500	1,250	—
Lewis & Clark Exposition, Portland, Ore.	1905	Indian Head cent	Souvenir encasement bearing painful puns	15	35	100
Larranaga Cigars (nationwide)	1906	Indian Head cent	Handmade Cuban cigars still sold today	15	40	100
Bob Harper's, San Angelo, Texas	1910	Lincoln cent	Many special-shape encasements were patented	200	500	1,500
Baltimore & Ohio Railroad	1933	Lincoln cent	Souvenir of the Century of Progress Exposition	2	5	15
Big Rock Candy Mountain, Utah	1955D	Lincoln cent	A lucky pocket piece, good for show-and-tell	—	2	12
Earl Fankhauser, Fort Wayne, Ind.	1958D	Lincoln cent	The man who revived the encasement after WWII	—	2	4

Encased Coins *(continued)*

ISSUER	DATE	HOST COIN	COMMENTARY	F	EF	MS-63
American Numismatic Association	2007	Wisc. state quarter	Souvenir of 2007 World's Fair of Money, Milwaukee	—	—	$3
Florida United Numismatists	2008	Jefferson nickel	Souvenir of the 2008 FUN show, Orlando	—	—	3

Capped Coins

Capped coins, most of which date between 1930 and 1980, were made on the same principle as encased coins, except the advertising was borne on a metallic shell or "cap" covering one whole side of the coin. Some even employed bottle caps as the shell, with the crimped edges tightly sealed to the coin—as a simple way to advertise soda and beer. (The examples shown here are not advertising caps, but historical commemorative pieces from a collectible series of eight different subjects made by the Tatum Stamp and Coin Co. of Springfield, Massachusetts.) Other 1930s cents bear the obverse legend MERRY CHRISTMAS and show Santa Claus at a chimney. Cents of the 1960s and 1970s were capped to promote the virtues of Zippo lighters. These scarce items are more likely to be collected as representatives of modified-coin novelties, rather than as a separate line.

ISSUER	DATE	HOST COIN	COMMENTARY	F	EF	MS-63
Unknown	1934	Lincoln Head cent	Commemorating Byrd's second Antarctic journey	$15	$35	—
Unknown	1934	Lincoln Head cent	The Lindberg baby kidnapping trial location	15	35	—

Stickered Coins

An easy way for a business to put its name into circulation was by placing a printed advertising sticker on a coin. In the 1930s, there was a craze for stickering silver dollars, and since then stickers have been placed on almost every coin denomination. The practice is catching on again in the 21st century, and the coin most frequently stickered today is the quarter. In this category, the numismatic interest of the underlying coin does have an impact on price. Over the years, the quantities of stickered coins encountered, in declining order, has been: dollars, cents, quarters, nickels, and dimes.[87] A 200-page guide to the subject, *Stickered Coins*, was written by Duane Feisel in 2003.

ISSUER	DATE	HOST COIN	COMMENTARY	F	EF	MS-63
McClintock's, Neosho, Mo.	1920s	Peace dollar	A supermarket "good-for" paid out in change	$17	$25	$35
Buck's, Guerneville, Calif.	1921	Morgan dollar	Souvenir of a wine-country steakhouse	17	25	35
Kau-Kau Korner, Honolulu, Hawaii	1921	Peace dollar	Early drive-in restaurant, open from 1935 to 1960	20	30	45
Butter Krust Bakery, Sunbury, Penn.	1921	Morgan dollar	1930s payroll piece, from the dawn of sliced bread	15	25	35
Arvada Stationery, Arvada, Colo.	1923	Peace dollar	Print-shop payroll piece from "Olde Town" Arvada	15	25	35
Club Homestead, Ketchikan, Alaska	1925	Peace dollar	Ephemeral reminder of a defunct Alaskan grill	25	50	75

25
CARVED COINS

The products of coin carvers, while criticized by some as "post-Mint damage" or defacement, offer the historian a unique window to America's past. Coin carving was first seen in the United States on the Liberty Seated coinage inaugurated in the late 1830s. The alterations probably did not begin until the 1850s, when some prankster took silver half dimes, dimes, quarters, half dollars, dollars, and trade dollars, carved away Miss Liberty's clothes, and fashioned her rocky perch into a chamber pot. Collectors of Liberty Seated coinage, in particular, enjoy occasionally acquiring one of these "potty liberties," just for fun. In the 20th century, the Buffalo nickel became the prime target of the coin carvers.

YEAR	ARTIST	HOST COIN	COMMENTARY	F	EF	MS-63
1876	Unk	Seated Liberty quarter	The lady can be found stripped on all Seated Liberty denominations	$125	$200	—
1878	Unk	Trade dollar	Quantities suggest these were popular; some were quite pornographic	200	300	—

HOBO NICKELS

The word *hobo* derives from the 19th-century term *hoe boy*, describing an itinerant farm worker who carried his belongings inside a bundle of fabric tied to his hoe. The term *hobo nickel*, describing the folk art of coin carving, honors certain hoboes who practiced it on Buffalo nickels in the 1910s through the 1940s.

The Buffalo nickel, designed by sculptor James Earle Fraser, debuted in 1913. According to Stephen Alpert, in his 2005 work *Hobo Nickel Guidebook*, the Indian Head bust on this coin was a natural for carvers to alter, because of its large size relative to the size of the coin. Even though the tough copper-nickel alloy was hard to work (especially with a pocket knife), the bust afforded plenty of room to add details such as hats, beards, amusing hairstyles, enlarged noses, and the like, and the buffalo on the reverse could readily be altered into another animal or anything else an imaginative carver could think of. The best-known early hobo carvers were Bertram Wiegand and his protégé, George Washington Hughes, known to today's collectors by their respective signatures: "Bert" and "Bo." Between 1913 and 1980, Bert, Bo, and other artists created somewhere around 100,000 "classic" hobo nickels. The 1913 date is the most prevalent. New carvings are still being made today, and already these outnumber the classic group. Some are close copies of famous classic pieces.[88] It can be a challenge to identify the origin of a particular carving.

Alpert separates them into three eras: classic, from 1913 to 1940; later classic, from 1941 to 1981; and modern, from 1982 to the present. (The year 1982, when Del Romines published the first catalog of classic pieces, *Hobo Nickels*, made a logical delineation.)

Classic hobo nickels generally had hat, hair, and feature alterations on the Indian bust, and if the reverse was carved, it was often to alter the buffalo into some other animal. Modern carvers have changed the Indian head into everything from a witch to a cartoon character, celebrity, president, or sports figure. They have broadened their art to include other coins, and some have used powered instruments to decrease the amount of time necessary to create a carving (classic nickels took days or weeks to complete).

Collectors grade the quality of the artwork with designations ranging from *crude*, for works done by amateurs, to *superior*, for the output of the most talented. Works by Bert or Bo will bring the highest prices, especially if they have initialed their carvings. According to Alpert, modern carvings of superior grade, such as those of Ron Landis of Arkansas, sell for about the same as classic nickels of the same grade by unknown artists. Coins carved on both sides fetch better prices than those with only one worked side, and those bearing just scratched-on grafitti or doodles have no value. There is a lot to know about this fascinating category, and anyone planning to specialize would benefit from joining the Original Hobo Nickel Society, located on the Web at hobonickels.org.

YEAR	ARTIST	COMMENTARY	SUPERIOR
1913	Bo	A hobo appearing on a hobo nickel—particularly desirable	$1,093
1913	Unk	Designs on both sides enhance the value. Derbies and beards are popular	1,000
1915	Unk	Lampooning "Little Eva," a suffragette statue at the Panama-Pacific Exposition	2,000+
1919	Bo	Said to be a portrait of Bo's brother, a World War I soldier	1,380
1936	Bo	The flower dangling from this clown's hat adds charm and value	1,265
1937	Bert	Letters deducted from LIBERTY reveal the artist's signature	1,840
1937	Bo	Said to be the artist's self-portrait	1,093
1937	Bo	No hat, no beard, and eyeglasses set this design apart	1,265
1938	Unk	The poignant inscription bespeaks the wayfarer's lifestyle	2,530
1948	Bo	Homage to a generation's sports hero, carved in cupronickel	1,840
1950	Bo	Emmett Kelly, the legendary clown; initialed and dated by the artist	2,763

Note: Specimens and prices shown here come from a 2003 Bowers & Merena sale of the Bill Fivaz collection, except for the "Little Eva" specimen, which sold privately.

26

ELONGATED COINS

Chicago's 1892–1893 World's Columbian Exposition saw the debut of many innovations, but few have maintained their popularity as long as the *penny machine*, a hand-operated roller press for converting pennies into souvenirs. The process is simple: feed a cent into a slot and turn a crank. As the coin is forced between the rollers under enormous pressure, it is simultaneously thinned, elongated, and impressed with a new design. One side remains smooth and flat, often with a ghost of the underlying design remaining visible.

The Columbian expo offered four different designs from machines stationed around the grounds. Since then, penny machines have been produced nearly continuously, and today, at amusement parks, museums, landmarks, famous restaurants, and myriad other public places around the world, multiple thousands of elongated designs are being produced. Designs on a machine's roller dies can be updated at any time, like the ones at New York's Empire State Building, which imprint a new year date each January.

Obtaining elongateds is easy and inexpensive. A collector encounters a new machine, rolls one coin for his/her own collection, and than makes a number of duplicates for trading with other collectors. The price of a single pressing operation is typically 50¢ to $1. Machines that press pennies are the most common, but models exist for pressing dimes, nickels, and quarters as well. (Using the wrong coin will result in a jam—don't do it.)

As always in collecting, the earlier the piece and the more historically interesting its place of origin, the higher its value (assuming good condition). Elongated pieces that reveal the date and mintmark of the underlying coin may have added value. The most recent reference by Angelo A. Rosato, *Encyclopedia of the Modern Elongateds* (1990), runs to 1,700 pages, giving an idea of the size of this entertaining series. *Yesterday's Elongateds* by Lee Martin and Dottie Dow focuses on the earlier pieces. The Elongated Collectors may be found on the Web at tecnews.org.

MACHINE LOCATION	DATE	HOST COIN	COMMENTARY	F	EF	MS-63
World's Columbian Exposition, Chicago	—	Small cent	The Cairo Street machine is the rarest	—	$1,000	—
World's Columbian Exposition, Chicago	—	Three-cent piece	Chicago machines could press any size coin	—	75	—
World's Columbian Exposition, Chicago	—	Canada five-cent piece	World visitors happily smashed their pocket change	—	300	—
World's Columbian Exposition, Chicago	1834	Silver quarter	This coin was 60 years old when smashed	—	300	—

Elongated Coins 277

MACHINE LOCATION	DATE	HOST COIN	COMMENTARY	F	EF	MS-63
World's Columbian Exposition, Chicago	1883	Hawaii half dollar	The specialist has many Columbian issues to pursue	—	$350	—
Pan-American Exposition, Buffalo, N.Y.	1901	Small cent	Two varieties; this is the "Buffalo head under AM"	$10	12	$15
Louisiana Purchase Exposition, St. Louis	1904	Indian Head cent	"On the pike" were stationed two machines	—	150	400
Louisiana Purchase Exposition, St. Louis	1904	Indian Head cent	Cents from this machine are by far the rarest	—	4,000	—
The Alamo, San Antonio	—	Lincoln cent	To preserve the date, ensure it faces the smooth roller	1	1	1
Permian Basin Petroleum Museum, Midland, Texas	—	Small cent	Texas oil struck 1901; oil museum opened 1975	1	1	1
Rose Festival, Portland, Ore.	—	Small cent	Famous festival held annualy since 1907	1	2	3
Toilet City Coin Club	1973	Lincoln cent	Individuals and clubs find these irresistible	1	1	1
The Elongated Collectors Club	2006	Lincoln cent	Of course this club hopes you'll take home a flatty	1	1	1
Times Square, New York City	2006	Lincoln cent	From author's visit with daughter and friend	1	1	1

27

LOVE TOKENS AND OTHER ENGRAVED COINS

When it comes to love tokens and other engraved coins, the concept of rarity takes on new meaning. Every one is unique! Talented artists took coins, smoothed their relief surfaces away, then polished and hand-engraved them with any monogram, name, statement, or pictorial scene specified by the buyer—for presentation as a gift to a loved one. Originating in late-18th-century England, love tokens first appeared on U.S. coins in the 1820s (the 1787 Nova Eborac engraving seen here, from the American Numismatic Society collection, was likely made in England). They reached the height of their popularity in the Victorian era, from the late 1860s to the late 1890s, and were produced at the shops of engravers and jewelers as well as at exposition engraving booths (while the purchaser roamed the exhibits). The majority of love tokens went to women, who hung them from charm bracelets or neck chains or pinned them on as brooches. For men, they took the form of watch fobs, cufflinks, and buttons. Therefore, many are holed or looped, have a pinback, or show traces of old solder from where a mounting has been removed.

Engravings made for people of average budget were most commonly done on Liberty Seated silver dimes, though some were fashioned from bronze two-cent and silver or copper-nickel three-cent pieces. Wealthier buyers could order works on gold coins, sometimes studded with jewels, or having carefully enameled design elements. Often it was the reverse of the coin that was smoothed away, leaving the obverse intact to indicate the year in which the gift was made. In other instances, a date was engraved as part of the design. To today's collector, pictorial pieces are the most desirable, though monogram designs having elaborate, ornate lettering are far more common.

Lloyd L. Entenmann penned the most recent reference, *Love Tokens as Engraved Coins*, in 1991. The international collectors' organization is the Love Token Society (located on the Web at geocities.com/lovetokenwebsite), which publishes the bimonthly journal, *Love Letter*. Members of this group collect only hand-engraved pieces, considering machine-made pieces to fall outside the genuine love-token category.

SUBJECT / PURPOSE	HOST COIN	COMMENTARY	F	EF	MS-63
Initial H / Jewelry piece	1787 Nova Eborac, facing right	An experienced engraver created this ornate charm	—	—	—
Louise and JJ / Jewelry charm	Liberty Seated dime	The initials of the giver make up the reverse design	$10	$20	$30
JHJ monogram	Indian Princess Head gold dollar	Difficult to carve on a tiny 15 mm coin	—	50	—
LG monogram	Indian Princess Head gold dollar	The addition of a loop creates a pendant	—	50	—

Love Tokens and Other Engraved Coins 279

SUBJECT / PURPOSE	HOST COIN	COMMENTARY	F	EF	MS-63
E. Knipe / Recognition	1859 Seated Liberty dollar	Recognition of service, presented with muster-out pay	—	$5,000	—
Roberts / Surrender medal	Mexico 8 Real	A proud Tennesseean's 1865 memento of service	—	5,000	—
Grandpa and Charles / Gift	1877 Trade dollar	A silver dollar became a birthday memento in 1907	—	200	—
Remember Me	1882 Morgan dollar	A pinback made this sentiment wearable	$50	100	—
For Louis' sister	1889 Morgan dollar	Elaborate bimetal twig-form design soldered to surface	50	200	—

SUBJECT / PURPOSE	HOST COIN	COMMENTARY	F	EF	MS-63
Bimetallic monogram	1893 Columbian half dollar	A beautiful souvenir of the World's Columbian Exposition	$25	$90	—
Atlanteans 1894	1893 Barber dime	Souvenir of an early New Orleans Mardi Gras krewe	20	75	—
Map of western hemisphere	1907 Liberty Head nickel	After being smoothed and engraved, it was plated in gold	25	125	—
1939 friendship gift	1899-O Morgan dollar	A keepsake with a welded-on dedication	30	70	—

28

CUT-OUT, ENAMELED, AND POP-OUT COINS

Coins have been cut, enameled, and otherwise altered for a variety of reasons. These processes turn a normal federal coin into a lucky pocket piece, a presentation piece or charm, a souvenir, or a memento. Enameled, cut-out, and pop-out coins are collected by exonumists with an eye for the unusual and historical.

Enameled Coins

The art of cloisonné enameling on metal, developed in the ancient near East and perfected in China and in Turkey during the Byzantine era, has, since Victorian times, been used to turn coins into novelty jewelry. (This art achieved a high degree of sophistication in England and France.) In the process, the blank fields and areas surrounding the relief design and lettering were deepened with a sharp tool. This turned the raised design into partitions between which various colors of powdered glass could be poured. A brief heat treatment in a kiln converted the powder to liquid enamel that hardened upon cooling. In the later-20th century, liquid enamel paints were baked on to add color to a coin design. (For examples of the use of colored enameling on modern medals, see the challenge coins in chapter 23.) In the case of the "colorized" 2001 Kentucky quarter shown below, a thin polymer sheet bearing a computer-printed design was applied to the entire obverse of the coin.

SUBJECT / PURPOSE	HOST COIN	COMMENTARY	EF OR BETTER
Jewelry charm	1878 Liberty Seated quarter	Deep-blue enameling carefully applied, then baked on	$250
A fun collectible	2001 Kentucky state quarter	Preprinted polymer sheet, baked on	5

Cut-Out Coins

The process here was simple: the artisan used a tiny jeweler's drill and saw to cut away a coin's blank fields. Without provenance data, these items have value only as novelties—because no matter what the date of the subject coin, it may be difficult to determine the era of the cutting.

Cut-Out Coins *(continued)*

SUBJECT / PURPOSE	HOST COIN	COMMENTARY	F	EF	MS-63
Pocket piece	1893 Columbian half dollar	A simple trick enhances an already interesting design	$50	$75	—
Helen / Presentation piece	1909 Mexican peso	Combining the arts of coin cutting and love-token engraving	50	75	—
Bicentennial pendant	1976 Bicentennial quarter	A wearable souvenir of the nation's anniversary	25	30	—
Liberty pendant	Walking Liberty half dollar	Adolph Weinman's beautiful design becomes jewelry	25	30	—

Pop-Out Coins

Pop-out coins or "pops" got their name from the way the featured design appears to burst through the flat plane of the original coin. Some even show the edges of the popped portrait as torn or fractured paper. The earliest pops seen by this author date to 1903 and were patented in June of that year by William A. Malliet of Hackensack, New Jersey.

In some cases, such as for the Indian Head cents seen below, the designs were amplifications of the original central device of the coin's obverse. In others, a completely unrelated design was added, as when Woodrow Wilson's face popped through Miss Liberty's on a Barber dime, or George Washington's protruded through Lincoln's on a Wheat cent. Malliet fashioned pop-outs by making a pair of coining dies on which the intended central device (a face, as seen below, or a moose) was thrown into very high relief. Since it was desirable to retain the host coin's date, border, and rim designs, the coin could not be impressed (as a planchet) between these dies. Only the facial portion to be applied to the host coin was struck in this manner. Then, the artisan cut away the head portion on the coin's obverse, leaving a head-shaped hole, and soldered the new, high-relief face into place. The Newark Museum of New Jersey has a watch-fob specimen, signed and dated 1904 by Malliet, that consists of "altered U.S. coins showing three assassinated presidents" (namely, Lincoln, Garfield, and McKinley).

According to Q. David Bowers, new pop-out coins were being made well into the 1950s. He remembers New York City dealer Louis S. Werner owned a Liberty Head die, and favored placing Miss Liberty on Barber coins. He also made Santa Claus pops on Lincoln cents, and sold these types and others at coin shows—sometimes in wholesale quantities. Early Indian Head pops have a tiny bar applied on the reverse bearing a patent date of August 11, 1903. Some Liberty Head pops (on Barber halves) are seen with a patent date of November 22, 1904. Buyer beware—as with all altered coins, the date on the coin is not necessarily the date of manufacture.

The fledgling collector organization for this category can be contacted by email at pop-up-coins@yahoo.com.

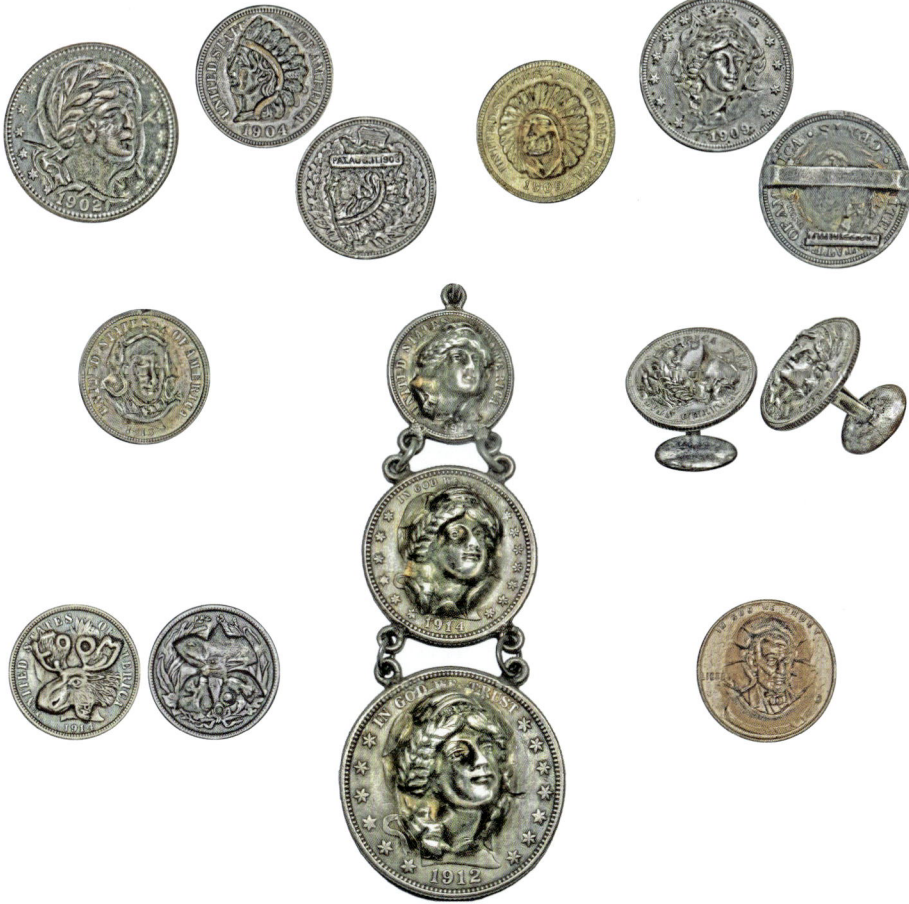

SUBJECT / PURPOSE	HOST COIN	COMMENTARY	F	EF	MS-63
Profile of pretty woman	1902 Barber quarter	The background arranged to look as if she's popped through	$30	$40	—
Indian Head pocket piece	1904 Indian Head cent	After the relief was applied, the piece was silvered	30	40	—
Indian Head stickpin	1909 Indian Head cent	Nice frontal portrait; gilded after popping	30	40	—
Lady Liberty	1909 Liberty Head nickel with cents	Popular design found in several sizes as jewelry	30	40	—
Wilson portrait	1913 Barber dime	Woodrow Wilson honored in the first year of his presidency	50	65	—
Moose FOOM	1914 Barber dime	Featuring a scary version of the brotherhood's mascot	60	70	—
Liberty trio	1912, 1913, 1914 Barber coins	Three dates and three denominations made a nice necklace	75	90	—
Pair of cufflinks	1916 Barber dimes	A perfect adornment for the coin collector's sleeves	50	65	—
Abraham Lincoln	1930 Lincoln cent	With the president no longer in profile view	—	15	—

BIBLIOGRAPHY

"A Brief History of the Counter," *TAMS Journal*, Vol. 12, No. 6, Part II, December 1972.

"About the APS: Background," Web site of the American Philosophical Society, http://www.amphilsoc.org.

Alpert, Stephen, "A History of Hobo Nickels," on Original Hobo Nickel Society Web site, http://www.hobonickels.org, 2003.

Alpert, Stephen, and Lawrence Elman, *Tokens and Medals, A Guide to the Identification and Values of United States Exonumia*, 1992.

American Numismatic Association, *The Dictionary of Numismatic Terms*, 1975.

Andes, Charles, interview, September 20, 2005.

Annaloro, Victor, "DeWitt Clinton's Big Ditch," *Numismatist*, January 2005.

Aqua, Herman M., *Pennsylvania Merchant Tokens*, Michigan Exonumia Publishers, Tecumseh, Michigan, 2000.

"The Art of Sinking Dies: A Talk With One of the Oldest New York Medallists," *New York Sun*, August 16, 1885, p. 10, col. 7.

Athearn, Robert, Ed., *American Heritage Illustrated History of the United States*, 1988.

Baldwin, Agnes, *Catalogue of the International Exhibition of Contemporary Medals of March 1910*, American Numismatic Society, New York, 1911.

Baxter, Barbara, *The Beaux-Arts Medal in America*, ANS, 1987.

Bishop, Lee and J. Robert Elliott, *American Society Medals, An Identification Guide*, 1998.

Bowers, Q. David, *American Numismatics Before the Civil War, 1760–1860*, 1998.

Bowers, Q. David, *A Tune for a Token*, 1975.

Bowers, Q. David, *Expert's Guide to Collecting and Investing in Rare Coins*, Whitman Publishing, 2005.

Bowers, Q. David, "Two Coins in One: Large Cents With Interesting Counterstamps," in *The Token: America's Other Money*, Richard Doty, ed., ANS COAC, 1994.

Bressett, Kenneth, ed., *A Guide Book of United States Coins*, 59th ed., 2005, and 60th ed., 2006.

Brouwer, Norman, "The Birth, Death and Rebirth of New York's Ferries," in *Seaport, New York's History Magazine*, Spring/Summer 2003.

"Charter of the Life Saving Benevolent Association of New York: Premiums Awarded, List of Managers, Donors, and Correspondence," New York, 1853.

Coffee, John M., Jr., *The Atwood-Coffee Catalogue of United States and Canadian Transportation Tokens, Fourth Edition, Volume Two, History and Encyclopedia of Transportation Tokens*, American Vecturist Association, Boston, 1984.

Cuhaj, George S., "Early Transportation Tokens and Tickets of New York City," in *The Token: America's Other Money*, Richard Doty, ed., ANS COAC, 1994.

Daub, Eugene, telephone interview, July 13, 2005.

DeWitt, J. Doyle, and Edmund B. Sullivan, *American Political Badges and Medalets, 1789–1892*, 1981.

D'Urso, Tony, "Andrew Jackson and the Bank War," in *From Revolution to Reconstruction*, University of Groningen, The Netherlands, http://www.odur.let.rug.nl/~usa/H/index.

Elder, Thomas L., "Display of Temperance Tokens" *New York Numismatic Club Yearbook, 1918–1921*, July 1919, pp. 60–64.

Gibbs, William T., "Collecting Encased Coins," *Coin World*, February 3, 2004.

Frudakis, EvAngelos, telephone interview, July 19, 2005.

Fuld, George J., "New Franklin Medal by St. Gaudens," *TAMS Journal*, March–April 1966, p. 39.

Fuld, George J., "U.S. Civil War Tokens," in *The Token: America's Other Money*, Richard Doty, ed., ANS COAC, 1994.

Fuld, George and Melvin, "Medallic Memorials to Franklin," *The Numismatist*, December 1956, pp. 1, 393.

Giedroyc, Richard, "Collecting Mardi Gras Medals," Web site of Professional Coin Grading Service, http://www.pcgs.com.

Golway, Terry, "Firefighters," *American Heritage*, December 2005, pp. 43–49.

Harkness, Andrew, "New York State Agricultural Society Award Medals," *TAMS Journal*, June 1987, pp. 88–91.

Hartzog, Richard, Web site, http://www.exonumia.com.

Harkness, Andrew, "The American Institute, Catalyst for American Greatness," *TAMS Journal*, August 1989, pp. 123–135.

Hibler, Harold, and Charles Kappen, *So-Called Dollars*, Coin & Currency Institute, New York, 1963 (2nd edition published 2008).

"History of Doubloons in Carnival," http://www.mardigrasdigest.com.

Homren, Wayne K., "Masonic Chapter Pennies," E-Sylum: Volume 8, Number 23, June 5, 2005.

Homren, Wayne K., "John Gault and J.C. Ayer: Encased Postage Stamp Maker and His Largest Client," in *The Token: America's Other Money*, Richard Doty, ed., ANS COAC, 1994.

Jackson, Kenneth T., *The Encyclopedia of New York City*, Yale University Press, 1995.

Jaeger, Katherine, and Q. David Bowers, *100 Greatest American Medals and Tokens*, Whitman Publishing, 2007.

Johnson, D. Wayne, "America's First Private Art Medal Series Grew Out of 1909 Lincoln Birth Centennial," *Johnson & Jensen Specialized Report*, September 1977.

Johnson, D. Wayne, "Series and Sets of American Medals, An Introduction," Web site of the Medal Collectors of America.

Julian, R.W., *Medals of the U.S. Mint, 1792–1892*, TAMS, 1977.

Kass, Murray, "Johnson Tells How Pantograph Aided in Minting Coins," *Heritage Villager*, July 17, 1992, Torrington, CT.

King, Robert P., *Lincoln in Numismatics*, reprinted by TAMS, 1966.

Krause, Chester, *Guidebook of Franklin Mint Issues*, 1981 edition.

Kuznick, Peter J., "Losing the World of Tomorrow: The Battle Over the Presentation of Science at the 1939 New York World's Fair," http://xroads.virginia.edu.

Laws, Rita, "St. Christopher: Collecting the Medals of the Man and the Myth," *Coin World*, December 26, 2005.

Leonard, Robert, Jr., "Collecting U.S. Tokens: Challenges and Rewards," in *Perspectives in Numismatics*, Chicago Coin Club, 1986.

Levine, Joseph, *Collectors Guide to Presidential Inaugural Medals and Memorabilia*, 1980.

Levine, Joseph, Catalogs, *The Charles McSorley Collection of 19th Century Political Campaign Tokens, Parts I and II*, 1997 and 1998, and *Exonumia Auction 74*, 2005.

Life Saving Benevolent Association of New York, "Annual Report 2004: Report of Committee on Donations and Awards for the Year 2003."

Lindesmith, Robert, "Medals of U.S. Agricultural Associations, Institutes, and Societies," *TAMS Journal*, February 1969, pp. 2–11.

Loubat, J.F., *The Medallic History of the United States of America, 1776–1876*, 1878. Reprinted by Flayderman, New Milford, Connecticut, 1967.

"Louisburg Memorial Medal," *New York Times*, June 16, 1895.

Luftschein, Susan, "Charles De Kay and the Circle of Friends of the Medallion: Aesthetic Taste in America," in *The Medal in America*, vol. 2, ANS COAC, 1997.

Luftschein, Susan, *One Hundred Years of American Medallic Art, 1845–1945, The John E. Marqusee Collection*, Herbert F. Johnson Museum of Art, Cornell University, Ithaca, New York.

King, Robert P., *Lincoln in Numismatics*, TAMS reprint of 1920s *Numismatist* articles, 1966.

MacNeil, Neil, *The President's Medal: 1789–1977*, Smithsonian Institution, 1977.

"Massachusetts Humane Society," on the Web site of the Hull Lifesaving Museum, Boston Harbor Heritage, http://www.lifesavingmuseum.org.

McSorley, Charles, "An Interesting Discovery," *The Political Collector*, September 1979.

"Medals and Tokens of Hayes and Tilden, Series by George H. Lovett," pp. 21–30. *New York Numismatic Club Year Book*, 1917.

"Medals Day at the Franklin Institute," *Science*, May 5, 1944, p. 367.

Mueller, Bob, "Paul Manship's Medallic Mythology" in *The Medal in America*, vol. 2, ANS COAC, 1997.

Mullins, Emily, "Be My Valentine: Love Tokens Once Expressions of Affection, Now Sought-After Collectibles," *Coin World*, February 13, 2006.

Mullins, Emily, "All the World's a Stage: Yankee Robinson Tokens Reflect the Great Entertainer and Entrepreneur," *Coin World*, November 28, 2005.

Newman, Eric P., "The Promotion and Suppression of Hard Times Tokens," in *The Token: America's Other Money*, Richard Doty, ed., ANS COAC, 1994.

New-York Historical Society: American Institute Manuscript Collection: Record Books for Medal Engravings, 1851–1892.

New-York Historical Society: "Historical Note to the Records of the American Institute of the City of New York for the Encouragement of Science and Invention, 1828–1983," www.nyhistory.org.

Noble, Dennis L., "A Legacy: The United States Life-Saving Service," U.S. Coast Guard Web site, http://www.uscg.mil/history/h_USLSS.html.

"Our Firemen: The History of the New York Fire Departments," Chapter 52, Part XII, on http://www.usgennet.com.

Prucha, Francis Paul, *Indian Peace Medals in American History*, 1971.

Rich, Paul and Guillermo de Los Reyes, "Classifying Masonic Medals: Interpreting the Incomprehensible," Coinage of the Americas Conference (1997). *The Medal in America*, vol. 2, edited by Alan M. Stahl, 1999.

Rulau, Russell, *Discovering America, The Coin Collecting Connection*, 1989.

Rulau, Russell, *Standard Catalog of U.S. Tokens, 1700–1900*, 4th ed., 2004.

Rulau, Russell, and George Fuld, *American Game Counters*, Iola, WI, 1972.

Rulau, Russell, and George Fuld, *Medallic Portraits of Washington*, 2nd ed.

Segel, Joseph, series of interviews August–September 2005.

Storer, Horatio R., *Medicina in Nummis*, Wright & Potter, Boston, 1931.

Storer, Horatio R., "The Advantages of Specialization in Numismatics," *The Numismatist*, Vol. IX, 1896, p. 8.

Storer, Malcolm, *Numismatics of Massachusetts* (1923), Quarterman Pubs., Lawrence, Mass., reprinted 1981.

Von Klinger, Eric, "Readers Ask," *Coin World*, October 24, 2005.

Weeks, W.R., "Obituary, George Hampden Lovett," *American Journal of Numismatics*, April 1894, p. 104.

Weinberger, Howard, "Robbins Medallions: Fact and Fiction," at Web site www.collectspace.com/resources/medallions_Robbins.

Notes

1. Bressett, editor of *A Guide Book of United States Coins* (the "Red Book"), in an April 29, 2006, email to the author.
2. Email from R.W. Julian to the author, April 19, 2006.
3. Numbered AL 1864-46 through AL 1864-66 in E.B. Sullivan's 1981 book, *American Political Badges and Medalets, 1789–1892*.
4. The "hub" bears the medal design in relief, and is used to make dies.
5. From a July 13, 2005, telephone conversation with the sculptor.
6. From a conversation with David Frent, July 16, 2005. Nixon ran for vice president twice and for president three times. Debs ran for president five times, the fifth time from prison.
7. See Part III.
8. Highly recommended for its wealth of detailed information on how to collect for investment and pleasure.
9. On his web site (exonumia.com), Rockford, Illinois, dealer Rich Hartzog provides a list of medals and tokens selling for more than $10,000 each.
10. The electrotype process was also used to make original pieces. The 1860 and 1861 shop tokens of Samuel H. Black, Electrotyper, listed in Rulau's *Standard Catalog of U.S. Tokens* (5th ed.) as NY 67 and NY 68, were struck in lead and electrolytically coated in a fine layer of copper. (Reference supplied by David Gladfelter.)
11. Listed in *A Guide Book of United States Coins*, 60th edition.
12. "Collecting U.S. Tokens: Challenges and Rewards," Robert D. Leonard Jr., in *Perspectives in Numismatics*, Chicago Coin Club, 1986.
13. Rulau, *Standard Catalog of U.S. Tokens*, 4th ed.
14. Charles Haswell, *Reminiscences of New York by an Octogenarian, 1816–1860* (1896).
15. For an in-depth look at the birth of the American collecting hobby, with biographies of A.B. Sage and other 19th-century numismatists, see Q. David Bowers, *American Numismatics Before the Civil War, 1760–1860*, 1998.
16. As pointed out by Bob Leonard, in a 2006 email to author.
17. Lists of known brothel and saloon token fantasies are available in Alpert and Elman, *Tokens and Medals*, 1992, and at Rich Hartzog's web site, http://www.exonumia.com.
18. Alpert and Elman, *Tokens and Medals*, 1992, gives guidelines for dating 20th-century tokens.
19. Rulau, *Standard Catalog of United States Tokens*, p. 113.
20. *A Guide Book of United States Coins*, 60th ed., p. 368.
21. For further discussion of satire on political tokens, see Part III.
22. *Expert's Guide to Collecting and Investing in Rare Coins*, p. 474.
23. Encased postage stamps are fully cataloged, by denomination and issuer, in A.L. and I.S. Friedberg, *A Guide Book of United States Paper Money*, 2nd ed.
24. Rulau, in *Standard Catalog of U.S. Tokens*, 4th ed, p. 432, states that Chicago diesinkers made the earliest war tokens in 1861, and that these issues were made not in response to the coin shortage, but for ordinary merchant use.
25. Q. David Bowers recalls a conversation with Catton in which he asked, "Do you collect Civil War tokens?" and Catton replied, "What are they?"
26. "Legend of 'Sixteen Tons,'" 1946, cited at http://www.tennesseeernie.com.
27. Birdie Blesoe Kyle, in April–June 1980 *Goldenseal*, cited at Rootsweb.com under West Virginia Coal.
28. For a catalog of these types, see Terry N. Trantow's *Lumber Company Store Tokens*, self-published, 1978.
29. The POG acronym came from a 1930s Hawaiian bottle-cap game. It stood for "passion fruit, orange, and guava," a juice flavor available at the time.
30. Information furnished by John Kallman.
31. Rulau and Fuld, "American Game Counters: Chapter XIII, Store Card Counters of California," *TAMS Journal*, v. 13, no. 1, February 1973.
32. Games listed are in the collections of the New-York Historical Society. Parker Brothers introduced Monopoly in 1936, supposedly the invention of a Pennsylvanian named Darrow.
33. Bob Leonard furnished this entry, from R.F. Clothier, *Play Money of American Children*, p. 7.

34. "Tips on Chip Collecting," http://www.antiquegamblingchips.com.
35. "Chipology," http://www.goallin.com/members/articles.
36. Historical background drawn from volume 2 of John M. Coffee's work, *The Atwood-Coffee Catalogue of United States and Canadian Transportation Tokens: History and Encyclopedia*, 1984.
37. Letter from William Constable to his parents in England, 1806, in J. Brian Jenkins, *Citizen Daniel (1775–1835) and the Call of America*, Aardvark Editorial Services, Hartford, 2000, p. 39.
38. Op cit., p. 5.
39. *Encyclopedia of New York City*, entry for "Dead Man's Curve."
40. Casey Ressler, "Prints Commemorate Anniversary," *Mat-su Valley Frontiersman*, January 21, 2005.
41. Hal Schindler, "The Jangle of Blood Money in Utah's History," *Salt Lake Tribune*, October 23, 1994.
42. "Readers Ask," Eric von Klinger, *Coin World*, October 24, 2005.
43. "Readers Ask," Eric von Klinger, *Coin World*, October 24, 2005.
44. For the 400th anniversary of Columbus's voyage, in 1892, diesinkers made up for the lapse with scores of medals and tokens featuring themes of discovery, exploration, and development of the New World, and many more have been struck for anniversaries since then. These are cataloged by Russ Rulau in *Discovering America: The Coin Collecting Collection* (1989).
45. Some later military and naval medals struck in the U.S. also carry the legend COMITIA AMERICANA, which is French for "American Congress." Only the medals struck in France in the 1780s are referred to when speaking of the Comitia Americana group. The Comitia Americana medal for Major Henry Lee might have been struck at the U.S. Mint in 1792. An in-depth reference, *Comitia Americana and Related Medals: Underappreciated Monuments to Our Heritage* by John W. Adams and Anne E. Bentley, was published in 2007.
46. Per a February 14, 2008, communication from Q. David Bowers, exceptions were a few were Indian peace medals, made in odd metals such as aluminum; and a few weird mulings of Assay Commission medals.
47. Peach Day, September 11, 1894, is remembered today for the infamous "Peach Day Massacre." Cattlemen, outraged at having to compete for grazing rights with western Colorado sheep farmers, drove a herd of 4,000 sheep off a cliff to their deaths.
48. Some contained only trace amounts of relic metal added to large quantities of coin material.
49. The complete series is depicted on the Medal Collectors of America Web site, http://www.medalcollectors.org/Guides/NASA/NASA_Balfour.html
50. Sale price reported on Rich Hartzog's web site, http://www.exonumia.com.
51. Henry Adams, *The Education of Henry Adams*, 1907, Modern Library reprint, 1996, p. 339.
52. They did include issues of many other types of civic celebrations, such as centennial jubilees and monument openings.
53. Catalog, Presidential Coin & Antique Co. Exonumia Auction 74, December 2005.
54. Information supplied by Dennis Tucker.
55. MS = Mint State, PF = Proof, AU = About Uncirculated. For more on grading, see the most recent edition of *The Official American Numismatic Association Grading Standards for United States Coins*.
56. At the time, U.S. Mint Director Eva Adams sought (but failed) to block Segel from using the word "Mint" in his company name!
57. Seth Lubove, *"King of the Startups,"* Forbes, November 8, 1993, Vol. 152, Issue 11.
58. Transcript, *CBS 60 Minutes*, November 12, 1978, Burrelle's Information Services.
59. Angela Peers, "Value of Franklin Mint Collections May be a Coin Toss," *Wall St. Journal*, August 3, 1994.
60. Terry Lefton, "Chasing Tigers in Unlicensed Woods," *Brandweek*, New York, June 19, 1997, and Paul Holmes, "From Both a Legal and PR View, Franklin Mint's Frivolous Lawsuit Is a No-Win Situation," *PR Week*, July 21, 2003.
61. Q. David Bowers, *Experts' Guide to Collecting and Investing in Rare Coins*, 2005.
62. *Maine Antiques Digest*, July 1998.
63. *Collecting Political Americana*, 1981.
64. *Collecting Political Americana*, p. 80.
65. 20th-century examples from Sullivan, *Collecting Political Americana*, and S.P. Alpert and L.E. Elman, *Tokens and Medals*, 1992.
66. Roger Fischer, *Tippecanoe and Trinkets Too*, p. 144.
67. Developed and maintained by the Coin and Medal Collectors' Asylum.
68. Letter from Robert Patterson, Mint Director, to William Merrill, Director of Indian Affairs, July 18, 1846.

69. Rulau and Fuld, *Medallic Portraits of Washington*, 2nd ed., 1999.
70. Per author telephone conversation with MACO chief executive Robert Hoff, March 23, 2006.
71. A number of bronze proofs were also struck.
72. Franklin quoted on the American Philosophical Society Web site, http://www.amphilsoc.org.
73. "Charter of the Life Saving Benevolent Association of New York: Premiums Awarded, List of Managers, Donors, and Correspondence," New York, 1853, p. 20.
74. "LSBA Annual Report 2004: Report of Committee on Donations and Awards for the Year 2003," furnished by Peter G. Scott of Atlantic Mutual Companies.
75. The address is http://www.titanic1.org
76. Terry Golway, "Firefighters," *American Heritage*, December 2005, pp 43-49.
77. Merritt interviewed by Major Jeanne Fraser Brooks for her story "Coining a Tradition" in *Soldiers Magazine*, August 1994, reprinted on the Web site of the U.S. Army, www.army.mil. According to Russ Rulau in an April 23, 2006, email to the author, unit countermarks on coins were also seen among the Special Ops forces based in Thailand and the Philippines after the U.S. pulled out of Vietnam in 1973.
78. Email from Michael McAllister to the author, September 2005.
79. http://www.challengecoinusa.com.
80. Cataloged in Rulau and Fuld, *Medallic Portraits of Washington*, 2nd ed., 1999.
81. Paul Rich and Guillermo de los Reyes, "Classifying Masonic Medals: Interpreting the Incomprehensible," COAC conference proceedings *The Medal in America*, Vol. 2, 1999.
82. A comprehensive list of fraternal acronyms is posted at the Web site of dealer Rich Hartzog, http://www.exonumia.com.
83. Citation from http://www.straightdope.com/mailbag/mcoin.html.
84. A 1790s silver teapot with a full-name Brasher hallmark sold for $8,625 at a Stack's auction in January 2001. Rulau, *Standard Catalog of U.S. Tokens*, 4th ed., p. 41.
85. Rich Hartzog, "Known Items Selling for Over 10,000," http://www.exonumia.com.
86. William Gibbs, "Collecting Encased Coins," *Coin World*, February 3, 2004.
87. Email, Clifford Mishler to the author, May 30, 2006.
88. It is considered ethical to create these only if the modern artist initials the piece.

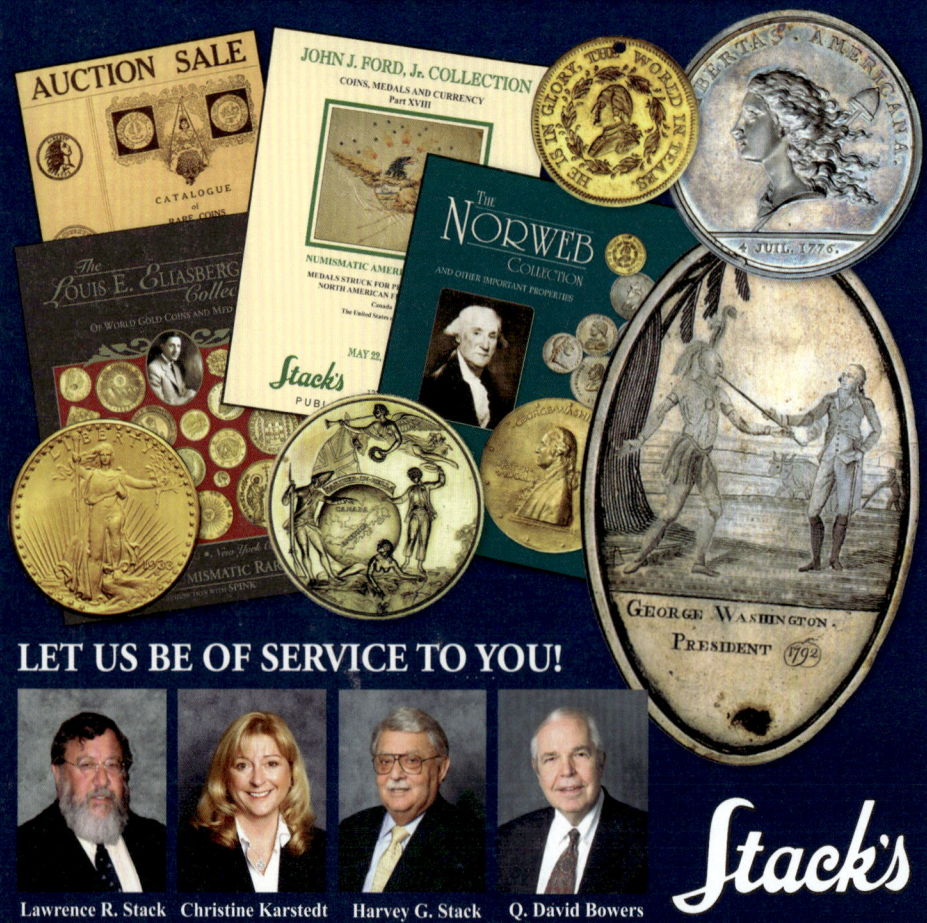